To Ray;

With Best Wishes

for your full attainment

of the high-calling

of the Ministry.

From.

Arnold Sowden

Tipton.
Aug.31.

"Press toward the mark, Etc."

(Phil. 3.14.)

CHRISTUS VERITAS

MACMILLAN AND CO., Limited
LONDON · BOMBAY · CALCUTTA · MADRAS
MELBOURNE

THE MACMILLAN COMPANY
NEW YORK · BOSTON · CHICAGO
DALLAS · ATLANTA · SAN FRANCISCO

THE MACMILLAN COMPANY
OF CANADA, LIMITED
TORONTO

CHRISTUS VERITAS

AN ESSAY

BY

WILLIAM TEMPLE
ARCHBISHOP OF YORK

MACMILLAN AND CO., LIMITED
ST. MARTIN'S STREET, LONDON
1930

PRINTED IN GREAT BRITAIN

TO

MY WIFE

PREFACE

THIS book is a sequel, or rather a companion, to *Mens Creatrix*, which was published in 1917. The earlier book was mainly philosophical in its aim; this is mainly theological. That is to say, I tried in *Mens Creatrix* first to set out a philosophic view, without any deliberate reference to Christian revelation or experience, and then to show that the Incarnation in fact supplied the one great need of philosophy. But I knew that I was moving away from philosophy and that *Mens Creatrix* would be my only serious attempt at the statement of a philosophical position in the usually accepted sense of the word. I always hoped, however, to follow this with a theological book which should begin where *Mens Creatrix* left off and work backwards from there.

The thought in this book follows that course. It is written with the Christian revelation full in view from the outset. But for purposes of exposition I have found it better to work in from the circumference to the heart of the Christian position, and then out again. I want to make it clear that this method is adopted for purposes of exposition only. I make no attempt to outline a philosophic approach to belief in God. That was done, as far as I can do it, in the former volume. Here I am trying to set out a whole view of the world and life as it appears to one mind at least from an avowedly Christian standpoint. The order employed was adopted because it was necessary to fix the meaning of certain terms before the central theme could be discussed. It has been my aim to set forth a complete outline, but it is worth while, perhaps, to point out that the greater part of the argument is independent of the particular doctrine of Value developed at the outset.

My desire to write a companion volume to *Mens Creatrix* was fostered by a suggestion from Bishop Gore that I should expand a footnote in that work into a treatise. The footnote in question is on page 360 and runs as follows:

"When the human mind tries to conceive the Eternal and Omniscient God, it always pictures Him as knowing all Time *at a moment of Time*,—as, for example, knowing *now* all the past and future. But the whole point of the argument is that while all Time is the object of the Eternal comprehension, the comprehending Mind is extra-temporal and therefore does not grasp it now or at any other Time, but precisely Eternally. Thus we turn the flank of Bergson's argument that Finalism is 'only inverted mechanism,' and that by means of a treatment of Time which is based on his own."

This footnote was connected in my own mind with another, which is on page 318:

"It is to be remembered that we have not the World-History without the Incarnation as one expression of the Divine Will and the Life of the Incarnate as another; for that Life is a part of History, though it reveals the principle of the whole, and it is through its occurrence in the midst of History that History is fashioned into an exposition of the principle there revealed. We have here a series which is part of another series and is yet perfectly representative of it. (Cf. the Supplementary Essay in Royce's *The World and the Individual*.) But here the series which is contained (the Life, Death, Resurrection of Christ) only becomes representative of the series which contains it (the entire history of the world) in virtue of the influence which by occurring within the latter it is able to exercise upon it. Therefore, though Transcendence and Immanence are fused into one, the Transcendent aspect is always dominant.''

Those two footnotes are a summary of what I have tried to set forth here in some detail.

I am convinced that one reason why comparatively few men of the highest ability and education are at present offering themselves for ordination is that the intellectual atmosphere is dominated by a philosophy which leaves no room for a specific Incarnation. This philosophy is not materialist or atheist; it is both spiritual and theistic; but the idea of God which it reaches is such as to preclude His ever doing anything in particular in any other sense than that in which He does everything in general. I believe that a very slight touch to the intellectual balance may make the scales incline the other way. Part of the trouble is that theologians have left the field of most general enquiry too largely to non-theological philosophers; they have tended to write either history or detailed discussion of particular doctrines. What is needed is the exposition of the Christian idea of God, life and the world, or, in other words, a Christo-centric metaphysics.

The building of such a scheme of thought out of the over-abundant intellectual material available in our generation must be the work of many minds, not of one—especially if that one is primarily occupied with administration, policy, and practical movements. My contribution must be a small one; I hope it may lead, even by the process of its own refutation if need be, to more substantial contributions from better qualified minds.

Most of my reading and a great part of my writing for three years past has been planned with a view to this volume. The first draft of Chapter I. was written as a paper to be read at a meeting of the British Philosophical Societies in Manchester in the summer of 1922, and afterwards appeared in *Mind*, N.S. 124. Chapter VII. and most of Chapter XIV. were first written as lectures delivered in Manchester Cathedral, and the former was published with others of the same series by Messrs. Palmer & Sons under the title *Fundamentals of the Faith*. Part of Chapter III. appeared in *The Pilgrim* for April 1921. To all who are concerned I offer my thanks for permission to republish.

My thanks are also due in a special degree to Mrs. Duff, whose delightful hospitality in the Isle of Wight during successive summer holidays provided the peace of mind and body without which the book could never have been either planned or written; to the Rev. L. W. Grensted, who has read the whole in typescript and made many valuable suggestions; to Canon Raven for searching comments on the first draft of Chapter VIII.; and to Canon Quick, who has read the proofs, and to whom I owe many improvements both in the argument itself and in its expression.

W. MANCHESTER.

BISHOPSCOURT,
MANCHESTER,
June, 1924.

PREFACE TO SECOND IMPRESSION

THIS is rather a reprint than a second edition, for I
have only made a few verbal changes and corrected a
few slips. But I am glad to take the opportunity of
making some observations on two criticisms which the
book has called forth.

(1) The first of these concerns the relationship of
Theology to Philosophy which is set forth both in this
book and in *Mens Creatrix*. It is said that this essay
is really just as philosophical as the former one, and
that what I ought to have attempted is a demonstration that Christianity is the only true philosophy ; it
is urged that by treating Theology as different from
Philosophy I have confused my own aim, and I am
recommended to emulate Aristotle for whom Theology
and Philosophy in its primary sense (πρώτη φιλοσοφία)
are identical.

Now, of course, I believe that there is only one
truth, and that the true theology in its completeness is
identical with the true philosophy in its completeness.
But I believe that in the limited state of our knowledge
there are two methods to be followed, and the ordinary
use of words suggests that one of them should be
called philosophic and the other theological. Since
the first edition of this book appeared, I have read
Mr. R. G. Collingwood's fascinating *Speculum Mentis*.
In a letter to me answering some comments which I
made to him he uses a phrase which illustrates my
point : " I strongly hold that to be intuited in religion,

and described as so intuited in theology, which is conceived in philosophy." As far as it goes, that indicates the distinction which I wish to draw, but I am compelled to go further.

Aristotle had not to deal with a specific Revelation ; indeed such a thing was impossible within his scheme of thought, and if accepted would have burst it. Now the mind can examine the whole field of its experience, including religious experience, without attributing to anything within it that predominance which must be attributed to what is accepted as a specific act of Divine Self-Revelation. This enterprise is what I mean by Philosophy. But some forms of religion, and most conspicuously Christianity, rest on the belief that such a Revelation exists. Those who accept that belief, and examine the whole field of experience in the light of it, are committed to an enterprise which is what I mean by Theology. From this it might appear that Theology is just one form of Philosophy ; but while that conveys part of the truth it obscures another part. For the belief in a specific Revelation, which I take to be the distinctive mark of Theology, is only justified when it has been shown that the Theology in which it is articulated supplies a conception of Reality which is more satisfactory, as a Philosophy, than any other. If the claim made on behalf of any supposed Revelation could be substantiated in isolation, the method of Philosophy and the method of Theology would be identical. But in fact Theology has to accept as a starting-point something which obtains its philosophic justification, if at all, only when the Theology is complete. It therefore adopts a course of argument which is not philosophically justified ; in popular language, religion is an affair of the heart more than of the head ; and the acceptance of its deliverances as decisive for our whole world-view is a leap only justified intellectually by its results. In Mr. Collingwood's language, Theology,

by describing what is intuited in religion, enables us
to conceive what would have remained inconceivable
so long as we made no assumption which was not
actually probable at the stage when we made it. The
contention of this book is that the leap is justified.
I cannot prove the existence of God or His Incarnation
in Jesus Christ ; Philosophy (in my sense of the
word) must not assume these doctrines, nor may it
build on them until they have been shown to be at
least probable ; Theology accepts them from Religion,
and shows them to be probable by exhibiting them as
the springs of a conception of Reality which, when
reached, commends itself as the most satisfying conception which is in·fact available. The method of
Theology is thus precarious, and is only justified by
the result; in the result it is justified, and that on
grounds acceptable to Philosophy. The method of
Philosophy is secure, but its result is comparatively
barren. One day, perhaps, the two will perfectly co-
incide ; but that day is not yet ; both philosophers
and theologians are concerned to hasten it, but meanwhile the motto of Theology must be *Credo, ut
intelligam*.

(2) The other criticism to which I would refer
takes the form of a complaint that in the opening
chapters I treat the relation of Fact to Value as that of
Symbol to Meaning, whereas in many cases it seems
to be that of Means to End. The critic takes the
instance of a musical instrument, where the value lies
in the music to be drawn from it, while this can hardly
be called the meaning of which the instrument is a
symbol. I think this is true ; and the relation of the
Symbol-Meaning relation to the Means-End relation
calls for inquiry. But while I admit a gap in the
argument at this point, I do not think it really affects
the coherence of the essay as a whole; for I am convinced that, at the level on which the argument seeks
to move, no relation so external as that of Means to

End can be normative. The work of God as a whole must be a true expression of the Mind of God.

The point at which this set of considerations becomes important is the relation of History to Eternity. Now I certainly do not think that this is merely a relation of Symbol to Meaning, if by History we mean terrestrial history. This is made clear on p. 211, where it is insisted that the Christian hope is not only the attainment of a point of view from which the problems of existence are seen to be solved, but rather a resurrection to a new order of being. This passage is intended to correct the insufficiency of the analogy from Drama which is employed elsewhere (p. 90). On the whole I think we may say that, seen from this end, that is while we are still in ignorance of the new order of being to which we hope to attain by resurrection, the relation of History to Eternal Life must predominantly appear as one of Means to End; but viewed from the other end, when the attainment of Eternal Life will itself be a fact of History, it will appear as one of Symbol and Meaning. We cannot apprehend it thus, but we can see that it must in principle be thus apprehensible.

I have said something about these two points because they touch the main principles of my argument. Beyond this I would only say that this is an Essay, not a Treatise—a sketch, not a picture.

W. M.

December 1924.

CONTENTS

PART I
OUTER CIRCLE

CHAPTER I

PART II
INNER CIRCLE

CHAPTER IV

xv

CHAPTER VI

PART III

THE CORE OF THE ARGUMENT

CHAPTER VII

CHAPTER VIII

CHAPTER IX

PART IV

INNER CIRCLE

CHAPTER X

CHAPTER XI

CHAPTER XII

PART V

OUTER CIRCLE

CHAPTER XIII

CHAPTER XIV

CHAPTER XV

PART I
OUTER CIRCLE

CHAPTER I

THE STRUCTURE OF REALITY

"Ὅδε ὁ κόσμος οὕτω, ζῷον ὁρατὸν τὰ ὁρατὰ περιέχον, εἰκὼν τοῦ νοητοῦ θεὸς αἰσθητός, μέγιστος καὶ ἄριστος κάλλιστός τε καὶ τελεώτατος γέγονεν εἰς οὐρανὸς ὅδε μονογενὴς ὤν.—PLATO.

" The world of reality, we may say in a word, is the world of values."—F. H. BRADLEY.

IT is abundantly clear that one of the chief characteristics of contemporary philosophy is the place which it gives to the concept of Value. There is nothing unprecedented in this. Indeed it is not possible to give a higher place to Value than Plato did when he made the Good the supreme principle in Reality, or required of Anaxagoras that, in order to illustrate the supremacy of Reason, he should prove the earth to be either round or flat by showing which it is better that it should be. Aristotle, whom no one has yet censured for sentimentalism, similarly clinches his argument for the Unity of God or the governing principle with the maxim and the quotation: τὰ δὲ ὄντα οὐ βούλεται πολιτεύεσθαι κακῶς. " οὐκ ἀγαθὸν πολυκοιρανίη· εἷς κοίρανος ἔστω." [1] But though not unprecedented, the prominence of Value in the thought of our time is characteristic. To the religious thinker, it is welcome. And yet there is a remarkable indefiniteness in the current use of the term, and the relation of Value to Reality or Substance is by most writers either not discussed or is very sketchily outlined.

[1] *Metaphysics, Λ ad fin.*

3

The structure of Reality, as it presents itself to us, seems to be as follows: It consists of many grades, of which each presupposes those lower than itself, and of which each finds its own completion or perfect development only in so far as it is possessed or in-dwelt by that which is above it. This seems to involve an infinite regress, and suggests an infinite progress. Whether there is in fact a lowest and a highest term in this scale of finite existences I do not know, and I do not greatly care. In a former book [1] I have tried to show that the infinite series is not necessarily meaningless in logic or futile in ethics. At present I am not concerned with the problem of lowest and highest terms, but with the facts before us, which may fall midway between such terms. Moreover, I am rather tabulating impressions than constructing a system, though the tabulation is of interest because it suggests the principle of a system. To make my present meaning clear it will be enough to take the broad divisions: Matter, Life, Mind, Spirit. These grades may be for our present purpose indifferently regarded as various entities or as different modes of action and re-action. Matter is itself a term covering many grades; so is Life. But each has sufficient identity in itself and sufficient distinctness from the others for the requirements of the argument.

The term Matter is here taken to cover the sub-stances, or the modes of action and re-action, which are studied in the sciences of Physics and Chemistry. It is at once quite clear that those sciences give no account of the self-movement which is one character-istic of Life, or of the comprehension of spaces and times which is one characteristic of Mind. The lower cannot explain the higher. But that is not all. The living organism has in its material constitution a unity of differences, a subtlety of co-ordination, a spontaneity of adaptation, that no knowledge of Physics and

[1] *Mens Creatrix* (Macmillan, 1917).

Chemistry would enable the observer to anticipate. The material only reveals its full potentialities when Life possesses and indwells it. The later development reveals what had all along been potential in the earlier; but no knowledge of the earlier apart from that development would have made possible a prediction of the development. Matter only reveals what it really is when Life supervenes upon it.

Similarly Life only reveals what it really is when Mind supervenes upon it. No study of zoology and biology will enable the student to predict the occurrence among living things of the mathematician or the financier. The use of faculties, which at first are used for mere survival, in the interest of ends that have nothing at all to do with survival, must occur in fact before it can be anticipated in theory. So, too, Mind as intellect only shows what it can be and do when it is guided by Mind as Spirit. I should find the differentia of Spirit in the sense of Absolute Value and therefore of obligation; this, at its height, is Love or personal union. Because Spirit is, or has, the sense of absolute value it also is, or has, the capacity for fellowship with God. The claim made upon Life by Art and Science cannot be accounted for in terms of calculation; still less can the self-sacrifice of the hero or the martyr. And, if Religion is to be trusted, even Spirit (as known in our experience) only reveals what it can be and do when it is possessed by that Highest Being, whom we call Spirit because Spirit is the highest grade of Reality known to us.

It is to be admitted, and indeed emphasised, that these " grades " taken singly are abstractions. Reality is a continuous whole within which the mind of each individual finds itself. The mind draws for itself the distinctions which it makes in this continuous whole— the distinction of Self and Not-self being one of the most fundamental. To treat either the Self or the

Not-self in isolation, or to speak of any of the distinguishable elements in Reality without reference to their setting, is to ignore some part of the truth concerning them, and will become a falsification unless we remember what we are doing. But abstraction is an inevitable phase of thought, and we need not shrink from it. Also we have to remember that Reality is either supra-temporal and supra-spatial, or else is continuous in time as truly as it is continuous in space. Consequently, in whatever sense we may consider the Past in abstraction from the Present and Future, in just that same sense we may consider Matter in abstraction from Life. Geology may legitimately aspire to the apprehension of truth concerning the world as it was before Life appeared.

We begin, then, with the conception of Reality as existing in many grades, each of which finds its own completion or perfect development only in so far as it is possessed or indwelt by that which is above it. But we then notice that each depends for its actuality upon those which are below it. Matter itself as experienced by us can be reduced to what is simpler than itself, whether to a, β, and γ particles[1] or still more ultimately to Space-Time.[2] Life is unknown apart from living organisms, which are Matter informed by Life. Mind is unknown except in reasoning, living organisms. Spirit is unknown except in conscientious, reasoning, living organisms. Whether the higher grades can exist apart, there seems to be no means of deciding; in our experience they never do.

Thus we see each grade dependent for its existence on the grades below, and dependent for its own full actualisation on the grade or grades above. Such seems, apart from any theory of its origin or *raison d'être*, to be in fact the structure of Reality.

---

[1] Or " emanations," if " particles " be regarded as an incorrect term.
[2] I must not be understood to accept this modern amalgam as really the ultimate constituent of the material universe.

Now, if we ask for an explanation of the Universe as a whole we are bound to formulate the answer in terms of Will. This is a dogmatic statement of a controversial position; its justification will be more apparent as we proceed. Here I would only submit that there is in our experience one, and only one, self-explanatory principle—namely, Purpose or Will. No doubt, if any one can believe in a purpose with no will behind it, we should have to say "Purpose" only, leaving "Will" as a precarious inference; but as it appears that Purpose and Will are terms that mutually imply each other, we may speak of either indifferently. There is a "problem of evil," but there is not in the same sense any problem of good. When we find as the cause of any phenomenon an intelligent will which chose to cause that phenomenon to occur, we raise no further questions, unless we fail to see how that will came to seek this occurrence as good. We may be puzzled by the way a man exercises choice; but our problem here is not, as a rule, a problem of efficient causation. When we sympathise, we are not puzzled. If I say of any one " I cannot understand acting like that," I do not mean that I cannot give a psychological analysis of the motives of the action; I mean that I cannot imagine myself doing it. When in the causal regress we arrive at a will, the regress is at an end, and to understand means, not to give a causal explanation, but to sympathise. We have reached an ultimate term. And when we do sympathise, our mind raises no more questions. The only explanation of the Universe that would really explain it, in the sense of providing to the question why it exists an answer that raises no further question, would be the demonstration that it is the creation of a Will which in the creative act seeks an intelligible good. But that is Theism. Theism of some kind is the only theory of the universe which could really explain it. Theism may be untenable; if it is, the universe is ultimately inexplicable. Merely to show how it fits together as a rational system does not fully explain it, for we are left still asking—Why does it exist at all? When once that question is asked, the answer must be found in Theism or nowhere.

I need hardly say that I do not advance this outline argument either as the only defence of Theism or as a sufficient intellectual basis for it. The whole body of argument that is articulated by Professor Pringle-Pattison and Professor Sorley in their Gifford Lectures, or by Dr. Matthews in his Boyle Lectures, is here presupposed.[1] But the point which I have just mentioned, and which deserves more attention in my judgement than it generally receives, is the one most germane to the group of considerations with which we are now specially concerned. Other arguments seem to establish the principle that the universe must be interpreted by spiritual rather than by mechanical or other materialistic categories. Other arguments tend to establish the ethical character of the spiritual power or powers that govern the world. Philosophically everything is ready for Theism. But actual belief in a living God rests primarily, as I think, on religious experience, and finds its intellectual support in the reflexion that this belief is capable in principle of supplying an explanation of the very existence of the Universe, which no other hypothesis available to us affords any hope of doing. That is no proof. It cannot be laid down as an axiom that there must be some explanation of the existence of the Universe. If the existing scheme of things be internally coherent, it cannot be said that the intellect imperiously demands more than this for its satisfaction.[2] It is true that we

---

[1] Pringle-Pattison, *The Idea of God*; Sorley, *Moral Values and the Idea of God*; Matthews, *Studies in Christian Philosophy*. I have attempted to state my own philosophical approach to Theism in *Mens Creatrix*; in the present essay Theism is assumed.

[2] Such a Universe would not be valueless; it would have intellectual value, but no moral value; and if Reason manifests itself (as I should maintain) in

have to choose between postulating a rational universe and accepting complete scepticism. It is not true that we have to choose between theism and scepticism. I should be very sorry to have to believe that Reality is what Mr. Bradley describes or even what Professor Pringle-Pattison describes. But I could not reject their accounts of it only on the ground that they do not explain its existence as a whole. For while it is an additional advantage in any theory if it can do this, it is not fatal to any theory that it should fail to do this, or even refuse to attempt it. It may be that there is no explanation of Reality itself, and that it is not self-explanatory except in the sense that all its parts support each other in constituting the whole. Or, again, it may be that there is an explanation of Reality, but that it is something wholly inaccessible to the mind of man. There seems no reason to suppose that mind, in its human manifestation, either includes, or itself is, the last term in cosmic evolution, and if there is more to follow, then, though human mind would comprehend the lower forms, it would not know at all what constituted the higher forms, and it would be in these, not in human mind, that the explanation of Reality might be found.

None the less, if there is an available hypothesis which is capable in its own nature of supplying the explanation of Reality, it is thoroughly scientific to experiment with it and see if it can make good its claim. Now, Purpose, as the expression of a Will, is such a principle. But to seek the explanation of the Universe in a Purpose grounded in a Will is Theism; it is the acceptance, provisionally at least, of the doctrine of God as Creator. From religion there comes abundant support for this doctrine. To some religions, and notably to the Jewish and Christian religions, it is essential and fundamental.

the apprehension of ultimate value whereby all other values are either found or brought to cohere with one another and with existence, then such a Universe would not be rational. (I owe this point to Canon Quick.)

Now, if we assume the structure of Reality to be such as I have outlined, and if we accept (at least for purposes of enquiry) the explanation of it which Theism offers, certain consequences follow, which it is our main purpose at present to trace out.

Will acts always for the sake of value, or good, to be created or enjoyed as a result of the action. It is precisely as so acting that it is self-explanatory and intrinsically intelligible. This would lead us to expect that whatever Will creates is either itself good or is a means to good. Moreover, if what is created is good not (or not only) as a means but in itself, this means that its very being or substance is good. I do not go so far as to say that good is the being or substance of all that exists, but we are entitled and even bound by the hypothesis adopted to say that whatever exists must either be a means to something which is substantially good or else be itself substantially good. We seem therefore to be led up to a new enquiry into the relations of value and reality.

Now, if I may take Professor Pringle-Pattison as an illustrious example of contemporary philosophy, and discuss, not the details of his argument, nor its claims taken as a whole, but the general impression created by it on my own mind, and also (as I find) on many other minds, I would venture to suggest that many of the anxieties with regard to it which that general impression arouses would vanish if he saw his way to a more thoroughgoing conception of God in terms of Will. For the general impression left on my mind by his great book on the *Idea of God*, and strengthened by his essay in the volume entitled *The Spirit*, is that he accepts the Universe as somehow existing, and then finds that it reveals values, which are regarded all the while as being adjectival to it. That they appear at all is a determinant consideration for the philosopher, and yet they appear rather as appendices of an other- wise existing universe than as themselves its constitutive elements; and when we reach the Being in whom all values are realised, He hovers uncertainly between two positions, being at one time the Ground of all existence and at another a characteristic of a universe which would apparently continue to exist (though shorn of its values) if He were to cease. And it is the latter position to which He seems to be ultimately relegated. I have no doubt that this summary is unjust to Professor Pringle-Pattison. Almost any summary of a theory elaborated with so delicate a balance and an argument so closely knit would be unjust. But at the end of *The Idea of God* I was left with a sense that this book makes God adjectival to the Universe, and the essay in *The Spirit* removed all doubt on the question. And yet I was sure that in the main the Professor was dealing with the matter on right lines and had rendered a great service to philosophy, and especially the philosophy of religion, by following the method which he had chosen.[1]

The question with which I am now concerned is this: should we conceive of things as existing independently, and possessing value as an attribute? or should we think of value as itself the true reality which realises its various forms through embodying itself in things—or through the creation of things for this purpose by the Divine Will?

Now, I believe that our difficulty arises from the fact that Philosophy, being an intellectual activity, always tends to depend more upon that search for an ultimate value which is conducted in science than upon the two kindred efforts of ethics and of art. In science the intellect is not only supreme but sole; it is natural for the intellect to take the methods and operations of science not only as its method but also

---

[1] I should add that in an article in *Mind* (N.S. 109) the Professor shows that he does not actually regard God as adjectival to the Universe, and does not desire his argument to suggest such a conclusion. But if it does suggest it, that only makes it clearer than ever that the foundations of the argument are incomplete.

as determining the subject-matter of its enquiry. That I take to be the essential feature of the heresy of intellectualism. Philosophy must be intellectual or it ceases to be itself. But the intellect always gets its subject-matter from outside itself; it is ready enough to accept it from the physical world, and from its own procedure and results in dealing with the physical world. It is less ready to accept as the material of its operations the procedure and results of human activities which are either not purely or not at all intellectual. Yet for a satisfactory metaphysic it must include these, and indeed (as I think) must give them a determining influence. The goal of Science is on the objective side Reality, on the subjective side Knowledge: the goal of Art is on the objective side Beauty, on the subjective side Creation and Appreciation; the goal of Ethics is on the objective side Society, on the subjective side enlightened Conscience and dutiful Action. No doubt both Art and Ethics presuppose Science or Knowledge, and the spirit of Beauty and of Morality is the same as the spirit of Truth. "Love is the mainspring of Logic."[1] But while Art and Ethics include the intellectual element, they contain also emotional and volitional elements, which Science omits with the single exception of the will to know. But these processes, while containing elements not intellectual in origin, are susceptible of intellectual treatment. Our plea is not that philosophy should cease to be intellectual, but that the material of its intellectual enquiry should be drawn as much from Ethics and Art as from Logic or Epistemology. It is apparent that whereas Science ends in Knowledge, which leaves the objective world as it finds it, Art and Ethics aim both at a comprehension of the object and at action which modifies the object. Now, if the intellect is led by its own process to the affirmation, or at least to the supposition, that the explanation

[1] Bosanquet, *The Principle of Individuality and Value*, p. 341.

of the Universe is to be found in the activity of a
Creative Will, it must go on to accept those human
activities which include some creative energy as surer
guides to the constitution of Reality than its own
special activity of science, which leaves its object as it
finds it.

Starting with the general outlook appropriate to
science, philosophers have generally made Existence
their substantive notion, while Value has become
adjectival. It is quite true that Plato spoke of the
Idea of Good as ἐπέκεινα τῆς οὐσίας—which the context proves to mean "above and beyond objective
being" (*Republic*, vi. 509 B); but he does not follow
this up by including ethics and politics in his pro-
paedeutic studies; he remains under the predominant
influence of geometry. Having apprehended the
Idea of Good, the philosopher is to return to practical
affairs and rule his city in the light of this supreme
principle. But the study of Ethics and Politics is not
called in to help in the apprehension of the Good.
So St. Thomas Aquinas is quite thorough in the
deliberate and reiterated identification of Good with
Being—"Bonum et ens sunt idem secundum rem:
sed differunt secundum rationem tantum" (*Sum.
Theol.* Pt. I., Q. v., A. 1)—yet he goes on to treat Being
as prior because it is the first object of the intellect, and
thereafter the whole concept of Value almost disappears.
Consequently his definition of Substance as that which
exists of itself—"substantiae nomen . . . significat
essentiam cui competit sic esse, id est per se esse" (*Sum.
Theol.* Pt. I., Q. iii., A. 5)—never leads him even
to consider whether this is not the same as to say
that Substance and Good (or Value) are synonymous
terms.[1]

But the identity of substance (so defined) with
Value follows inevitably from a thoroughgoing acceptance of the Theistic hypothesis. The Universe is to

---

[1] Hence the chief difficulties of his sacramental theories.

be conceived as deriving its origin and unity from a Creative Will. But the correlative of Will is Good or Value; therefore the most fundamental element in things is their Value. This is not a property which they have incidentally; it is the constitutive principle, the true self, of every existent. Aquinas says that a thing is perfect in so far as it exists: " In tantum est autem perfectum unumquodque in quantum est in actu "[1] (*Sum. Theol.* Pt. I., Q. v., A. 1)—and that everything is good so far as it exists: " Omne ens, in quantum est ens, est bonum " (*Sum. Theol.* Pt. I., Q. v., A. 3).

The inversion of this is the fertile truth; everything exists so far as it is good.[2] The ultimate Reality and the primary ground of existence for all else is the Creative God, in whom all value is eternally real. Value, being the immediate object of the Creative Will, is itself the secondary ground of existence for all created things. Value is thus, in the order of being, prior to existence. But Value is not Existence, and must receive (or come into) existence in order to be a part of Reality; on the other hand nothing is brought into existence except as a means to, or as a vehicle of, Value.

This view of Value as prior to Existence and as the ground of existence is not easy to express in terms adapted to the opposite conception. It is not indeed a novel view, for, as has been said, it dominates the thought of Plato. But language has not been fashioned to accord with it, and even those thinkers who have wished to give a primary place to Value have often failed to escape the entangling suggestions

---

[1] Cf. p. 34.

[2] Hocking argues strongly and (I think) convincingly that " the value of any object of attention is nothing other than the entering of the reality-idea into the thought of the object," so that " the use of the God-idea . . . will be the chief determinant of the value level in any consciousness " (*The Meaning of God in Human Experience*, pp. 130 and 136). Edward Caird used to urge his pupils to avoid the common phrase " too good to be true." " If anything is not true," he would say, " it is because it is not good enough to be true."

of the language which they had to use. Thus Ritschlianism is (on our view) right in so far as it contends that all religious doctrines are Value-judgements, but is wrong, and even hopelessly wrong, in so far as it regards these as other than metaphysical and ontological judgements. Perhaps we may help ourselves to avoid a similar entanglement by considering some senses of the term " Substance," already referred to, which on our view it is specially important to distinguish.

If it were possible to ignore all former use, I should urge that Substance be used for Real Thing;[1] in that case Substance = Value + Existence. But we cannot ignore the fact that, according to one familiar use of the word, the Substance of a thing is something other than the whole real thing, being distinguished from some elements in the whole real thing, as, for example, from the Accidents. Now I submit that if the word is used in this way at all, Substance is and can be nothing but Value. Value is the element in real things which both causes them to be, and makes them what they are, and is thus fitly called Substance in so far as this is other or less than their totality. But in this sense Substance is to be distinguished from actuality. Eternally all Values are realised in God; but in the process of time not all Values are actual here and now.

It is certainly true that Value is only actual in the various things that are valuable: and it is only fully actual (though the discussion of this point belongs to a later stage of the argument) so far as it is appreciated by some conscious being. It is tempting to separate the Good from the good thing, and to demand either

[1] So Bishop Gore writes: " Let us proclaim to all the winds of heaven that by ' substance ' the Church means no more and no less than ' real thing,' so that when we speak of the Son and of the Spirit as ' of one substance ' with the Father, we mean that they belong to that one real being which we call God; and when we speak of Christ as ' of one substance ' with us, we mean that He took the real being of man, and is that real thing, in all respects that a man is " (*The Holy Spirit and the Church*, pp. 233, 234).

some account of it in such separation or else a method of apprehending it in separation. But to do this is to repeat the mistake made by the Hedonists in Ethics. When I am hungry, I want food and not (except incidentally) the pleasure of eating. Desire is not of some one general thing, such as pleasure. And yet it is true that when I am hungry what I want is the value or the good of food; but this is not separable from the food, and is not even properly distinguishable from it, though it is distinguishable from other aspects of any particular food which are irrelevant to my hunger.

So Will aims at Good in all its forms; and as God makes the world, He beholds it as very good. There is the problem of Evil, of course, and it may be that it will wreck this whole fashion of philosophy; but we cannot embark upon the discussion of it here.[1] Our concern just now is with the method which philosophy must pursue if it adopts this principle that only Value has substantial being.

It is clear at once that Ethics and Politics and Aesthetics will be exalted alongside of Mathematics, as the typical activities of Mind, and that on the whole they will be the more normative for Metaphysic. The Universe will be approached less as a problem (or theorem) in Geometry, more as a Drama or Symphony, and as a Society in process of formation.

Now if the structure of Reality is such as we described, and if the problem of Metaphysics is to be approached along the lines now indicated, we begin to see a great unification take place. The lower grades, we said, only attain to the fullness of their own being so far as they are indwelt and dominated by those above them. They exist then, ultimately, to embody or symbolise what is more than themselves. The universe is sacramental. Everything except the Creative Will exists to be the expression of that Will,

[1] I made an attempt to deal with it in *Mens Creatrix*.

the actualisation of its values, and the communication of those Values to spirits created for the special value actualised through fellowship in creation and appreciation of values. Men can do some of this work themselves. Speech is a manipulation of sounds for just such communication and fellowship. By this doctrine the reality of the objects in the world is not divorced from our sense of their significance. A friend gave me during the war an illustration to show how familiar a fact is the transvaluation, which on this theory is the only true transubstantiation: Suppose a man comes to see me, finds some strips of coloured calico on the floor, and amuses himself by dancing on them to show his contempt for what he takes to be my interests; I may think him a tiresome fellow, but that will be all: now suppose those bits of calico have been sewn together to make my national flag, and he dances contemptuously on it; I shall kick him out of the house.

That is comparatively a trifling instance. In any case the symbolism of a flag is purely conventional. Yet even here it seems absurd to say that the reality of the flag is the same as the reality of the strips of calico. The accidents (as the schoolmen would say) are the same; the substance is changed.

Beginning with such a conventional symbol we may go on to fuller symbolism such as that of great Art. Here the principle emerges that to be a true or (as I have named it elsewhere) an essential symbol, a thing must be itself an individual instance of what it symbolises. So Macbeth can symbolise ambition because he is a very individual ambitious man. In great art, at least, the symbol is unique, and there is no other way of saying what the artist has said. In Emerson's great phrase " The word is one with that it tells of." If after reading *King Lear* or hearing the Fifth Symphony a man asks what either means, we can only tell him that each means itself; but that

c

is the extreme opposite of saying that either is meaningless.[1]

In that highest sphere of creative art which we call human conduct, the good or value sought is that of Personality (or Character) in Fellowship, with all the varieties that this implies. Actions have their value as symbolising and as producing this.

Of course symbolism and value involve a subjective element. For symbolism this may be a limitation, for the subjective element is specially concerned with interpretation, and if the symbol is to be really expressive, or, in other words, if it is to be a real symbol, it must be such as can be understood by those minds for whom it is created. But into value the subjective element enters not as a limitation, but as a constituent. Value exists in order to be appreciated; and though the appreciating mind finds rather than creates the value, yet the value is dormant or potential until appreciation awakes it to energy and actuality.[2] Value, in short, is actual in experience. And it is one of the advantages of a philosophy which makes Value its central principle that it thus in its central principle holds objective and subjective together. If a philosophy can be constructed on this basis at all, it will at least be free from the divisive claims of the objective and the subjective. Whatever may be true of knowledge and fact, there is no doubt that in actualised Value subject and object are united on equal terms.

[1] For a full discussion of the symbolism of Art, I must refer to the chapter on "The Nature and Significance of Art" in *Mens Creatrix*. This is one of the points where language becomes a source of great difficulty. A symbol is (properly) something which means or signifies something else. But the perfect symbol *is* (in a focal manifestation) what it symbolises. Thus words are sounds in the air or marks on paper; they symbolise a meaning which is not on paper or in the air. But a poem can itself be the very embodiment and vehicle of a value which is found *in* (not only on occasion of) the apprehension of the words. See further Chapter XIII.

[2] Value is found by the appreciating mind, not imported into the valuable object. Yet the object is actually valuable, in the sense of contributing to the sum of good, only when it is appreciated. Dr. G. E. Moore holds it "better" that a beautiful world should exist than an ugly one, even if no one ever appreciated it (*Principia Ethica*, p. 84). I can attach no meaning to this. But if value is not purely objective, no more is it purely subjective. It arises in a subject-object system when subject and object are perfectly co-related to each other.

Moreover, it brings them together at the point where they ought to meet. For it is in man that the first manifestation is found both of conscious appreciation of value and of clear distinction between subject and object. The division between subject and object is therefore, on this view, bridged in the very moment of its appearance. As we rise to the grade or level of Mind, where appreciation first becomes possible, that is, of Man (though animals show the beginnings both of thought and of appreciation), the problem and its solution appear together. For, if our whole theory is sound, value determines existence, but value is only actual when it is appreciated; therefore Man's appreciation of the world is the first instalment, so to speak, within the Time process, of the realisation of that for which the world was made, though in the eternal Mind which comprehends all Time this is actual eternally. It is Man who first rises to the question why is there a world at all. It is in Man's appreciation of its Value that the answer begins to appear; for the solution of the problem of existence is found in the experience of what is good. Thus the whole universe is created to reflect the manifold goodness of the Creator, and to produce within itself beings who may share with the Creator His joy in the goodness of the created thing. Symbolism is thus the supreme philosophic principle. The universe exists to reveal the goodness of God so far as it evolves intelligences capable of receiving the revelation.

It is clear that as we advance from the purely conventional symbolism, represented by the flag, to the essential symbol of great art or of ethical conduct, the subjective element is reduced in importance, at least so far as it is variable. The Union Jack has value only for those who are familiar with a particular convention; and to those who do know this it may have very different values—for Lord Carson and Mr. de Valera, for example. Yet even here the value is constitutive in so far as the flag is only made for the sake of the value. But in the symbolism of Art and Conduct there is no such variability. Men may still react in varying degrees of intensity to the different embodiments of value; some are more stirred by colour; some more by line; some are more stirred by heroic energy, some more by patient humility. But at this level there is no doubt what is the value expressed in the work of art or the moral action.

If we start with this principle of symbolism as our basis, we shall not, I think, be led to any system very different in the greater part of its structure from such as is set out, for example, by Professor Pringle-Pattison. The difference will be mainly one of emphasis and of detailed expression; but the difference of this kind will be all-pervasive. In ways innumerable the statement will be (as I think) more luminous in detail, more sympathetic. There will be more understanding of the different phases of Reality from the inside. For it is the characteristic of aesthetic and moral appreciation that in them we become absorbed in the object itself, as a single whole, and understand it by letting it take possession of us, whereas in science we understand partly by setting the object in an ever-widening context and learning what forces mould it from without, and partly by breaking it up analytically into its own constituent elements. Of course our method will not dispense with the processes and results of science; but it will depend quite equally, or rather more, on those of art and morality. We shall not dispense with the psychologist or sociologist; but we shall expect to learn still more of philosophic value from the dramatist and the statesman. We shall still seek rational coherence, but shall interpret it more as realised in the *Civitas Dei* than as represented by the solution of logical contradiction.[1]

[1] This essay does not profess or attempt to supply, even in outline, the system of philosophy here desiderated; it deals with a small part of the field—the part which I believe to be of central and pivotal importance.

We said earlier that contemporary philosophy manifests a high degree of tension between Value and Existence. Perhaps no writer has expressed this with so great vehemence as Miguel da Unamuno in *The Tragedy of Life*. It will be among the advantages of a Value-philosophy that, if it can make good its position at all, it will remove this tension. But it must rest on real values and not on any general theory of Value. It is here that the intellectualist tradition has most damaged philosophy. Discussions of Good in general carry us but a little way. Light comes from the study of the actual good things. This involves an element of unwelcome dogmatism, for our estimate of the various good things cannot claim universal acceptance. It is partly for this reason that philosophers have shrunk from taking their stand firmly on certain traditional scales of Value, such, for example, as that of Christianity. But when we find a philosopher who does this we are at once aware of a greater solidity and richness in his treatment of his problem; it is enough to cite in illustration Solovyof's great book *The Justification of Good*. The philosopher who makes value his central principle must take the risk of dogmatism and base himself on some selected actual values, vindicating his selection as fully as he can; he will gain in concrete fullness enough to justify the risk.

Above all he will avoid two difficulties that are inherent in the more traditional method of philosophy. We shall not try to treat the merely physical as self-subsistent, leaving values to attach themselves to it in a rather vague manner, while still declaring that the explanation of the lower is in the higher; but making this declaration, we shall insist that the higher are the more nearly self-subsisting, while only the Highest is altogether so. And we shall not leave God to hover uncertainly between His function as the universal ground of existence and His adjectival attachment to the universe as the sum or realisation of its values, but we shall confidently affirm Him as the sole self-subsistent Being, existing in absolute independence of all else, for whose pleasure and by whose creative activity all things are and were created.

CHAPTER II

THE APPREHENSION OF VALUE

Ὁ δὴ διώκει μὲν ἄπασα ψυχὴ καὶ τούτου ἕνεκα πάντα πρ.ίττει, ἀπομαντευομένη τι εἶναι.—PLATO.

IT is in Man that the sense of Value seems first to become distinct. Other animals have appreciation, and even a rudimentary sense of duty. But it seems certain that only in Man is there a distinct awareness of good and evil as principles, and not only of particular good and evil things. If our whole position is sound, then all things exist either for their own value or else for the sake of something else that has value. Whether that is so or not, certainly human conduct is all directed to the attainment of value. Many of men's activities have indeed no value in themselves, but these are undertaken for the sake of value which it is hoped to realise by means of them.

The distinction of means and ends in this connexion must be employed with some caution. It appears to suggest that what is classified as " means " is irrelevant to the good desired, except as a completely external condition. So it sometimes is. Thus a man may take up an occupation which he dislikes, and which he believes to do no good to any one, in order to make money which he may spend either on his pleasure or on work which he does believe to benefit mankind. Such an occupation is for that man a mere means, having no value in itself, and not affecting the value of the end. More commonly, however, there is some value inherent in the means; and even when this is not so, the value of the end is affected by the process of its attainment. It is commonly said that men do not value what costs them nothing; and though many applications of this principle are rather ludicrous, it is a sound principle. It may be true that many people enjoy a concert more if they have paid for their seats than if they have not; if so, this is only because the fact of payment has suggested an expectation of enjoyment and has thus stimulated sensitiveness. But where the cost is not a mere payment as a condition of the experience, but an effort or sacrifice directly undertaken for the sake of the desired end, it is found to affect very intimately the experience in which the desired end consists. Perhaps a part of the secret of maternal love is to be found here. But the principle is certainly true. No one can really see the view from a mountain top who has not actually climbed the mountain; the man who goes up in a mountain-railway may enjoy the view in his own way, but it is a different way.

To this group of considerations we must return when we come to discuss the relation of the Time-process to our apprehension of Value. At present it is enough to make clear the danger of separating means and ends in our estimate of the value of ends. The means may have no value in itself, and yet may increase the value of the end which is reached through it.

It is, of course, in ends alone that value actually resides. Many activities or experiences which are chosen as means to others also have value in themselves; but to this extent they become ends. To ask, then, what are the various kinds of Value and to ask what are the possible ends of life is to ask the same question in different words. To that question we now turn.

Value is recognised by a sense of kinship or "at-homeness" which we may call satisfaction. Where a man claims to find this, his claim cannot be disputed. To every man his own sense of value is final. This does not involve anarchy or chaos, as will become plain shortly; even if it did, the fact would stand.

But though value is recognised by a sense of satisfaction it does not consist in this satisfaction. Satisfaction is an indispensable element in the experience of value, but its prominence is very variable, and the amount of our nature affected by the satisfaction is also very variable. In Pleasure (as ordinarily understood—that is in isolated moments or periods of satisfaction) the subjective element is extremely prominent, and the area of satisfaction is comparatively small; if it is Pleasure pure and simple, the good experienced *is* the feeling, and the satisfaction is of feeling only. No doubt most pleasures are also something more than pleasure pure and simple, and all forms of value are pleasurable when appreciated. But there are some forms of good, deliberately adjudged to be good and deliberately chosen, in which the element of pleasure is almost non-existent, while pain is very prominent. Of such a good we may say what George Eliot's Romola says of the highest happiness, " We only know it from pain by its being what we would choose before everything else, because our souls see it is good."

Pleasures of sense afford the minimum of satisfaction though they may occasion the maximum of excitement. Very different are the pleasures of Pride. Here the subjective element counts for less and the objective for more; but the subjective is still conspicuous. The objective element is here dependent on a comparison or a contrast. The value in pleasures of sense is absolute in the sense that it is wholly independent of other experiences; it is made comparative by circumstances, when we have to choose between such a pleasure and some other end in comparison with which the value of the pleasure may be great or small. But the value of a bodily pleasure in itself is what it is. The value of the pleasures of Pride is comparative essentially; or rather, the occasion of such pleasure is a comparison. A man enjoys being richer than some one else, or cleverer, or better skilled in some game or art; or not being one of these he aims at it, knowing that to achieve it will bring him pleasure. Here again, the good or value is the subjective state, or feeling; but it is (or may be) the self as a whole that is satisfied. Ambition is, as a rule, very largely the desire to reach this kind of good. People who, when they play games, care very much whether they win or lose, show that in their games at least they are seeking a comparative value. These values are in their influence anti-social, because the success of one must involve the failure of others.

Of the values of Pleasure or Pride it cannot be said that they represent the end for which the world was made; nor can it be supposed that the Creator finds satisfaction in the attainment of them by His creatures. Pleasure indeed may find a subordinate place in a perfect life, adding to it a certain flavour; the pleasures of Pride may stimulate a sluggish soul to activity, but are really the product of that perverted use of self-consciousness which is called the Fall of Man. We have not yet reached the type of Value of which we could say in the first chapter that it is the real cause of the world's existence. This is Absolute Value, which is known to us in the three forms of Truth, Beauty, and Goodness (of character).[1]

If a man says that he does not see why he should want to know the Truth, or to appreciate Beauty, no argument can persuade him; if a man says he does not see why he ought to be good, no argument can persuade him. "Good" and "ought" are correlative terms: good is what a man ought to be, and a man's obligation is to be good. And "good" in man

---

[1] I keep the familiar trio of terms, but Truth is here a confusing word, as Canon Quick has pointed out to me. Truth is the perfect correlation of mind to reality, and is not itself, therefore, apprehended as an object in the same way as (e.g.) Beauty. What is really intended is that there are three forms of absolute value—intellectual, aesthetic, and moral.

includes at least some adjustment towards Truth and Beauty. Value includes more than the characters of good men, so that these other two must be named side by side with Good. But they are not three Absolute Values; they are three forms of the One Absolute Value, which is Love; this uses each of the three as its channel to reveal and communicate itself. " The effort of the soul to attain unity with other souls, and supremely with God, is the final value or reality possible to that soul." [1]

Truth is the end of the intellect; man does think, and he may think right or wrong; to think right is to attain truth so far as his thought has gone. Men always desire to reach some truth, for their plans will break down if they are calculated on a basis of error; but this is to desire truth as a means, not as an end. To desire truth as an end is to desire the perfect correlation of the mind to Reality. And this is a good in itself, so clearly a good as to impose upon all who have understood its nature an obligation to seek it. The end is not to acquire masses of information, though that may be a means to the end and must be included in it, if it is perfectly attained; the end is perfect intellectual correlation with Reality.

The general nature of Beauty I have discussed elsewhere and can only give here a dogmatic re-statement of the position there reached.[2] Beauty is the perfect (*i.e.* truly adequate) expression of the value of any truth or fact. Thus it is closely related to Truth and has the same logical structure. It appeals, as Truth does not, to feeling; and this appeal may be so predominant that there is no intellectual element traceable at all at first sight. But in fact this element is always there in the shape of proportion, or rhythm, or grouping, or some other kind of diversity in unity. To make Beauty the end

---

[1] I owe this sentence to my friend the Rev. L. W. Grensted.
[2] See the chapter on " The Nature and Significance of Art " in *Mens Creatrix*.

of any activity is to seek a perfect correlation of feeling with the various values of what is apprehended by consciousness. The Value may be in the thought rather than in the expression as such, as it is in great poetry; but apart from the expression there is no beauty—indeed the thought only becomes fully actual in the expression. Hence Beauty, strictly speaking, concerns what is apprehended by means of the senses, though what is so apprehended may be far more than sensuous.

Goodness (of character) is the perfect correlation of all the elements of personality into one whole, and of that whole with its environment, especially its personal environment. This also I have discussed at length elsewhere,[1] and must handle again repeatedly in later chapters.

The mere statement of what Truth, Beauty, and Goodness are as ends of action is enough to show that their Value is both inherent and absolute. It is inherent inasmuch as they are plainly good in themselves, it is absolute inasmuch as it depends on no comparison. Also it is social, for its attainment by one does not hinder but greatly helps in its attainment by others. Self is here a mere receptivity; any emphasis on it or concern about it will assuredly prevent a full apprehension of Truth or Beauty or Goodness. But this does not mean that the self is merely passive. On the contrary, it is intensely active; but its activity is mainly receptive, at least in its apprehensions of Truth and of Beauty, and its attention is concentrated utterly on the object, not at all on itself. But the satisfaction is of the whole self, entire and complete.

Thus we reach a principle of great practical and theoretical importance; the self is capable of complete satisfaction in proportion as it is left outside the field

---

[1] See *Mens Creatrix*, Part III. But there I based duty far too exclusively (as I now think) on social relationships. I should now contend that obligation is the correlate of value—absolute obligation of absolute value.

of its own attention.[1] Value exists for subjects; but the subject finds the value only when completely absorbed in the object.

It may seem that although ideal Truth, Beauty, and Goodness are absolute values, yet they can never be actually experienced as such by us. To some extent this is so with Truth, but it is not so with Beauty. To see this we have only to consider the methods of Science and of Art. Science is discursive and analytical. It seeks to understand the object of its study either by breaking it up into its component parts and showing how these fit together, or by setting it in an ever wider context, asking Why? and of the answer asking Why? again. But no limit can be set to either of these processes, and therefore completeness is never reached. If all Reality is one, this means that no knowledge of any department can be absolute.[2] An apparent exception is Mathematics; but Mathematics reaches its perfect cogency by an abstraction so complete that it may be said to have turned its back on Reality and to be a science of notions only. The internal angles of a triangle are equal to two right angles; that is absolute truth, but only because the meaning of " triangle " and " right angle " is fixed by definition. To know this does not give us any absolute knowledge of any object existing in space, it gives us absolute knowledge only of the implications of our definitions. Only in this sphere of abstractions is absolute knowledge attainable. Truth claims our allegiance but always eludes our

---

[1] In other words, joy is the fruit of humility. But I use the word " joy " in its Christian sense, which is not always that associated with it in psychological works.

[2] In *Mens Creatrix* I pressed this to the paradoxical extremity of allowing no finality to any knowledge at all, short of omniscience; this I should now repudiate. But it remains true that the search for Truth leads to the apprehension of an ever-widening context, so that it never affords the finite mind any such repose of satisfaction as may be reached in the search for Beauty. I should like to take this opportunity of recommending readers of *Mens Creatrix* to consider the searching criticism of some of its positions contained in Professor A. E. Taylor's review of that book in *Mind*, N.S. 106. Some of his objections are due to misapprehension of my meaning: some now seem to me to be valid.

grasp; but the intellectual correlation with Reality can be perfect in the sense that the mind is always ready to apprehend rightly even though there is much which is in fact not yet apprehended.

The apprehension of Beauty proceeds by another method. Here attention is narrowly concentrated upon some one object; the understanding of it that is sought consists in intimacy of acquaintance, not in completeness of analysis. For this reason the artist must select. We cannot achieve an intimate acquaintance with a vast range of facts. Selection must go to the point where apprehension is possible in one act—however prolonged—of concentrated attention. We must be able to see the whole picture at once, and not have to piece it together by a deliberate mental construction. This limits the scope of apprehensible Beauty, but it also means that an absolute apprehension of absolute Beauty is possible for us. For though there may be a richer Beauty apprehensible to beings with a wider range of faculties, yet because concentration and not discursiveness is the essence of aesthetic method, there can be an experience of Beauty which is perfect in its own kind. Homer's material is less rich and varied than Shakespeare's, but Shakespeare has not made Homer out of date; that simpler material will only exhibit its value to him who concentrates his attention on it alone. There is, therefore, possible to us an absolute apprehension of absolute Beauty such as is not possible of absolute Truth.

The same is true of Goodness; but here our task is not so much to admire Goodness elsewhere as to create it in ourselves. Man's obligation is not chiefly to admire goodness but to be good. And this consists, as has been said and as will be set forth at more length shortly, in the achievement of internal and external unity. If a man's whole being is organised to the fulfilment of one purpose, and that purpose is the fulfilment of his contribution to the universal good, he has reached perfect goodness. He has no need to be omniscient for this. If he can regard his life not from the standpoint of self-interest, but from that of God who looks upon the whole society of men from without, so that he is perfectly just not only in conscience, but even in desire, and can perfectly control his impulses to live according to such a view of his place in the scheme of things, he is a perfectly good man.

Thus the whole Truth of God could not find expression in a human life, but the perfection of intellectual virtue[1] can do so; the whole of apprehensible Beauty could not be concentrated in one human consciousness, though perfect Beauty of many kinds and grades can be realised there; the whole Goodness of God can in its completeness be expressed in a human life. We do not now discuss what conditions are requisite for this to happen; we are only concerned at present to assert its possibility in principle.

Truth, Beauty, and Goodness are all absolute Values; they are good in themselves, apart from all consequences. But they may in experience become rivals through force of circumstance; there may be insufficient time for the fulfilment of some apparent social duty as well as for complete dedication to Science or to Art. Where such a choice has to be made, no man may judge his brother. But in principle Goodness has a priority over the other two because it is the distinctively human type of value and we are human. Indeed when we follow after Truth and Beauty with an absolute devotion, if we are not neglecting some other and yet stronger claim, we are manifesting Goodness. But it is possible to pursue these selfishly, not for their absolute value but for our own pleasure alike in the pursuit and the attainment; and then our

---

[1] *I.e.* the readiness of the mind to apprehend rightly whatever it may have the opportunity to apprehend.

conduct is wrong; for we are not responding to any absolute obligation but to our own desire for our own enjoyment. Goodness cannot be so pursued. We may do the acts of goodness from selfish motives— desire for admiration or fear of censure. But goodness of character itself must be sought for itself or it is not sought at all. Truth and Beauty are absolute values, and it is good that we should seek them; but they are not distinctively human; Truth we apprehend but do not create; Beauty we both appreciate and create, but appreciation predominates, for much of the Beauty of the world exists apart from our production of it, and so far as our activity creates Beauty, it is largely imitative. It is true, indeed, that appreciation is a very real activity, and I believe that it is in fact an activity of discovering in Art or in Nature the kindred spirit of the Artist (Divine or human) there self-expressed; and the essential moment in creation and appreciation of Beauty is this expression and recognition of spirit.[1] It remains true, however, that appreciation is not creation. But Goodness, in the whole world so far as we know it, is a human creation; here, too, we appreciate and imitate. But each man must live his own life; imitation should never predominate; and moral goodness is an achievement of mankind, so that if we take mankind as a unit we find here an original contribution to the scheme of things, where no imitation is possible except of God Himself.

We have now considered various types of Value, and must proceed to ask what is the nature of Value itself. If our whole position is sound, no definition is possible; you cannot state the *Genus* and *Differentia* of your highest principle. But characteristics can be stated. We find, then, that for any actual Value or Good there must be two factors in a certain relationship—the " valuable " object and the apprehending

---

[1] Cf. Balfour, *Theism and Humanism*, pp. 55-94, specially 77-81.

and appreciating subject; and these must meet in an experience which "satisfies" or is fit for permanence. We shall see later that only the " good " character affords the inner condition of permanence on the subjective side, so that the apparent actualisation of Value represented by base pleasures is illusory. We shall further see that the " good " character is one which has achieved inner and outer totality or comprehensive unity; the objects which such a character accounts " valuable " are found to have this same quality; they are all marked by totality. Science seeks a totality of perpetually wider extension; Art seeks a totality of perfected inner unity; Goodness is the achievement of inner unity in the individual and extended unity in the society—totality in both. Value, in short, is a system of experience in which a subject free from inner causes of change finds satisfaction in an object which (therefore) it does not seek to change. Its type is God's eternal contemplation of His perfect work. It is not a relation of subject and object or of object and object; it is a unitary system of experience in which such relations have their place. Because it is a subject-object system, perfectly co-related, the object must reveal the characteristics of Mind and the subject must be absorbed in the object. Hence springs the demand for intellectual or logical structure in works of Art. Mind discovers itself in the Real, and in the discovery becomes its full self: that is Value or Good. But Mind will only perfectly discover itself in other minds; therefore Fellowship is the true norm of Value, and Love its perfect realisation.

One other consideration claims attention — the relation of Value to the Time-process. Many of the highest values are found in activities or experiences lasting through considerable periods of time—presumably the highest of all is in the experience which comprehends the whole range of Time and Space.

D

When we study the experiences in which our finite minds can apprehend Value and which require a process of time for their actualisation—such as a drama or a man's life or a nation's history—we find that the value of the whole is by no means the same as the total or the average of all its stages. Thus we may consider two plays in three acts: in one the first act is cheerful, the second neutral, the third depressing; here the total effect is depressing. In the other the first act is full of gloom, the second shows a dawn of hope, and the third is joyful; here the whole effect is triumphant. The Value of an experience lasting through a period of time depends on its tendency and conclusion, not upon the stages in isolation.

This carries with it the supremely important principle that, though past facts cannot be altered, their value can, so that the presence of evil in the world at any moment or through any period of time is not in principle any argument against the perfect goodness of the Whole.

That is a consideration of supreme importance, because of the close relationship that exists between Value and Totality. In all Value, as we saw just now, Totality is the distinguishing feature. Totality is the very form of the Good; this is the " perfection " of which St. Thomas speaks in the words quoted above.[1] But the Whole, for us, is the Will of God and what it has created; therefore every apprehension of Value is in principle a religious experience. Hocking[2] argues that in our sense perception of Nature there is already an apprehension of God. I think this is true. Certainly there is no apprehension of Value which is not an inchoate apprehension of God —and no human experience is utterly without value.

[1] Cf. p. 14.
[2] *Op. cit.* pp. 268-300, specially pp. 297, 298.

CHAPTER III

> Those obstinate questionings
> Of sense and outward things,
> Fallings from us, vanishings;
> Blank misgivings of a Creature
> Moving about in worlds not realised,
> High instincts before which our mortal Nature
> Did tremble like a guilty Thing surprised.
>
> WORDSWORTH.

To be conscious of absolute value and the absolute obligation which it imposes is plainly a direct awareness of something ultimate in the universe; and if the position already taken up with regard to Value is correct, then it is a direct awareness of what in all creation is most fundamental. It is a consciousness of the very object of the Creative Will; it is thus of itself a knowledge of God.

But for a vast multitude of people it not only is, but is directly experienced as being, a knowledge of God. All men have conscience; that is, all men to some extent judge their actual character and conduct by comparison with an ideal formed from their sense of absolute goodness. Many men experience this ideal as God's will for them; and so conscience becomes the channel of religious experience. It is so that religious experience comes to most men, at any rate to most men born and brought up in a Christian civilisation. Among primitive peoples, perhaps, it is the sense of vastness rather than the sense of value that chiefly leads to a sense of the divine power; man

35

finds himself very small and helpless in face of a world vast and unaccountable, and he imagines spirits, mostly hostile, who must be endlessly placated. He is not utterly wrong; he is applying very crudely the conviction that only Will adequately accounts for anything. And the influence of his mental attitude still persists; in face of great manifestations of natural forces, especially in face of great calamities, men begin to speak of the Hand of God, who never use such phrases about small events or trace His Hand in the movement of the tides or the phases of the moon. But when once the influence of that ethical mono-theism, which came to the world through Israel, has taken possession of men's minds, the normal channel for religious experience is conscience.[1]

It is necessary to insist on this, for some psycho-logists have tended to confine the phrase " religious experience " to moments of personal awareness of the presence of God. Of course they are perfectly at liberty to study such momentary experiences in isolation; but they must not suppose or suggest that these moments constitute the whole or even the chief part of the " religious experience " on which religious men rely as part of the confirmatory evidence for their beliefs. William James, in his celebrated *Varieties of Religious Experience*, is a conspicuous offender in this matter. Philosophers have encouraged the same bad tendency, for they have often drawn their illustrations of religious experience exclusively from the mystics. Mysticism is indeed the extreme development of

---

[1] Conscience, at its fullest development, passes into Love, but stages below that level of supreme attainment must be included here.

This book was already in proof before I read Rudolf Otto's important study of *The Idea of the Holy* (*Das Heilige*). I think he makes good his contention that there is something ultimate in religious experience, of which the nature may be expressed in the phrase " Mysterium Tremendum." Deity presents itself as in one aspect " wholly other " and thus utterly unintelligible; and the human response is " awe " or " dread." But my own experience of this, which Otto calls the Numinous, is chiefly occasioned (apart from the Gospel story) by the Vastness of the Universe and the Authority of the Moral Law. So it was, of course, for Kant; and so it is, I believe, for most persons in a reflective age.

religion pure and simple; but just because it is religion pure and simple, it is on one side unrepresentative of religion. For religion is not departmental; it takes life as a whole for its sphere; and " religious experience " is not an affair of isolated moments, it is a whole experience of life and the world, permeated through and through with religion. In certain moments, no doubt, the whole significance of this is gathered up; but those moments derive the greater part of their importance from the fact that they neither are, nor are thought to be, isolated or unique in kind; they are important precisely because they bring to clear and vivid consciousness what is permanently present as a background to all experience.

To the religious man every activity is religious. He eats and drinks religiously, of which " grace " at meals is the symbol; he works religiously, for his work is his life-service to God; he plays religiously, for his recreation is with thanksgiving; but above all he sins religiously. To do wrong is for an irreligious man to abandon his ideal and perhaps to lower his self-respect. For the religious man to do wrong is to defy his King; for the Christian, it is to wound his Friend. It is here that for many people the distinctively religious experience is most acute.

But the validity of this experience is challenged as the validity of other experience is not challenged. The validity of sight is not challenged, though we do not always believe that a man actually saw what he seemed to himself to see. Here, however, it appears that the whole validity is challenged; we are told by some that the religious experience is purely subjective and has no counterpart in the objective world at all, while others, who stop short of that, would say that, though the experience has an objective counterpart, this is not in the least what religious people have supposed it to be.

It is not possible here to discuss the psychology of

religious experience; but it is necessary to describe the attitude adopted towards it in this argument. First, then I would say that in all perceptive experience there is an apprehension of a given somewhat; we do not have experiences and infer the object which occasions them; the experience *is* the apprehension of the object. But this does not tell us beyond all question what the object is; that is a matter for a reflective and critical process, which always goes beyond what can be said to be immediately given in perception. But though it goes beyond what is immediately given, it does not go away from it; on the contrary it interprets what it truly is. Moreover, all our experience contains this element of interpretation from the outset. We never experience a mere " This." The reflective process may be very elaborate, as it is in a fully developed science; but it is not a process of theorising about a given and unchanging fact at an ever greater distance from it; it is the ever fuller articulation of what the fact has been from the first. In these respects there is no difference in principle between religious experience and any other experience which claims by its nature to be an apprehension of reality.

Secondly, however, we have to admit that this experience has to vindicate itself against the charge of illusion, which is brought here and is not brought against the experience of sight and hearing. Psychologists are ready to provide a variety of accounts of the process whereby the religious experience is generated in the soul. And if the weight of the general philosophic argument were plainly adverse to the theistic interpretation of the world, I should, for myself, consider that a case for it could hardly be made out from the data of specifically religious experience alone. But in fact the weight of the general philosophic argument tells, in my judgement, decisively the other way; I should say this even if the specific religious experience were excluded from consideration in the formulation of this general philosophic argument, though to exclude it is plainly unscientific. When we find that the general argument points to the existence of God, we are naturally more ready to pay a specially serious attention to such experience as seems to those, to whom it comes, to be a direct apprehension of the divine. The true case for Theism does not rest upon general philosophy alone nor upon religious experience alone, but upon the coincidence or convergence of these two.

Our general position, then, with regard to religious experience will be that it must, indeed, be examined and tested like any other experience for which the claim is made that in it we apprehend reality, but that there is no objection in principle to this claim when made for this type of experience.

The objection is usually based on the supposition that some men have no religious experience at all. But this is very doubtful and seems even to be false. There are many men who pay little attention to their religious experience, and in whom (often for that reason) it is rudimentary; there are many who do not recognise it for what it is. But it is doubtful if any man can go through life without ever feeling reverence for something which is morally so high above him as to be out of his reach, or awe before the great Reality on which he is utterly dependent. And it may safely be said that no one escapes, though he may to his own satisfaction explain away, the sense of absolute obligation. All of these are in their true nature religious experiences—the recognition of an Absolute. To understand them fully will of itself carry a man far into theology. If his reverence and his awe are justified, they imply a Reality fit to be their occasion. If he is genuinely subject to the obligation, that implies a universe in which obligation has a place. Of all the various forms of undeveloped or unsophisti-

cated religious experience, this sense of absolute obligation is the most certainly universal and the most
commonly recognised. It is on this, therefore, that
our argument will chiefly rest.

The absolute obligation due to the absolute Value
of Truth and Beauty is a command of God and a
means of access to Him; but it is in the claim of
Goodness that this command is most universally found
and the access to God most fully effected. Truth has
its necessary place, for all religious life involves some
belief, and that belief is a theology and philosophy.
Beauty has its place, for there must be expression of
our faith and adoration; and what adequately expresses
these must be beautiful. But Goodness comes first
because we are men, and Goodness is the value which is
actualised by men alone, and is therefore the specific
human value; thus it is the Truth or Reality of man,
and may be described as Truth expressed, and so made
beautiful, in human life.

That does not mean that religion can rightly
become an affair of well-doing only. If a man has
found God as his King and Father, or rather has been
found of Him, God becomes the chief factor in his
environment, and there must be activities directly
expressive of relationship to Him. Worship comes
first, then service inspired by worship; prayer first,
then conduct. It will help to make clear the nature
of religious experience and its relation to some kindred
forms of experience if we set out this point more fully,
though in doing so we must draw on forms of religious
experience which imply theological or metaphysical
beliefs which have still to be justified.

Prayer is often regarded, even by genuinely religious
people, as chiefly a means to various ends; it is a way
of getting things done. That is true, so far as it
goes; but, like so many half-truths, it is in practice
as misleading as a complete falsehood. Prayer which
is mainly occupied with a result to be obtained is

comparatively powerless to obtain results. The real significance of prayer lies in the fact that it is the effort and attitude of the soul which makes possible the unity of the human spirit with God; it is therefore itself the supreme aim of human existence. Only when it is experienced and valued as itself the goal of life is its secondary quality, as producing results beyond itself, fully operative. For it is only then that the human spirit reaches the maturity of its powers; it is only then that the infinite resources of omnipotence can play upon the world through human instrumentality.

The essence of prayer is intercourse with God; and that is the goal of human evolution. By means of prayer we may sometimes obtain for ourselves or for others temporal benefits; we may lift ourselves or others above the range of some perilous temptation; we may help forward deserving causes; we may increase the volume of goodwill. But all of these, even the last, are secondary in nature and in importance. The primary and fundamental matter in every real prayer is that a human soul is once again, or perhaps for the first time, holding intercourse with its Father.

Religion thus comes into close contact with much that is seldom called religious. Science in its greatest phases is an intercourse of the mind of man with the Mind expressed in the universe. In philosophy a deliberate effort is undertaken to reach some degree of communion with the Absolute Mind or Spirit. A pupil of Edward Caird can confidently testify that the philosophic life may have in it more of real prayer than is to be found in very many devotional exercises. The artists and the poets perpetually rise to heights of spiritual achievement which supply a model to the religious aspirant.

Communion with the Eternal is probably not quite unknown to any human being. Whenever a man feels the constraint of moral obligation, he is in touch with the Eternal; for the maxim " because right is right to follow right " is no creature of Time.   But to most men the sphere in which, outside religion, this highest experience is most often reached is the sphere of art.   As one looks upon the picture, held fast in concentrated peace by its compelling beauty, he enters eternity; the whole period of his contemplation is, in Browning's phrase, a " moment eternal ": a moment, because there is no sense of duration; eternal, because the meaning of such an experience is a completed whole, which asks for no explanations from past origins or future destiny.   As we surrender ourselves to the surge of a great symphony, floating upon oceans of sound wherein the intertwined melodies and rhythms vanish in the mighty mass they constitute, the same experience is ours.   Not in spite of the storm and tumult but even because of it, we are at peace in our unity with the inner reality of all things.   In the climax of artistic endeavour—tragedy—this is most abundantly true.   The vast conflict rages, the over-powering emotions topple and sway, the catastrophe crashes down and crushes out the hero with both his ambitions and his agonies; but terror is redeemed by beauty, and the reader or spectator is established in a final peace which is not only untroubled but knows that nothing now can trouble it, because it has faced the worst and found therein occasion for its solemn joy.   In such an experience man shares in his tiny measure the august pastime of the Eternal.

In prayer that fulfils its function the religious man by his own methods scales those self-same heights. But there is a difference which makes the work of prayer more difficult, but also, when it is perfect, nobler.

The " cosmic consciousness," as it is sometimes called, may be induced by art in such a way as to omit all ethical or social content, and even so as to make us forgetful of moral obligation.   The man who is

entranced by music does not find himself brought by
his rapture into charity with all men; rather he finds
their vulgarity and obtuseness at such a time peculiarly
repellent. And though the aesthetic ecstasy is not
self-centred or selfish (for the initiate is far too absorbed
in what he contemplates through eyes or ears to attend
even to his own joy in contemplation), it is not social;
it is sub-personal. The qualities which make fellowship
a possibility are not exercised. There is no need for
human companionship in those moments; for comedy
we need companionship, but not for tragedy; the
heights to which we are called are austere in loneliness. And on these we find no one waiting for us.
Beethoven, perhaps, composed the symphony that
carries us into the sublimities; but we do not meet
him there and hold intercourse with him. Nothing
at all occurs to call our social qualities into play, nor
is there any place for the action of our wills.

In prayer the exact contrary is the fact. Not as
mere appreciative intelligences do we pray, but as
children who want to be with their Father, as friends
who must mark off certain times to enjoy the company
of their Friend. This Father is the composer of the
music of the spheres; this Friend is the author of the
tremendous drama of history. To enter into His
mind is to be on the high places to which art aspires;
but it is to be there in company. This method only
leads us to its goal as we become one in moral character
with God; for this is partly the meaning and partly the
result of being in the company of God. Only the
pure in heart can see Him; only by longing for Him
do men become pure in heart; only by His own impulse do men begin to long for Him. Prayer is a
correspondence with the impulse of God to draw us
to Himself.

If God were merely the Mind which grasps the
universe as a single intelligible whole, prayer and
philosophy would be indistinguishable. But even

philosophy knows that He must be more than that.
If He is to supply the principle whereby the universe
is an intelligible whole at all, He must be the source
of righteousness no less than of truth and of beauty.
Correspondence with His impulse therefore involves
righteousness of will.   This is one reason why prayer
is a harder way of ascent to the spiritual heights than
philosophy or art; it is also one reason why the achievement, if attained, is nobler.   A completer humanity
is carried to the lofty regions.   By this method there
can be no ecstasy that is devoid of charity.   For God
is Love; and only by love do men draw near to Him.
None can come into that Presence for his own benefit
alone.   The key that unlocks the door of the presence-
chamber is love, without which all vitality of understanding and sensibility is accounted death.

From this two conclusions follow.   A self-centred
devotion, or a religious life which has self-perfection
as its goal, can never reach the innermost shrine of
divine communion.   Rather there is required of us
a love so intense that it will not let us enter that shrine
and dwell there until all others are won to enter also.
Here is one of the divine paradoxes.   To be in heaven
is to be with God; and God is Love; so that whoever
loves most is most in heaven.   Yet love, which admits
to heaven, will not let us dwell in heaven while there
are still men on earth who have no desire for heaven.
In the crucial instance we know that this is true.   God
is never so much God as in the moment when, accepting
the world's load of evil, He feels Himself to be deserted
by God.

And secondly, because there is work to do in
bringing others to desire the Life Divine, true prayer
is always accompanied by appropriate conduct.   Indeed,
if prayer and conduct are both perfect, no distinction
can be drawn between them.   But those who live
at various levels of imperfection know from their own
experience the difference between the times when

their whole attention is concentrated on God Himself and the times when their attention is concentrated on some task which is believed to be appointed them by Him.

The Western mind sets great store by doing; and it is right. But it is not so wholly right that it can afford to ignore the witness of the East to the primacy of Being. We tend to test all energies by their results in conduct. If prayer makes men lead better lives—by which most people mean, do better deeds— then it is justified; if not, it is a harmless occupation, provided that the time allowed to it is not excessive. So men often think, and sometimes say. But in simple truth, prayer—the corresponding of men with God's impulse to draw them to Himself—is the highest occupation in which a man can be engaged. That is not to say that endlessly " saying prayers " or joining in forms of worship is of this dignity. It may be so; and where the spirit of true prayer breathes through the words and ritual acts it is so; but there are many who in their worship are not opening their souls to the divine influence, and are rather indulging a religious sentiment than conforming their wills to God. Such worshippers correspond to the sensualists who make their artistic skill play pander to the baser passions. " By their fruits ye shall know them." Does their religious emotion leave them in charity with all men? A man or woman who has merely been indulging a religious sentiment will be censorious towards what clashes with that sentiment—coarseness, vulgarity, blatancy. A man or woman who has been in communion with perfect Love is filled with love— at least in greater measure than before—towards all to whom the Love Divine goes forth.

So the proper relation in thought between prayer and conduct is not that conduct is supremely important and prayer may help it, but that prayer is supremely important and conduct tests it. If the prayer is real,

the conduct inevitably follows.   Indeed, in many cases
the very reality of prayer will shorten the time allotted
to prayer, so strong will be the impulse of love to act
for the well-being of others.   But let any man who
finds it thus with him take heed.   The life with God
is the supreme concern, and the source of all power
to serve.   It is only the man who loves God with all
his being who will be able to love his neighbour as
himself.

PART II

INNER CIRCLE

CHAPTER IV

THE NATURE OF MAN

" What a piece of work is a man! how noble in reason! how infinite in faculty! in form and moving how express and admirable! in action how like an angel! in apprehension how like a god! the beauty of the world! the paragon of animals! " —SHAKESPEARE.

THE structure of Reality as outlined in our first chapter is most fully illustrated—within our experience—by Man. It is possible, or at least arguable, that Man does not represent the fullest development hitherto of one line of evolution, but is rather the representative of one among several lines. Thus it may be that Bergson is right in refusing to regard intelligence as in any way superior to instinct, and in maintaining that these two terms express different and largely incompatible lines of evolution.[1] The higher animals should in that case not be regarded as of necessity " lower " than man; they may be, at least biologically, at an equally advanced stage on another line of development. Yet it still remains true that, within our experience, human nature is the fullest illustration. In our bodies we belong to the physical, chemical, vegetable, and animal worlds; these bodies are largely directed by our minds or intelligences; our minds are capable of being directed by spirit, or, in other words, of exerting themselves in ·the fulfilment of obligation. We shall therefore learn more about the true nature and meaning of Reality from the study of

[1] *L'Évolution créatrice*, pp. 146 ff.

E

man, in all his activities, than from any other study; and human nature will be more capable of expressing the Creative Will than any other created thing known to us. How far it may be capable of this, our study of man must help us to determine.

As we ascend in the scale of complexity or richness of being, the most important transition is that from Thing to Person.[1] The Thing has these three characteristics: (*a*) it has no significant individuality, (*b*) it acts only as it is impelled from without, (*c*) it has no sentience or point of view. It is easy to illustrate these points: (*a*) no doubt every brick in a heap has some real *differentia*, whereby it is distinguished from every other brick, but this is (so to speak) external and irrelevant—it is the third or the ninety-seventh to pass through its particular mould as compared with the sixth or the eighty-fifth. Its material or the fashion of its baking may have made it a bad brick— porous or in some other way defective; but even then its badness is thought of as typical rather than indi- vidual. One brick does as well as another of the same pattern, unless it be faulty; and then it is only *a* bad brick. The individuality of the brick does not count. (*b*) Similarly it cannot direct its own motion. If the billiard-table is flat and the ball round, the ball will remain still until it is struck and will then follow the line imposed upon it by the impinging body— the cue or another ball; and if the ball rolls without being struck, it must be either because the table is not flat or because the ball is not round, and its motion is a mere instance of the general law of gravitation. (*c*) Consequently, having neither individuality nor self-direction, the thing has no sentience or point of view. A cricketer feels no moral obligation to keep his bat out of the way of a fast ball for fear lest the violent impact may hurt the ball. He takes it for

[1] Cf. my lectures on *The Nature of Personality* for a more detailed exposition of this point.

granted—not that he is under no obligation to consider the ball's point of view but—that the ball has no point of view which even could be considered.

As we pass from the purely physical and chemical world to the vegetable world, we find the beginnings of self-motion in the phenomenon of growth. There is in the vegetable a principle which determines its reaction to environment, so that from the same soil and the same water two plants draw the nourishment of quite different forms of foliage and the like. As we pass to the animal world, the power of self-motion is completely present, and variety in modes of reaction is still richer; moreover sentience has appeared, and with it a " point of view "—both of which are generally assumed to be lacking in vegetables. We assume (rightly or wrongly) that a plant suffers no pain when its flowers are picked, and it seems certain that any sentience there is must be quite rudimentary;[1] but the animal is capable of pleasure and pain; which immediately involves the obligation to consider its point of view in the treatment of it. A man may pick a flower off a plant solely to please himself; but he must not pull the head off a kitten or even the wings off a fly. And with sentience appears the beginning of real Individuality. Of course in a purely logical sense every existent thing is an individual—that is, it is a particular instance of some general kind. And every division of reality will always leave individuals; no process of analysis can get behind individuality. But in the lower stages the particular or distinctive element is almost negligible; in the extreme instance it is reduced to mere This-ness. Among animals the distinctive character of the particular animal may be as marked as its generic qualities. Every one who has enjoyed the friendship of a dog or cat knows this.

---

[1] In the border cases—such as the Rotifer or the Fly-catcher—we generally assume some rudimentary sentience as a concomitant of the rudimentary power of self-motion.

Certainly among human beings the distinctive qualities of each are fully as important as the generic qualities. It is only ignorance or laziness that leads people to speak in generic terms about groups of individuals, as if in that way something very important could be said. There is a real group consciousness; but this does not mean a uniform type of consciousness endlessly reproduced in all the individuals of the group. Individuality is one of the dominant elements in the Nature of Man; and the more that any one is truly individual, so much the more is he truly human. The justification for this proposition will become apparent as we proceed; the proposition itself is of fundamental importance for ethics and politics.

The greater prominence of individuality in human nature as compared with other types of existence known to us corresponds with, and is largely due to, the increased " time-span " possible from the " point of view " of a human being. We agree that an animal, being sentient, has a " point of view," involving a claim to consideration. But this seems to be limited to the present. A dog is indeed capable of something very like a " purpose " in his loyalty, which may rise even to devotion; but it seems likely that this only becomes apparent in the activities which it prompts, and is never present to the consciousness of the dog as a principle fitted to control all possible actions for an indefinite period of time. Consequently, while a dog may fairly be said to have a " character " and even " moral qualities," he cannot reasonably be said to have " moral principles." He has a memory, and can have hopes; but he has not (one supposes) an ideal towards which he constantly strives.

This capacity for forming ideals is distinctively human. In man we find not only a character which does in fact express itself in appropriate actions, but also an apprehension of principles by which it is recognised that conduct ought to be guided even if

in fact it is not so guided. This is made possible by
the capacity of the human mind to contemplate in
one act unlimited stretches of time, so that its generalis-
ations with regard to its own possible reactions to
circumstance can be really universal principles. Moreover, inasmuch as the mind both can and does apprehend
principles far beyond its present actual achievement,
the future (which we generally suppose to be present
in the vaguest form or not at all to the minds of
animals) becomes to man the predominant interest.
It is a distinguishing mark of full Personality that for
persons the future is more interesting and more
important than the past, or even the present.

It is because man is capable of ideals and principles
that he becomes a subject of Rights and Duties as
distinct from mere claims and counter-claims. The
sense of Obligation carries a man beyond the calculation of means devised for the realisation of ends which
are fixed by instinct or desire. It leads him to think
of himself as a person in a society of persons. Consequently the same qualities which make him supremely
individual stamp his individuality as fundamentally
and inherently social. If by the term Fellowship we
may denote the deliberate association of free persons,
then it is true to say that " Personality is the capacity
for Fellowship."

The uniqueness of individuality must not be interpreted as even a relative independence of environment.
Neither the mind nor the spirit of man has such independence. All our growth proceeds by reaction.
The word education means Nourishment.[1] Mental
like bodily nourishment depends upon the reception
of food from without, and the subsequent assimilation
of it. The mind quite as much as the body depends
on supplies from without. The main part of education is always the work of direct experience, and the
part of the educator is to select and, in some degree,

---

[1] *Educat nutrix.*

to mould the sort of experience by which the growing mind is to be influenced. Thus a good school is a highly artificial social organisation designed to promote full participation in social life, with its discipline of responsibility, at an age when apart from such a deliberate organisation real membership in a society is impossible. A child is not a full " member " of its family, for the child cannot have, and ought not to have, a responsibility similar to that of its parents. By deliberately constructing societies of children or of adolescents we make possible an educative experience that would otherwise be lacking. In addition to learning or growing by what may thus be described as in a special sense " its own " experience, the mind grows by intercourse with other minds more mature than itself. This intercourse it finds in its relations with parents, teachers, and the authors of books. But in all cases the two stages of the process are equally indispensable; nourishment must be both supplied and assimilated.

Every human mind is potentially a focussing point for the whole range of possible experience, that is of the whole universe. It will have its own angle of vision, its own dominant interests to guide its attention, its own order of experiencing different aspects of the world. But it is in potency a mirror for all reality; and it grows, not by isolation, but by receiving and assimilating perpetually greater wealth of experience.

Greatness of mind is therefore primarily a matter of receptivity. There is an average capacity for assimilating experience, and when there is some divergence from this, otherwise than by relative defect, we have originality. Sometimes this takes the form of special sensitiveness to a particular aspect of reality; then we have a one-sided development which, if it is sufficient, produces both the " genius " and the " freak." Sometimes it takes the form of a greater general sensitiveness, and then we find all-round " greatness."

The great man is not less dependent on his environment than others; he is dependent to exactly the same extent; but the environment on which he is dependent (or to which he is responsive) is greater. So he seems independent of circumstance, because he is comparatively unmoved by those changes and chances which profoundly disturb his neighbours. But the truth about him is a deeper and wider dependence, not a comparative independence. The great individual is not the man who grows in the nearest approach to isolation; whoever does this will remain the nearest approach to a perfect idiot; the great individual is the man who is reacting to the greatest number of the elements in Reality, the greatest variety of its aspects. If he could become apprehensive of all its Truth, appreciative of all its Beauty, worthy of all its Goodness —conducting a corresponding range of activities in perfect accord with his receptivity, he would be the ideally great man, the perfect individual.

It is clear that the relative importance and interest of the various elements in experience depend upon the other elements with which they are compared. To a child the smashing of a toy may cause sorrow that almost breaks the heart; for attention had become fastened on the toy, and it was the centre of all interest. The grown man will not (or should not) have such intense emotion over a similar misfortune, because he sees it in relation to other interests which make it seem trifling. So the hero comes to think of his own death as relatively unimportant, and the saint becomes indifferent to the greatest of temporal calamities: " I have put my trust in God," he says; " and will not fear what flesh can do unto me." [1]   So Christ teaches His disciples to see all things in the context of eternity: " Fear not them which kill the body, and after that have no more which they can do." [2]

It follows that every element in Reality, as it is

---

[1] Psalm lvi. 4.   [2] St. Luke xii. 4.

focussed in any finite mind, derives its tone or colour from the elements already apprehended and assimilated by that mind. So in its finite centres of consciousness the Universe perpetually realises new types of experience due to the fresh blending in new combinations of the old elements. In every mind there is some peculiarity of experience; and inasmuch as the process by which we reach any mental or spiritual result not only colours that result but is truly conserved in it, this peculiarity and distinctness of one mind from another will endure for ever, even though as they develop they are found to have received and assimilated identical material.

From what has been said in the last few paragraphs it might be supposed that Determinism is a true account of the formation of character. But it omits a vital part of the truth. Indeed, if taken quite strictly Determinism is sheer nonsense. It declares that of all the entities composing the universe, each is what it is *solely* as a result of the influence of the others. But this is true of each of the others also, and if everything is made what it is *entirely* by the influence of other things, the process of mutual determination can never start. Every entity—every section into which Reality can be mentally divided—contains something that is unique, its own underived contribution to the sum of things whereby it becomes capable of action and reaction. This element of distinctness makes the core of every object.[1]

The failure of Determinism as an explanation of everything in general and of human conduct in particular involves, of course, the acceptance of real Indeterminism as part of our conception of Reality. The element of Indetermination at the mechanical level is negligible; when Life appears, it increases. In Man it is at its height so far as our knowledge goes. But, as we shall see when we come to consider the

---

[1] Cp. *The Nature of Personality*, p. 15.

relation of history to eternity, this is not to assert
blind chance or some gap in the rationality of the
whole.   It is impossible that things or persons should
wholly constitute one another, so there must be a core
of original being in whatever can be called individual—
from a grain of sand to Shakespeare.   And as new
forms of being come into existence more fully representative of the principle to which all things owe their
being, we rise further and further from such external
determination of character and action.   That principle
is, plainly, one of growth; and the forms of being that
most fully represent it are characterised by some
measure of self-directed growth.   Just as, in the
whole system of things, the biological and ethical
stages could not be predicted from knowledge of
physical and chemical nature, so in the beings who
actually exhibit this principle it is impossible to predict their later character and conduct from knowledge
of their earlier lives.   There is a real self-directed
growth.   But the growth as a whole may be a rationally
intelligible unit, in which all the stages fit together.
The extent to which that happens depends on the
extent to which Reason controls the whole life.   We
escape from the rational scheme of external determination, which may make a chaos of personal life, in the
degree in which we rise to the rationality of inward
self-direction.   To that we must return; meanwhile
it is man's individuality, the fact that his reactions are
not merely generic, but are his own, which is the root
of moral responsibility.

But it is not this which constitutes moral freedom
in its completest sense and its most precious form.
What is required for responsibility is that an act
should be genuinely the act of a certain person, who
acted as he did because he was that kind of person
and not because he was physically compelled or morally
terrified.   That is all the " freedom " required to
make a man " responsible " for his acts; it is enough

to make him the real origin of those acts and their consequences. No doubt his environment has had a great deal to do with forming his character, and it is never possible to begin to separate the contribution due to his own distinctive being from those due to heredity and circumstance. But if the act expresses what in fact he is, then he is responsible. No one who likes to use the great word " freedom " to express this connexion between character and act can be prevented from doing so. But it is no great privilege. St. Paul once called it " this body of death."[1] It is the freedom of men to destroy themselves, most vividly represented by Shakespeare's tragic characters. " They are free, for the origin of their actions is themselves; they are bound hand and foot, for from themselves there is no flight."[2]

But there is another freedom besides this; it is found when a man not only recognises that an action is his own, but when he feels that he has truly expressed his whole nature in it and can whole-heartedly rejoice in it. For this freedom the absence of external coercion is indeed a necessary condition; but freedom from internal compulsion is its essence. How can there be such internal compulsion? and how may a man escape from it if it exists? The consideration of these questions will lead us to a more ultimate and radical conception of human nature.

We have so far pictured man as an individual over against all other existent things, so constituted that all Reality may find a focussing point in his consciousness, and capable therefore of apprehending universal principles which are applicable throughout the range of space and time. Because he is an individual he brings with him an original contribution to the sum of things, which in part determines his reactions to the circumstances in which he is placed (though how far it does so can be known only to omniscience); and

---

[1] Romans vii. 24.   [2] *Mens Creatrix*, p. 144.

because he is a unique focussing point for Reality—
and in principle for the entire range thereof—he is of
strictly infinite significance and value.

Yet he does not commonly behave as one in whom
all Being finds a focus; he commonly behaves as one
with strictly local and contemporary interests, even
as one for whom the animal desires which are limited
to the immediate present count for more than the
spectacle of all time and all existence. This happens
because Man's animal Life is not yet wholly possessed
and informed by Mind and Spirit.

The fact is that the unity of the human soul is
at first—and sometimes throughout life—formal only.
It is real in certain senses: thus the various ingredients
cannot be acting simultaneously except in combination;
a man cannot be at the same time in full pursuit of
altruistic and egoistic aims with reference to the same
act of choice; one or the other must give way, or the
two must combine in a mixed product. Moreover,
the man will only be altogether himself if he can succeed
in so organising his nature and his activities that all
his various capacities and impulses have scope in the
maintenance and promotion of a life through which
they find their expression.

As Plato plainly saw, the ethical and the political
problems are really the same — the production of
harmonious unity out of a great number of diverse
constituents. There is some difference of emphasis.
The problem for the individual is to unite in one
coherent scheme all the different tendencies of his
nature—" out of many to become one." The problem for society is to give full scope to all its citizens
without breaking up the unity of the whole. At
present our concern is with the individual.

At birth he is a whole congeries of instincts,
impulses, and capacities. Almost any one of these
may be called into play by the appropriate circumstance.
But he has besides a capacity carrying the potency of

wonderful achievements: this is the capacity for selective attention. What determines the selection of objects to which he will attend is never fully known. No doubt it is partly the balance of his inherited temperament; but it is here that his original endowment plays its greater or smaller part. The training of this capacity, both its strengthening and its direction, is the main business of all education, and is almost the only business of the earliest stages of education. This capacity to fix the attention on one object to the neglect of others is the foundation of what is called Will.

We laugh at the physical science which explained heat by means of a substance called caloric, and defined caloric as that which makes bodies hot. There is no instance of this procedure so disastrous as its application to the phenomena of Choice. Choice itself is a familiar fact. It has been accounted for by the supposition of a "faculty" of choice, called Will; and Will is just the faculty of choosing. But being supposed to exist, people have gone on, quite ridiculously, to ask—Is the Will free? This means—Has the power to choose got power to choose?[1] The only reasonable questions would be either Is choice a reality? or Has man any power to choose? or Has man a will? Further, the Will, being supposed to exist, has been regarded as existing by itself side by side with all the other "faculties" of the soul; and those who believe in its "freedom" seem to imagine it as hovering over the various motives or inducements to action which nature or circumstance suggest, and arbitrarily choosing one by which it shall be directed. The so-called "faculty" psychology has survived here, at least in popular thinking, though in other departments it has been utterly exploded.

But Will, conceived as the seat of Purpose, is not a separate faculty, except in the sense that man has

[1] Cf. the celebrated chapter on "Power" in Locke's *Essay on the Human Understanding*.

the capacity to form a Purpose; rather it is the co-ordination of his whole psychic nature for action.   It is therefore something which every one is capable of having, but which no one actually has in perfection. The degree to which Will in this sense is formed varies greatly from one individual to another, and a relative completeness is achieved at various stages.   If any one interest is from the first predominant, unity is reached without great difficulty; so it is also if the impulses which might tend to conflict with one another are comparatively feeble; but in this latter case the resultant Will is likely to be ineffective.   Where there are strong and volcanic passions the unification of the personality is far more difficult, but the result when attained is far more potent.   To the end, however, the Will is incomplete.   The forces which modern psychology describes as located in the subconscious regions of the soul can never be all brought into the harmony which is the Will.   The very fact that they are part of the unconscious prevents this; and the existence of these forces renders nugatory any attempt to identify Will and Personality.   Will is so much of a Personality as is consciously co-ordinated for action [1]— the co-ordination being effected by selective attention and the pressure of environment; it can be, though it seldom is, the whole of conscious Personality.   Yet because there is more in every human being than has come within the sphere of consciousness, Personality is always more than Will.

With a view to some of the discussions which follow, we must here relate our enquiries to a method of speaking which has ceased to be employed by either philosophers or psychologists.   We have used such terms as Nature and Personality; we have spoken of men and of Man.   It is necessary to determine more

---

[1] " The basis and character of freedom " lies " not in simple initiations but in an equipment capable of embodying extraordinarily delicate responses to extraordinarily varied environments " (Bosanquet in *Contemporary British Philosophy*, p. 68).

precisely the significance of these terms both in themselves and in relation to each other.

In earlier times men believed in a universal Humanity, which was called Human Nature, and which was distinguishable from all particular Persons, and could be rightly conceived apart from all individualisation. Most of what makes up any human being was this Human Nature; Personality was the distinguishing point whereby one individual was differentiated from another. I have heard it expressed by a scientific parable thus: Human Nature is a continuous fluid into which Personalities are set like drops of acid, each Personality forming about itself a crystal out of the fluid into which it comes. It is only in theology that this use of terms now persists, so we may turn to theology for an illustration. According to the traditional terminology there is in God one Nature and three Persons; as Will belongs to Nature and not to Person, there is in God only one Will. On the other hand there is in Jesus Christ one Person and two Natures; and as Will belongs to Nature and not to Person, there are in Jesus Christ two Wills, one divine and one human.[1]

Such discussions seem to most people of our time utterly divorced from reality; but this is only because habits of thought have changed, and with them the accepted meaning of words. The problems are still familiar and still important; they are the problems of man's relation to God and of the individual's relation to society.

First, then, we have to ask in what does the unity of an individual Personality consist? Does the unity of a Person depend on, and consist of, an organic relationship between the constituent elements, or

---

[1] The difficulties of this position are indicated by the fact that Dr. Weston, the Bishop of Zanzibar, when engaged in defending orthodoxy, is, through his adherence to the traditional use of terms, brought as near to an explicit adherence to the Monothelite heresy as a man could well come without an avowed acceptance of it. Cf. *The Christ and His Critics*, pp. 115, 121, 125.

is it some point of reference which remains fixed while these change? Is the Ego such a point of common reference or is it the living and energizing whole?

Broadly speaking, European thought has tended to take the view that personal unity and identity depend on some one point of reference. Probably this is because the early theologians took this view, so setting the tradition for theology, the sphere in which this question has most importance. But there is another strand in our tradition which can be traced back to Plato and Aristotle. Those supreme thinkers chiefly approached the problem from the side of Ethics, and they make it clear both that there is a formal unity of personality from the outset and also that substantial unity is an achievement. The aim is ἕνα γενέσθαι ἐκ πολλῶν—to become one from being many.[1] There is in every man a many-headed Monster (Desire), a Lion (Pride), and a Man (Reason); the aim of all education is to ally the Lion with the Man in the control of the Monster;[2] so according to Aristotle an act of Will is a union of thinking and desiring—νοῦς ὀρεκτικός or ὄρεξις διανοητική;[3] and sins of weakness (ἀκρασία) occur precisely because that union has not been effected.[4] In such a case we should not say that the Will has been overcome by a Desire, but that the Will did not exist, or at any rate did not perfectly exist. This is also the view of St. Augustine, who insists that the solution of the problem of moral weakness is to be found in the fact that there is no complete volition. If I entirely will to be good, I am good— not as a consequence, but because the two phrases mean the same thing. Consequently, when there is a true act of will there is no sense of struggle; the struggle, when it occurs, is the struggle of a partly formed will to complete itself. We may conveniently

---

[1] *Republic*, iv. 443 E.
[2] *Republic*, ix. 589 A, B.
[3] *Eth. Nic.* iii. 1113 a 10; vi. 1139 b 4, 5.
[4] *Eth. Nic.* vii. 1147 a 25-b 19.

use the term Will as correlated to a general Purpose by which our life is guided, and contrast with it a Desire which cuts across that Purpose; it is so that we experience Will as a rule either in ourselves or in others, and Will is most of all manifest in an inability to do things contrary to the character that has been and is being formed, in spite of desires that may be stimulated by circumstance or suggestion; [1] but if, and when, and in so far as, any such Desire is found to exist, the Purpose is not yet completely formed or accepted, and the Will does not yet wholly exist.

Yet there is a real unity from the first, and we assume some measure of continuous responsibility. Indeed it is in connexion with moral responsibility that this unity first becomes of practical importance. And it consists at the very least in the continued identity of the physical organism.

But this is itself a problem. The constituent parts of the body are constantly changing; and its form is also changing. In what sense is my body now the same body which my mother nursed? Plainly the identity consists in continuity of history. Wherever we deal with what is alive we find this form of identity. And it supplies the clue to the unity of personality. For some purposes we take bodily identity as sufficient. Thus all that the police or the judge is concerned about is bodily identity. If the body of the criminal is produced in court, it is of no use for the prisoner to say that he is Dr. Jekyll, while the crime was committed by Mr. Hyde. Personal identity is assumed where bodily identity is established. But the spiritual director cannot content himself with a method so rough and ready. He will indeed assume some degree of personal identity; he may have to attend quite as

[1] Of course this " inability " is objective only. Subjectively, the good man knows that he can sin but does not want to do so. Only from the objective point of view is it true to say " he can't." But this objective inability is most important. What it all comes to is that nothing except his own character prevents him; but that does.

carefully to a real personal difference. The commission of the crime may itself create a revolt in the soul of the criminal, so that while he is the man that did it, he is also a man who could not (being what he now is) do any such thing; or he may have subsequently undergone conversion, with the same result. St. Paul is to all eternity the persecutor of the Church as a matter of historic fact; as a matter of spiritual effort and sacrifice he is its foremost missionary.

Even the Law allows for these considerations in dealing with children. They are not regarded as fully responsible, partly because no one expects them to have fully formed wills, and partly because in early life the change of character may be so rapid.

How, then, are we to express the unity and identity of personality? It must be in such a way as to recognise the variety of grades at which it may exist. First there is the mere numerical identity of a man with himself as distinct from all other persons and things. This appears in the consciousness of an abiding Self through manifold experiences. Here is the " point of reference." But it is easy to misunderstand its significance. Philosophers, enquiring into the nature of self-consciousness, are liable to attribute to it the characteristics of their own enquiry. The ordinary man is conscious of himself, or is aware of his experiences in such a way as to compare them with other possible experiences; but this does not mean that he is conscious of his consciousness of himself, or aware of his awareness of his experiences. This is a later stage, a product of deliberate reflexion; in such reflexion we distinguish between the subjective and objective elements in self-consciousness and tend to regard these as separable entities, as though there might have been the same " self " (*qua* subject) with other experiences. But the self *is* the self-conscious system of experience. If the self *qua* subject is abstracted from all its experiences, it becomes a mere

F

possibility of experience and no actual entity at all. If there is no experience, there is no " self "; if there are other experiences, there is another " self." The ease with which we imagine the " self " and its experi- ences to be separable is due to the fact that we can imagine one or another of our experiences to be changed, while we ourselves remained unaltered; and so we might be, for all practical purposes; but we should not be entirely and absolutely unaltered; indeed, the only reason why we do at times think of such changes in our experience is that we should be different (as *e.g.* happier) if the change were made. A change in my experience is a change in me; but this does not destroy my personal identity, because this consists in continuity of growth and not in immutability.

From this it follows that if the ego is regarded as consisting in the mere point of reference or subjectivity, it becomes a pure abstraction denoting only the possibility of experience; it possesses no quality, no character; these belong to the experience which it merely makes possible. The ego so regarded is a focussing point in which nothing is focussed.

We cannot, then, find the ego, or principle of unity and self-hood, in any psychological point of reference which acts as a pivot for the experiences, active or passive, of any one Person. The unit is the whole psychic life. This reveals itself as a unit in a variety of ways.

(1) First, there is the unity of the physical organism. My body is part of the physical universe, subject to its laws. But it is a relatively independent part, having a life of its own. In Bergson's phrase, " the living body has been separated and closed off by Nature herself. It is composed of unlike parts that complete each other. It performs diverse functions that involve each other." [1] The Ego or Self, whatever

---

[1] Quoted by Hoernlé, *Matter, Life, Mind and God*, p. 95.

else may be said about it, manifests itself through the organism which is called its body. And this organism, just because it is an organism, is a single whole of many different parts, which passes from birth to death through a continuous process of change, but maintains throughout its identity with itself and its distinctness from all other objects.

(2) Secondly, there is the unity consisting in the fact that of the various constituents of the psychic life, no two can normally be active simultaneously except in combination or else by a conscious division of attention; such a division is plainly a manifestation of a unity which holds together the two fields of attention. A " person " may reveal one set of qualities to one group of acquaintances, and a quite different set to another; and these sets of qualities may be such as to prompt directly contrary types of action. But he cannot reveal both of these at once; if they act together, they must coalesce. Two " persons " may act simultaneously in contrary ways; one " person " may have the impulses that prompt both kinds of action, but he can only act in one way at one time; in choosing the way that he will act, which he does by fixing attention on the stimulus to one group of impulses, he exhibits the beginnings of Will, though if the other group of impulses remains active his will is still incompletely formed. Thus this first manifestation of personal unity points forward to the complete unity of a perfectly harmonised life.

(3) The unity of the Person also, and most fundamentally, consists in the completely organised and harmonised self which it is capable of becoming. Here, as in every true instance of growth, the end contains the explanation of the process and declares its true nature. When all the divergent and even warring impulses of a richly endowed personality have been wrought into the harmony of a noble purpose devotedly pursued, there is seen the true personal unity which is

only potential in the earlier stages of development and discipline.

So a man is one person partly because his body is one, partly because his " soul " is a distinguishable group of psychic forces which can only be all active so far as they combine, but most of all because there is possible for him a unity which it is his life's business to achieve.   In achieving it he reveals the full nature, not only of his psychic endowment, but also of the bodily organism which is its physical basis.

A " Person," then, is a self-conscious and self-determining system of experience, and human persons are in process of achieving the complete unification of the experience which constitutes them.   This " experience " is itself a product of and a reaction to the Universe.   Man tends to set himself in opposition to all the rest of the Universe, and of course he finds a ground for this in his own peculiar characteristics. But he is a part of it none the less and his whole being is rooted in it.   As has been already pointed out, greatness of individuality does not consist in independence of environment, but rather in responsiveness to an unusually large and rich environment.   For every " person," just because self-conscious, is the universe coming to consciousness of itself (or of some part of itself) in a particular focus.   The range of receptiveness varies from one individual to another.   It is in part, at least, determined by the physical organism. A deaf man can never appreciate the beauty of music. Some people are plainly more sensitive to various aspects of existence than others.   Some have special powers of co-ordinating ideas.   It is seldom that the same person has both scientific and artistic gifts in a very high degree.   This may be because of the conformation of the brain required for these two activities of the spirit.   Until we know far more than is known yet about the relations between Mind and Body, it is impossible to say wherein consist the conditions of

genius, of ability, or of limitation of capacity; but
whatever these may be, a human person is the Universe
coming to consciousness of some part or range or
aspect of itself through the means of a specific bodily
organism. It is for this reason that the mystic, who
more than others experiences direct fellowship with
the ground of his being, is more and not less aware
than other men of his kinship with beasts and flowers
and even the products of natural forces in which life
is not yet manifest.

But Man is also more than this. Just because he
is self-conscious he is no merely passive plaything of
external forces, nor of combinations of forces within
himself. Impulses to action must commend themselves to the judgement which is itself a part of his self-
consciousness. For this does not take the form of
watching inertly a process independent of consciousness; to suppose that is to set up again the absolute
opposition of subject and object which we have already
seen to be untenable. There are not two entities—
subject and object; but there is one self-conscious
entity. Therefore what moves this must move it as
self-conscious. And man, as self-conscious, com-
pares himself as he is with himself as he might be;
his self-consciousness is inherently judicial. Before
he can himself be truly called the agent of any act, his
judgement must have assented to it.

Thus he is self-determining. There is not a little
piece of him, called a Will, which determines the
rest of him. But the system of experience which he is,
with its *nisus* towards the complete unification of itself
which is very imperfectly understood until it is accomplished, determines his course at every stage. This
self-determination is the activity of will, so far as will
is yet formed, and also its development towards completion; it is his freedom in process of perfecting itself.

At this point, if no sooner, emerges the fact of
obligation. It has three roots. First, the fact that a

man is the Universe coming to self-consciousness in a particular focus makes it essentially unnatural that he should pursue his own course in isolation from other men in whom also, as in other *foci*, the same universe is in process of coming to self-consciousness. When we concentrate attention on some narrowly human concern, such as commercial profits, we may seem to be rivals with no common interest; but that is to think meanly of ourselves. So soon as a man realises the vast common background—the stellar spaces, the evolutionary aeons, the seas and mountains, the historic movement of humanity—of which he and his neighbours are the product, he must realise that enmity is essentially unnatural.

Secondly, as he looks forward to his own course of action he becomes aware of claims upon him which do not in any sense arise out of his individual convenience but which he recognises as binding upon him, and that never so forcibly as when, in fact, he violates them. His exercise of freedom can only bring him satisfaction so far as he accepts and meets them.

Thirdly, he finds that his own unity and peace can only be found in a purpose to which all his energies are given. But because he grows from the same stock as his neighbours, and is therefore social in the roots of his being,[1] the purpose to which all his energies are given must be a social purpose; if it is anything else it will leave no place for the social impulses, and they will not be dedicated to it; there will still be division and distraction in his life; the quality of his soul imposes obligation upon it.

Thus both from the origin out of which he emerges, and from the goal to which he advances, and from the facts of his nature as he stands, there springs the

---

[1] Of course this does not mean that he attains to fully social being at any point short of complete development; but from the beginning that is his destiny, though he may need years to learn it. "The development of personality is development into unity through ever-growing personal relationship." (I owe this sentence to the Rev. L. W. Grensted.)

reality of obligation.   Its content must be determined
by experience, and a man may make honest mistakes
about what he ought to do.   But to be aware that
there is a course which he ought to take—whether he
likes it or not, and whether it serves his interest as an
isolated individual or not—is part of the very form of
his self-consciousness.

As there is no one point of reference in man's
nature which is the source of individual distinctness
and unity, so there is no such thing as human nature
existing by itself apart from all individualisation, or
capable of being rightly so conceived.   But this does
not mean that human beings merely exist side by side,
or that humanity is a word denoting the mere aggre-
gation of them.   On the contrary, all the grounds of
obligation just set out involve the solidarity of the
human race, and all the more so inasmuch as the most
important and significant part of his environment to
which a man is receptive and reactive is that part which
consists of other human beings.[1]   From his parents
he derives the body, which is the physical basis of his
being; from his family—its traditions, outlook, circumstances, hopes, fears—he derives the main direction
of the impetus which carries him out into life; from
his country, and his social class in that country, he
receives the influences which either modify or stereo-
type that direction.   His whole being is a condensa-
tion of society.   He *is* his fellow-men's experience
focussed in a new centre.   There is no impenetrable
core of self-hood which is his, and his alone; his
distinctness is his angle of vision.   That is the core of
self-hood which, along with his own principle of self-
directed growth, he brings as an original contribution
to the scheme of things.

As the experience of any group of men expands,

[1] To the religious man God is the most important factor of environment; and
religion is the effort, by the direction given to attention, to make Him all-important.
But this is a highly developed stage, and at present we are dealing with the elementary
stage.

its content becomes more and more common to all of them. This does not lead to any merging of their individualities or separate selves in a common self; nothing can obliterate their past history; the route by which each has reached his stage of apprehension leaves its influence; even if all of us became omniscient, we should still be many *foci* of an experience common to all in its content, and should appreciate differently the values of the world that we all apprehended, for appreciation depends on subjective factors which are themselves largely dependent on personal history. But though humanity exists only in individuals who are eternally distinct, it is a unity itself. It is a unity, because human nature exists to be the coming to self-consciousness in many centres of the one universe;[1] it is a unity because only in the harmony of a united human race can any one human being find the satisfaction of his own nature; its unity is apparent in the indisputable fact of influence. Again, alike the origin and the goal and the present fact of human nature demonstrate its unity.

It has already been said that the form of human self-consciousness includes both the capacity to compare and contrast the actual state or experiences of the self with others that are possible though not actual, and the realisation of absolute claims. In other words, it involves an apprehension of good and evil in their various forms, or, in one word, of Value. In the animals this is already present, but not, as it would appear, consciously present in such a way that an unattained, and even *de facto* unattainable, good may be conceived as a goal of ambition. A dog has a sense of duty, but shows scarcely any signs of a divided consciousness. In man this is fully apparent, and carries with it four main results:

---

[1] I am not here concerned with the question why the Universe comes to self-consciousness in many centres rather than in one. The answer to this question is hinted at above; it is partly because all the values can only be appreciated if all angles of vision are taken. Cf. *Mens Creatrix*, pp. 82-86.

(*a*) As clearly apprehending and appreciating Value, man begins to bring to full actuality the Value or Good which is the *raison d'être* of the Universe; through his experience it begins to find its end.

(*b*) For the same reason man is capable of fellowship with God, for he can share the motive of Creation—" ye shall be as God, knowing good and evil."

(*c*) For the same reason man himself becomes creative. Everything that can be named represents some original contribution to the totality of things; and this individuality increases as we rise from the purely mechanical, through the various forms of life, to the dawning self-consciousness of certain animals. But only in man is there the clear apprehension of Value which brings with it deliberate, purposive action, so that by his sense of Value man tries to change the world about him.

(*d*) For the same reason also man is involved in deliberate selfishness. The Value which he seeks is focussed in his own individual consciousness, and comes to actuality through his individual appreciation; and it is only with effort that he comes to learn that his good is essentially a part of the universal good; and that only by seeking and assisting the realisation of the universal good can he find his own. Thus the arrival of man at full self-consciousness makes possible deliberate sin, makes it indeed so probable as to be almost certain.

" It is very unhappy," says Emerson, " but too late to be helped, the discovery we have made that we exist; that discovery is called the Fall of Man."[1] With that discovery human history begins.

[1] Essay on *Experience*.

NOTE TO CHAPTER IV

THE FALL

THE profound wisdom of the Myth with which the Bible opens sets before its readers the following truths:

(1) God made the world and saw that it was very good;

(2) Man arrived at conscious realisation of Value (Good and Evil) by doing what was in fact forbidden, but was (*ex hypothesi*) not realised as wrong; in breaking a rule he discovered a principle;

(3) Thereby he became a conscious sinner;

(4) But thereby also he became capable of fellowship with God.

This is a true analysis of all natural human progress. Man stumbles, by the impulse of his nature, into something which, by his misunderstanding of it, is first a source of new evils, but is the condition of a hitherto impossible good.

CHAPTER V

HISTORY AND ETERNITY

" I have seen the travail which God hath given to the sons of men to be exercised therewith.   He hath made everything beautiful in its time;   also he hath set eternity in their heart, yet so that man cannot find out the work that God hath done from the beginning even to the end."—ECCLESIASTES.

So far we have considered Man in himself; we have now to consider Man in action.   His destiny is fulfilled in the achievement of two unities, unity of individual personality and unity of universal fellowship. So much has become clear from our enquiry into the nature of man.   We have seen also how near to inevitable was the failure to realise without preliminary error and struggle all that the form of human self-consciousness makes possible.   Certainly that failure is a fact.   Man was made for unity but has chosen division; and as each man is by his nature in large part a focussing point for his environment, it is not possible that, when once this false start has been followed by any, there should be others who are totally unaffected by it, unless indeed some power coming into human history from outside should make this possible.   In so far as human history is a continuous process, where each stage proceeds from the one before it, there can be no perfecting of individuals except by the perfecting of the race; and as the race consists of individuals, and is what they make it, the outlook is gloomy enough.[1]

[1] Karl Marx scarcely overstates the dependence of the individual on his environment, though he does leave out of sight the spark of creative energy that is in every human soul; his error is that he misconceives the environment; he takes this to

Some progress indeed is possible, for every individual is in a small degree original and creative; no one is utterly the prey of circumstance; and by pressure of experience man learns something. Human history is, in the main, the effort of men to achieve individual unity, and the groping of men, sometimes conscious, more often unconscious, towards the unity of universal fellowship.

At a first glance the fundamental issue of history seems to be a struggle between the two unities which we have seen to be the true goal of human life—between liberty and order. It is true that this issue is at stake in a great part of history, and that the main conscious effort of civilisation is to achieve both in a harmonious balance. Man's incapacity to satisfy the cravings of his nature leads him to associations of various kinds; from the beginning the human race is organised in social units. There is no evidence whatever that Rousseau's noble savage ever existed—individual, free, uncorrupt. The first effort of civilisation is not to create a social unity, but to find room within the close-knit social unity for any particle of individual freedom. The savage is utterly bound by the conventions of his tribe; probably he has been driven by necessities of self-defence to sink his individuality in the social habits and customs of his people. The savage is not always fierce; he is always intensely conservative. In fact, one may define the savage as one who is hostile to new ideas or new practices as such. In a community of savages, progress is impossible. But even among savages, some conventions will prove their superiority over others by the greater prosperity which comes to those tribes which follow them. These tend to conquer or absorb the less prosperous, and to impose their superior conventions. In this way

---

consist chiefly of institutions and social organisation; these are important; but far more influential are the individual men and women, and (if He exists) God. To trust to organisation only for reform of character is a fearful error.

great empires may grow up, which reach an advanced
stage in the ordering of life, without ever grasping the
idea of progress or even feeling its impulse.   Such
were the empires of ancient Egypt, of Babylonia, of
Persia; such was the empire of China.   In every one
of these culture reached a high level of development, without any general principle of progress; and
as soon as outside circumstances gave no further
impetus, stagnation set in.   And in all of them
there was little enough scope for individual freedom
or originality.

The quest of freedom first appears in ancient
Greece—the nation which first "used deliberate
reflexion on past experience to modify future experience."[1]   There was still no general principle of
progress; Plato himself can only suggest a plainly
impossible kind of revolution as the means by which
the transition can be made from the actual society of
his experience to the ideal society of his argument.
But the determination to escape from tyranny is plain,
and the purpose to establish something like political
liberty for those inhabitants of a city who were fortunate
enough to be " citizens."

Watching the course of this purpose we see at
once that it follows a curve.   So long as there is
danger from the foreign enemy—Persia—liberty can
be practised without breaking up the social unity;
but as soon as the external pressure is removed by
the conquest of the Persian forces on sea and on land
the temptations to selfishness which are incident to
liberty prove too strong; the last hundred years of
Greek independence are a period of endless conflict,
city against city, faction against faction.   In the great
Peloponnesian War some principles and ideals are
involved: after that there are none; it is all an affair
of " hegemony "; the one motive is the desire for
power over others and at their expense.   At last order

---

[1] I owe the phrase to Mr. Lionel Curtis.

is restored at the cost of liberty under the Macedonian conquerors.

Rome exhibits exactly the same curve. The greatness which made possible the Roman Empire was already declining when that empire began to exist; we see it in the early struggles, and above all in the Hannibalic War. But as soon as the pressure of external danger was removed the temptations to selfishness which are incidental to liberty began to be too strong; the last century of the Roman Republic is a period of perpetual civil war, until order is restored at the cost of liberty under the military despotism of the Caesars.

Modern European history tells much the same story, though here a new influence is making itself felt. The same tension between liberty and order is apparent in the early history of the United States of America; and though there a balance in fact was reached, it is doubtful if this could have been accomplished if the new nation had been perfectly safe. As it was, Lincoln's struggle had to follow upon Washington's before the foundations of American civilisation could be secure. Judged from the point of view we have been taking, the United States and the British Commonwealth of Nations are no doubt the culmination of human history hitherto; and if they can themselves be associated in a League of Nations which includes all civilised countries and has in itself the secret of permanence, this line of historical development will have reached its conclusion.

But it may be predicted with some assurance that this will not happen unless other conditions are fulfilled, to which at present men pay little attention in forming their political opinions. For this first view of human history as consisting in the struggle between liberty and order and the adjustment of it does not take us to the roots of human conduct. We must go down to the elements. There are three, and only

three, primary relations in which one human being, as
agent, can stand to another; he may ignore him or
compete with him or co-operate with him.[1] (*a*) So
far as he lives for the satisfaction of elementary desires,
he is ignoring other people in the planning of his
life; he may need them as means to his end, but the
end is conceived in complete detachment from them.
Such an end is sub-personal; it does not include any
welfare for the whole self; and experience proves its
incapacity to satisfy. (*b*) So far as a man lives for
honour, fame, power, wealth, or anything else in
which the value is comparative, he is aiming at a
satisfaction of his whole self, but he is involved in
competition with others.   Wealth indeed is never a true
end; it is a means to the satisfaction of desire, or else
to power and honour; the other ends in this category
are those goods which cannot be enjoyed in common
and are diminished when they are shared. If the
former be called the life of Desire, this is the life of
Pride. Here success is to excel; and equality of
achievement is fatal to success. All desire for social
precedence, for a place in the best society, for conspicuous ability, even for conspicuous service, is of
this type; the success of one involves the comparative
failure of others. All " greatness " as distinct from
goodness belongs to this class.[2] (*c*) So far as a man
lives for an end of which the value is inherent and
absolute he will co-operate with others; there is here
no conflict between one man's success and his neighbour's. If his aim is that Truth may be known (and
not that he may himself be the discoverer), he can
rejoice in the discovery of another as much as in his
own. These are the true social goods, because the
search for them promotes social unity.

The three principles of life so indicated are dis-

---

[1] This is the ethical value of Plato's analysis of the soul into ἐπιθυμία, θυμός,
and τὸ λογιστικόν.

[2] Cf. " Beneath the Good how far—but far above the Great " (Gray).

coverable in every man, and they pass (as Plato has
shown) from the character of the citizens to the ordering
of the state.   The satisfaction of desire is necessary
to the maintenance of life; if hunger and thirst are
unsatisfied, the life of the individual ceases; if sexual
desire is unsatisfied, the life of the race ceases.[1]   Desire
becomes lust, and is evil, when attention is fixed, not
on its direct object, but on the pleasure connected with
its satisfaction.   I must eat to maintain life; and I
may as well eat what I enjoy (provided it be wholesome), partly because the pleasure as far as it goes is
good, partly because enjoyment assists digestion and
so conduces to the end for which I eat at all.   But if I
eat, not to satisfy hunger, but for the mere pleasure
of eating, that is wrong in principle, and the desire is
now lust, or evil desire.[2]   Similarly the element of
Self-respect or Pride has its place, first in assisting the
interest of the whole Self against particular Desires,
which tend to seek satisfaction beyond that to which
a harmonious economy of life entitles them, partly as
claiming for the individual his right to live his own
life and to find scope for the exercise of his abilities.
But so soon as this principle becomes not only a
demand for justice but an impulse to acquire whatever
may be available, it becomes evil and a source of evil.
This can never be true of the rational principle, which
aims at absolute values, and sees the individual as
what he is—a whole personality, but one among
others in the community.   But reasonableness, while
always a good, is not a sufficient equipment for the
perfectly good life; there must be the energy of desire
and the assertiveness of Pride—both directed and
controlled by Reason—if the full richness of human
life is to be realised.   Even the humility and forgiveness, which are the choicest fruits of reasonableness,

---

[1] This is not necessarily a disaster, as Solovyof forcibly points out.
[2] Of course the evil may be so minute as to be practically negligible; but the
principle holds.

are thin and poor if there is no pride behind them; for a man conscious of power to accept subordination is a finer thing than the same act in a man who has no such consciousness; forgiveness is nobler in a man who keenly feels an injury than in one who overlooks what he has never deeply felt.

We have here a psychological analogue to the stratification of Reality which was described in the first chapter. Desire (like Matter) is the indispensable foundation; but it does not display the purpose of its own being until we see it organised by Pride and controlled by Reason. Similarly Pride, which cannot be active unless life is maintained through the satisfaction of desire, shows an aspect when controlled by Reason so different from that which it presents when it usurps dominion over the soul, that the name is usually confined to this perverted form of the quality; but the quality (however named) is only seen in its true nature where Reason takes control. And Reason can never take control, can hardly indeed exist, in a soul distracted by a chaos of desires undisciplined as yet by that concern for the whole self which we have called Pride.[1] Each grade exists for the sake of what is made possible when the higher grade possesses it; and each higher grade requires the lower for the possibility of its own existence.

The history of mankind—the story alike of individuals and of nations—is the working out of these principles in their interaction on each other. No doubt we seldom find any one of them operating in history quite unaffected by the others; but they are all at work. The various impulses of Desire alone will give rise to some sort of social order, for the desires of any one man are various, while his capacities are few; therefore it is obviously prudent that each shall exert his own capacity beyond his own needs, sharing the superfluous product with his neighbour

---

[1] That is why the Man in us must make an ally of the Lion to control the Monster.

in return for the superfluous product of that neighbour's industry in another direction. So arises the barest minimum of a State.[1]

Such a society must be lacking in heroic virtue, but it can, in principle, be quite innocent. Moreover, it is the indispensable economic basis of every conceivable society. But in its purity it does not exist. In all actual societies there is a superstructure, due to the activity of Pride or Reason or both. If Pride or Self-assertion became the sole dominating principle for all that goes beyond the bare minimum required for the maintenance of life, the result would be a state resting in principle (though not in history) upon the Social Contract of Glauco and Hobbes. Each is at first for himself against all others; so the " life of man is solitary, poor, nasty, brutish, and short ; "[2] consequently men make a contract neither to inflict nor to suffer injuries,[3] and the State arises armed with authority to restrain men's self-assertiveness against each other and with force to uphold its authority. That is not the history of the origin of any state, but it is the true analysis of every actual society so far as that society depends upon the existence of a police-force or anything resembling it. Within civilised states this principle is still at work, but becomes manifestly less fundamental as a deeper foundation resting on Reason grows beneath it; at present the relation of civilised states to one another is still mainly determined by Pride which, in this connexion, is usually called self-interest.

The course of progress as the growth of the dominion of Reason can be traced in both the internal and external relations of communities. From the first, men live in communities. The primitive society allows little freedom to its citizens; but it succeeds in

---

[1] ἀναγκαιοτάτη πόλις, also called the City of Pigs. Plato, *Republic*, ii. 369 D, 372 D.

[2] Hobbes, *Leviathan*, Pt. I., Chap. xiii.

[3] συνθέσθαι μήτε ἀδικεῖν μήτε ἀδικεῖσθαι. Plato, *Republic*, ii. 359 A.

normal times in supplying them with the necessaries of their simple life. As freedom develops it gives new scope to the Pride or Self-assertion to which it owes its own origin. As the mere existence of the society becomes secure against foreign attack or failure of supplies, there is at once less need to repress individual initiative and more need for an outlet for the aggressive impulse which had been exercised against enemies. So Pride, no longer exercised in war or crushed in peace, demands and obtains freedom. At first it abuses what it has won. The temptations to selfishness (which is Pride become dominant) are too strong for any available resistance. Society becomes increasingly competitive; initiative is stimulated and thus development of resources of all kinds is accelerated. But distribution tends to become more and more accidental; the question begins to be asked whether it may not be worse to starve as a free man than to be well fed as a slave or serf. The depressed classes then find a common interest against the possessing classes, and a conflict begins to arise, not of individuals against individuals nor of nations against nations, but of group against group. This is the Class-war, announced as a fact by Adam Smith and proclaimed as a crusade by Marx and Engels.

Meanwhile the freedom, which Pride creates, affords an opportunity to Reason; and in so far as men learn to care about the social goods which have absolute Value—Knowledge, Beauty, Fellowship— they find a common interest, which rests upon their mutual recognition as selves or persons, and therefore by implication does justice to what is wholesome about Pride. In this community of the higher goods, which the development of civilisation makes possible, there is found a corrective to the class-war which is the necessary outcome of pre-occupation with the purely economic sphere. As men rise to the capacity for caring chiefly for what unites them to one another rather than for what separates them from one another, they find a fellowship which is not attainable by means of any outward ordering of life, though the outward order must inevitably be changed as the direction of the citizens' chief interest is altered.

Still more fundamental in creating a national unity which underlies all class-divisions is the reinforcement of the primitive tribal consciousness by mutual inter-course continued through many generations. It has already been said that each man's consciousness is a focussing-point for his environment, wherein human society is the most important and influential factor. The mutual influence of individuals is, of course, strongest where intercourse is closest; this is facili-tated by geographical neighbourhood, by common language and common education. So long as nations are isolated in any degree from one another by seas or by hostility, divergencies which have once appeared tend to develop. In times of international peace the tension between the classes tends to become pre-dominant, but war has hitherto always shown that this division is strictly subordinate to the national unity. It is possible that if internal conditions remain unaltered, a long period of peace in these days of rapid communications might lead to a consolidation of class-interests in all nations, so that the class-war would take the place of international war. In so far as the demand of class-conscious labour is for justice— as it largely is—the battle-cry " Workers of the world unite " is justified. But it must be noticed that ethically the class-unit is inferior to the national unit because its basis is narrower. The " class " is united by common economic interest only; the nation is a fellowship of many divers types in a common heritage of tradition, sentiment, and purpose covering every phase of human existence. To substitute class for nation as the primary object of loyalty is ethically retrograde; those who advocate it, and still more those who, by maintaining an unjust social order, cause many to tend in that direction, are the worst enemies of true progress.

The same Reason, which promotes unity and fellowship within the nation by directing attention to the " social goods," also insists that the nations stand on an equality and that to seek the interest of one at the cost of others is as much an intellectual blunder and a moral fault as to seek the interest of an individual at the cost of others. It points therefore to an international organisation of the world, such as the League of Nations, to which our consideration of the historic conflict between the principles of Liberty and Order had also led us. That it is right to work deliberately for the achievement of that goal there can be no doubt, but in doing so we must take stock of our resources.

At first sight it appears that there is in the process of history a power at work which will carry it to its destiny of a perfected civilisation — the complete realisation of the two unities at which man aims, personal unity and social unity, perfectly harmonised with one another and affording each other mutual support. The only question that arises on this view is whether our planet may not have become too cold to sustain life before the goal is reached. But that question at once raises others. First, is the goal of history one that is only enjoyed by those generations who are alive after its attainment?[1] And, secondly, is that a rational view which regards moral achievements as ultimately dependent on astronomical or other purely physical processes?

Moreover, this first view has its own difficulties. It is true that everywhere it presents the issue as one not between naked good and naked evil, but between higher and lower. Desire and Pride have their place

[1] A similar question led to one of the earliest assertions of immortality. Cf. Isaiah xxvi. 19 (with context).

in the perfectly good life. Pride, claiming dominion, is the ultimate source of all strictly spiritual evil, for the incursions of Desire are rebellions of the not yet perfectly controlled animal nature. Therefore it was in principle possible that the development of man's life should be perfectly harmonious from its simplest origins to its sublime attainment. But it has not been so, and (as we saw) the dice were heavily loaded against such a contingency. All human history springs from the fact that man is the centre of appreciation in whom the values of life come to actuality; and each man knows (quite rightly) that precisely his values can only be realised in him; therefore the very form of man's self-consciousness gives an initial bias to self-seeking or pride, at least until experience proves that the welfare of the individual is part and parcel of the welfare of the race. But in fact the difficulty is greater than this. In the animal world there is some appreciation of value, with all the perversions that so easily arise from it, and the history is continuous from animals to men. We may illustrate this by a vivid passage in which Professor Gilbert Murray expressed the bitterness of his soul many years before the Great War came to give new point to his words: " Consider the fowls of the air. A very pretty small bird, the great tit, when hungry, will lift up its beak, split open its brother's head, and proceed to eat his brains. It might then be satisfied think you? Not at all! It has a moral nature, you must please to remember, which demands to be satisfied as well as the physical. When it has finished its brother's brains, it first gets very angry and pecks the dead body; then it flies off to a tree and exults. What is it angry with, and why does it exult? It is angry with the profound wickedness of that brother in consequence of which it was obliged to kill him: it exults in the thought of its own courage, firmness, justice, moderation, and domestic sweetness. That song is its equivalent

—poor innocent thing—of a patriotic leading article in the *Kreuz Zeitung* or the *Daily Telegraph* or the *Petit Journal.*"[1]

Perhaps the Professor personifies the tit too much. Perhaps a psychologist would say that there is no sham-morality in its conduct, but that having (to satisfy its hunger) done what might be also done from hostility, its emotions of hostility are stimulated by association, so that it acts as against an enemy and triumphs as a conqueror. But even so, who will deny the reality in animals of selfishness, sometimes expressed in vicious attacks where no attack is justified, or of that enjoyment of power for its own sake which is the purest form of Pride? Man's trouble is not only a sin of his race; it is, in the precise Johannine phrase, a " sin of the world (cosmos)," which comes to maturity in him. It is worse in him; for he knows another course that he might follow. He not only acts wrongly; but he acts wrongly with knowledge that his act is wrong and that nothing but himself prevents his acting right. Moreover, it is perfectly clear that man has, in fact, not only deepened the intensity of evil already active, but has deliberately chosen and created further evil. He is not—nothing is—totally corrupt or depraved; but he is " very far gone " from what was possible for him. Can he recover? Are the forces which we have watched at work in the ordinary process of history sufficient to carry him to his goal?

The forces of which we have spoken are all centred upon self-interest. The Voluptuary is driven to self-respect by the discovery that in mere momentary pleasures there is no satisfaction. The individual learns good citizenship by the realisation that his welfare depends on that of his family and his country.

---

[1] Gilbert Murray, *Essays and Addresses*, p. 163; quoted by Prof. W. H. Moberly in his (most admirable) paper on " Moral Indignation," read to the Oxford Philosophical Society in March 1923.

Even when in war he gives his life for his country, there is likely to be the sense that it is for *his* country in its struggle with a country that is not his. The arguments which mainly lead to the League of Nations are grounded on the impossibility of security for any nation on any other ground. It is the small nations which actually show most concern about the League. There are other forces at work also: the truly disinterested love of parents for children—a heritage, like our selfishness, from the animal world; the similar response of children to parents; devotion to righteousness for its own sake, whether in a life-time of service or in the death of the soldier who fights not chiefly for his country but for the right; the fellowship in all spiritual goods, Knowledge, Beauty, and Love. These things exist; they could become the dominant factors of human life; yet it seems clear that the other considerations which find their centre in self are not being weakened in comparison. The higher life appears in occasional freaks of nature against all the probabilities and in defiance of all circumstances, as every slum parson knows; [1] so it proves its own possibility. Otherwise it exists mostly as a superstructure, after certain elementary claims have been made good. Mainly our progress is the extension of the Social Contract according to Hobbes and Glauco, the agreement not to inflict or to suffer injuries; it is the substitution of enlightened selfishness for stupid selfishness. Of any emancipation from selfishness itself, or any attainment of perfect fellowship in self-surrender to the absolute good, our historic progress hitherto gives no promise whatsoever.

Man needs education; but still more he needs conversion. Man needs political progress and social reform; but still more he needs redemption; man needs peace and security, but still more he needs eternal life.

---

[1] Perhaps then it is always dependent on the forces liberated by religious faith, with which at present we are not dealing.

The nature of Man is the chief instance hitherto
of that stratification which is the structure of Reality;
but his own nature and history prove that if left to
himself he is incomplete.   But inasmuch as he can
appreciate absolute values he is ready for fellowship
with the Highest; his completion will come when
God indwells him.

Before going on to consider whether or by what
process this completion is being wrought out, we
must pause to ask what is required to give real meaning
to human history whether or not it ever comes to a
triumphant conclusion on earth.   The significance of
any process may lie either in its result or in its whole
course, or in both.   The meaning of history must lie
partly in its result; and indeed we shall see that it
lies mainly there, though the result may not be any
consummation achieved on this planet.   On the other
hand, if the meaning of history lies in its result only,
its rationality is precarious, and in any case, if this
result is any terrestrial event, those who have died
before the result appears are denied any share in
that significance; and this in another way makes
the process itself morally irrational.   But if the meaning is even partly in the process itself, then it is
only apprehensible from a point of view outside
and above the process, whence the process can be
regarded as a single whole.   In other words, history
is fully intelligible only in the light of eternity.
But, on the other hand, eternity must be conceived
as requiring the actual historic process as part of its
own content; for otherwise we render history unmeaning by the very means through which it is thought
to secure its significance.   If history exists merely
in the movement of its process it is unmeaning; if,
on the other hand, it is the temporal presentation of a
self-subsisting eternal Reality, it is unmeaning.   As
we must regard history in the light of eternity, so we
must conceive eternity in the light of history.   History

and eternity must be so conceived as to interpret each other.

It must be laid down categorically that the human mind cannot form any adequate conception of infinity or eternity; we can only conceive it by means of analogies which are known to be inadequate. But even in such a survey of the course of history as we have attempted, we are approaching the eternal, for we have considered the process as a single fact and have tried to formulate the unchanging principles which govern its changes. This analogy, however, is inadequate in a way that we can correct; for it suggests that the eternal comprehension is of principles which govern change in abstraction from the changes which they govern; and this, we saw, is fatal, for instead of explaining history by endowing it with significance it reduces history to a merely endless repetition of illustrations of one theme. As I have suggested elsewhere,[1] we come nearest to any real analogue to the eternal if we consider our own experience as we watch a play with which we are already familiar. We watch every incident in the light of its known consequences. The Greek tragedians derive the whole of their celebrated irony from this fact; the character in the play speaks or acts with an intention which the audience knows will be frustrated by the event. The process is essential; its meaning cannot be extracted from it and expressed in a formula; the story is the only expression of its meaning. Moreover, the movement of the story internally is free. Its opening does not necessitate its middle or end. And the Value of the opening and the middle is dependent on the end which, while they hold the field, is still not yet. The story of the drama is a self-determining system, where the parts are explained only by the whole which they constitute.

To make this analogy adequate we should have to

---

[1] *Mens Creatrix*, pp. 357-61.

introduce elements which by our capacity are not to be combined with the others. We must conceive the characters as literally creating their own parts as the play proceeds, instead of merely enacting a part created in advance, while none the less, eternally regarded, the story is a unity apprehended as such. This baffles our understanding; but we are baffled at the very point where we ought to be baffled, for it is at the point where the finite seeks to comprehend the infinite.

CHAPTER VI

THE NATURE OF GOD

" The relation of the Spirit to the world is that of a lover to his beloved, or of a creative artist to a wild mass of unpromising material, out of which he is perpetually evolving, by a divine and loving art, the most surprising and beautiful combinations —anything but the relation of a power-loving potentate to his subjects, which is the very last thing that should be thought of in such a connexion."—L. P. JACKS.

WE have seen that Reality consists of distinguishable grades whose nature is such that the higher require the lower for their existence, but the lower require to be possessed by the higher in order that their whole potentiality may be realised.[1]   We have found, further, that if there is in our experience any principle which explains the Universe as a whole, so that not only is it rational within itself but that its very existence is rational also, it is the principle of Will; but a Will which is thus the origin of the Universe is plainly the Creator, *i.e.* God.[2]

Now Will emerges within the system of the Universe in Man, who is the highest grade hitherto in the stratification of Reality, and who is first able to raise the question of the rationality of the Universe. This is natural enough, for it means that the capacity to raise the question is one aspect, while the capacity to answer it is another aspect, of one nature.[3]

When we passed on to consider that one nature,

---

[1] Chapter I., pp. 4-6.
[2] Chapter I., pp. 7-9.
[3] Of course " to answer it " means to give the answer in principle, not to supply a detailed solution of the question as regards all particular facts.

we found that the Will is a completely unified activity
of the whole nature in all its parts, so that in fact no
human act or effort perfectly fulfils the whole ideal
of Will; moreover, an act of pure Will is one wholly
determined from within, as no act of a finite nature
can ever be, for every finite nature must be itself in
part determined by its environment.[1] But for the
Will that Creates the Universe there is plainly no
environment. It must supply entirely the grounds
of its own action and remain independent of what it
calls into being.

Further, Will acts for the realisation of Value.
But the actual Value of the actual world largely consists
in the process of history—the moral struggle and
progressive effort both of individuals and communities.
And the significance of this process, we saw, must be
in the whole course of the process itself, that is in
eternity conceived as the completed totality of the
temporal. Therefore the Creative Will must be the
active energy of a Nature enjoying in literal fact the
spectacle of all time and all existence.

Now, if we think of the Time-process as a whole,
we may regard the Creation as one act, and the divine
apprehension as one act; God's thought externalised
itself in His work, and His work is comprehended
in His thought. Into the experience of that omniscient
comprehension it is not possible for us to enter. From
the nature of the case, only omniscience can know
what omniscience feels like. For every mind that is
not all-comprehending is conditioned throughout its
experience by its limitations; and in principle this
remains true however widely the limits are extended.
Infinity is not a very big finite; it is always something more, and, still more, something other. We
have enough of knowledge to know that our knowledge is limited and that an all-comprehensive Mind
is in principle possible; into the experience of such

[1] Chapter II.

a mind we cannot enter at all. Before the awful sublimity of absolute Godhead, man can only adore in wondering humility.[1]

Now if God does not apprehend the historic process as a process, then either that process has no meaning, which we saw to be unreasonable, or else there is some significance in creation which evades the omniscience of the Creator, which is absurd. Therefore we must suppose that He apprehends the process not only as a block in its completeness, but as a movement in its changes. But what He thus apprehends is the creation of His own Will. Consequently it is reasonable to hold that God Himself is active in the process itself. Indeed, this seems to be necessary. For our view is not that God once made the world, and thereafter watched and watches its course, but that its course is itself the object of His creative Will and comprehending Mind. Hence it is necessary that just as He contemplates His own act in History as a whole, so in that same History as a process He is enacting that which eternally He creates and contemplates.

And this rather highly abstract argument finds support in a department of human experience on which hitherto no part of our argument has rested, though we have attempted some account of its nature, —religious experience. This form of experience is, to the religious man, as much its own witness as is the experience of sight or hearing, of enjoying or knowing. But it is no more explicable to the irreligious man than colour is to the blind man. Moreover, it involves, as sense experience does not, a special kind of philosophy. Consequently in this department as in no other the validity of experience is challenged. But it is as real as any other form of

---

[1] Here assuredly we confront Otto's Mysterium Tremendum—something which to us is " wholly other," with a remoteness which our partial apprehension only serves to emphasise.

experience,[1] and the fact that it supports, and finds
support in, the general course of our argument is
evidence for both; indeed the strongest intellectual
foundation for theism is, as was said earlier, neither
purely philosophic argument in itself nor purely
religious experience in itself, but the coincidence of
these two.   We have seen that on the side of Knowledge there can be no complete fellowship of man
with God, if by knowledge we mean intellectual grasp
of an articulated system of fact: here man is subject
to limitation and all his experience is relative.   But
in another direction man reaches a true finality—he
can appreciate absolute Value.

We have already seen that man has actual fruition
of absolute Beauty and Goodness, such as he cannot
have of absolute truth except in so restricted a sphere
as only to indicate what the apprehension of absolute
Truth would be.[2]   But it is not on this for the moment
that the argument rests.   Man appreciates absolute
Value mainly through the sense of absolute obligation
which it imposes, and this is as real in relation to
Truth as it is in relation to Beauty and Goodness.
And it is through this chiefly that man first actually
experiences God.   For if there is an absolute obligation, and if there is a Will on whose act all existence
depends, then that obligation must be the injunction
of that Will; just as, taking another point of view,
if there is a Creative Will, the end of its action must
be absolute Value.   Therefore to be conscious of
absolute Value is already to be in some form of intercourse with God;[3] and this form of intercourse with
God comes to every human being.[4]

This religious experience in its more developed

---

[1] See Chapter III., where, it will be remembered, the apprehension of absolute
value is regarded as the primary form of religious experience.   I should maintain
that absolute value (when apprehended as such) always has the character described
by Otto as Numinous.

[2] See Chapter II.

[3] Cf. Genesis iii. 5.

[4] Cf. Chapters II. and III.

form is emphatic in its witness in two directions. First, it is emphatic in its witness that God genuinely cares what men do. Even if we suppose that God is not only the Creator but also the perpetual energiser of the world and its history, we might still suppose that He is Himself unmoved by its occurrences—though if we think out to the end the implications of such a divine Apathy we shall find that it makes the act of creation irrational.[1] Men have shrunk from the belief that the Almighty is really concerned about the doings of men. Probably this is due to a radically false estimate of greatness and of the relative importance of things; if man is spiritual and the stars are not, then God is vastly more concerned about the selfishness of a child than about the wreck of a solar system. Anyhow, the witness of religious experience is overwhelming. All those who have such experience of fellowship with God as commends itself to the conscience of other men as genuine, agree in depicting God as at once exalted above all the tumult and anxiety of life, and also suffering grief and indignation at the conduct of man. " Thus saith the high and lofty One that inhabiteth eternity, whose name is Holy: I dwell in the high and holy place, with him also that is of a contrite and humble spirit, to revive the spirit of the humble and to revive the heart of the contrite ones. For I will not contend for ever, neither will I be always wroth: for the spirit should fail before me, and the souls which I have made. For the iniquity of his covetousness was I wroth and smote him, I hid my face and was wroth: and he went on frowardly in the way of his heart." " And now, O inhabitants of Jerusalem and men of Judah, judge, I pray you, betwixt me and my vineyard. What could have been done more to my vineyard, that I have not

---

[1] A parallel difficulty besets the characteristically Greek conceptions of God; cf. the God of Aristotle, who, just because His knowledge is perfect, is wholly unaware of the very existence of this imperfect world!

done in it? Wherefore, when I looked that it should bring forth grapes, brought it forth wild grapes?"[1] These utterances, though separated by a century and a half in their composition, reflect a similar experience of God; they are characteristic of the higher religious experience, as distinct from philosophic speculation, in all ages.

Secondly, religious experience is emphatic in its witness to a positive activity of God in history, and that in two forms. It asserts an activity of God within the souls of those who in any degree try to serve Him, so that they become aware of His presence urging, sustaining, and pressing them forwards. "The Spirit helpeth our infirmity: for we know not how to pray as we ought; but the Spirit himself maketh intercession for us with groanings that cannot be uttered":[2] that is plainly a record of frequently experienced fact; and most religious people have an experience which, though less vivid, is similar in kind. But religious experience also asserts the action of God's Providence in History. This often appears in small things, which any one who likes can describe as mere coincidence—meaning (I suppose) that the concurrent events are each and all the blind product of unknown causal processes. But experience enables us to say that by the "method of concomitant variations" we are entitled to affirm a causal connexion between the cultivation of the devotional life and the events which surprise us by their apposite occurrence. Nor, if we believe in God at all, is this surprising; if we are sensitive to the divine influence and responsive to the divine will it is natural and even probable that we should become instrumental to the divine purpose even beyond our knowledge of it.[3]

---

[1] Isaiah lvii. 15-17; v. 3, 4. No doubt this form of religious experience is most typical of Hebrew religion; but in the Greek religion it is present, and even in Hinduism and its daughters, though there the philosophic doctrine has so depreciated it as to reduce it to a minimum.
[2] Romans viii. 26.   [3] Cf. Chapter XI., specially pp. 195-196.

A further extension of this experience is also natural and probable. The fact of men's influence upon one another is unquestioned; and if so, intercessory prayer may be expected to be powerful for influencing the conduct and character of men, as experience seems beyond all reasonable doubt to show that it does.

But one part of the witness of religious experience is vehemently challenged; for it claims to find in historic occurrences an activity of God over and above the influencing of the human spirit. This appears both in the " raising up " of men to do certain work needed for the accomplishment of the providential purpose, and also in the occurrence of natural convulsions or other phenomena in the physical world. Yet the testimony is clear. If Isaiah was wrong in regarding the destruction of Sennacherib's army by plague as due to divine activity, it is very hard to attribute any authority to his view of life at all; for if history is not subordinate to the divine will in such a way as to make possible that interpretation of that event, then not only is he mistaken here or there in his understanding of God's will, but the whole orientation of his thought is false.

The objection to this view of things is twofold.[1] First, it is objected that, while human conduct may be self-determined in such a way as to leave room for real contingency, physical nature is governed by invariable laws (or, to be more accurate, displays invariable uniformity) so that if God intervenes in the way suggested He contradicts the principle of His own creative act. But it is impossible to " cut the universe in two with a hatchet " in this way. The object of the creative act is the whole universe, in which man is a part, and (as we have seen) the part which most fully reveals the principle of the whole. Moreover, if there is indeterminism in the conduct of

[1] I omit the objection that God cannot will physical calamities, as I must return to that whole class of considerations later (see Chapters X. and XI.).

man, it affects all else.   If I throw a stone or a cricket-ball, or if I walk across the room, I affect the movement of the earth in relation to its own centre of gravity. The fact that the amount of difference which I can make is too minute to be measured or taken into calculation does not affect the principle.   The position of the earth in the stellar system and its own rotation are not fixed unalterably by the laws of motion; they are also affected (though not appreciably) by the variable action of human wills.   No argument can be drawn from the " laws " of the physical world to discredit the notion of such divine activity in that world as will seem to us to be " intervention."

The other objection to such a belief depends on the view that it is inconsistent with the divine constancy. God is immutable, for if He changes it must be to something other than perfection; and that, being perfect, He cannot will, nor can He change except by His own will.   But it is characteristic of Purpose that, while constant in itself, it prompts diversity of actions according to the circumstances in which the purpose is from time to time to be fulfilled.   If, then, there is any element of indeterminism in human conduct, we shall expect to find a perpetual adaptation of the divine activity to meet the varied circumstances created by man's free conduct.   The Will is un-swerving, the Purpose unchanged; but the very constancy of the fulfilment of the one purpose requires variations in the method of activity, if the other con-ditions of the activity are variable.

This is a point of first-rate importance.   If the unifying principle of the Universe is not a system of intellectual principles but an active Will, this provides for elasticity in the unifying principle itself.   We can easily imagine a great statesman, whose aim is to weld a congeries of conflicting clans into a harmonious unity.   At first he may insist on a strong centralised government, to the indignation of " Liberals."   Later, when appreciation of common interests has become established, he may follow a policy of devolution, to the horror of " Tories." Smaller men will call him inconsistent. But he may be taking at each stage the next step in the fulfilment of a constant purpose. Purpose exhibits its own unity in the adaptations to changing conditions of which it is capable. We should therefore antecedently expect, what religious experience is found to affirm, that God not only controls all the world by the laws of its own being, inherent in its elements by His creative act, but that as He made it for the realisation of certain values, so in pursuit of those values He acts directly upon its course as occasion in His all-seeing judgement may require.

Now in the corresponding activity of men we find a suggestive parallel. Just in the degree in which a man achieves that unity of personal life which is the completion of Will in him, he reveals himself in some of his activities more than in others. A great part of his life—far the greatest in the mere " clock-time " which it occupies—is covered by a routine which he has partly accepted and partly constructed, and which tells his neighbours very little about him. The attempt to interest a company by the story of how the great Duke of Wellington used to eat figs was a failure: " it turned out to be the ordinary way, quadrisection down the stalk and then four licks."[1] There are, however, events which show that the Duke could react to circumstances by methods not at all familiar, such as the tactics of Salamanca or the carrying of Catholic Emancipation; and it is these which reveal the real man. Two brothers may grow up side by side, sharing the same education and following the same routine; their friends may come to think of them as exactly alike; then some sudden emergency may arise, and the two react to it in utterly different

[1] Beeching, *Pages from a Private Diary*, p. 258.

ways, which are yet both quite consistent with all that had previously been made known of their characters. So a man sometimes acts in such a way that even those who have known him well exclaim, " I never knew he had it in him." The whole of a man's conduct is expressive of his character and purpose in some degree, but these exceptional acts are the true revelation of him.

So it may be with God Himself. The routine of nature manifests His Will; but there may come occasions where action of a special and specially characteristic quality is required and the action so taken may be in an especial degree revealing; such acts are commonly called miracles.

We reach, then, a conception of God as at once comprehending the entirety of things in the whole range of space and of time, and also as constantly at work within the process of His own creation, shaping it as a master-artist till in its completeness—not its result only but its whole course—He finds the good for which He made it. As He so works, He follows for the most part the routine that is apparent to us as the uniformity of nature; but there are also occasions when His own constancy requires that in face of special emergencies He should act in an exceptional way; such action will be in a special measure a revelation.

He made the world for its value; this comes to actualisation in man, and for what man can give Him —loyalty and obedience and even love—He cares more than for the splendour of starry heavens or the delicacy of insects' wings. But man, through his very sense of value, has chosen a way which is not God's to pursue his own good. The evil or sin of the world—in any case a problem worthy of divine solution —culminates in the self-will of man, in whom most of all, hitherto at least, the joy of creation was to be sought. Here is an emergency sufficient if any could be for a special and specially revealing act.

PART III

THE CORE OF THE ARGUMENT

CHAPTER VII

THE GODHEAD OF JESUS CHRIST

" Our Lord is the crown, nay, the very substance of all Revelation. If He cannot convince the soul, no other can. The believer stakes all faith on His truth, all hope on His power. If the man of science would learn what it is that makes believers so sure of what they hold, he must study with an open heart the Jesus of the Gospels; if the believer seeks to keep his faith steady in the presence of so many and sometimes so violent storms of disputation, he will read of, ponder on, pray to, the Lord Jesus Christ."—ARCHBISHOP TEMPLE.

WE have been led by the argument to a view of the universe which requires for its confirmation a divine act in the midst of history. We have found that God is such as to act in a special way if occasion demand; we have found an occasion which demands such an act. If there is no such act, we must either compose ourselves to await it as the Jews were taught to await the coming of the Christ, or else we must abandon our whole view of life and the world.

But there is record of a divine act such as the need requires. It is the story of the Birth, Life, Death, Resurrection, and Ascension of Jesus of Nazareth, and the consequent coming of the Holy Spirit.

For this act the record tells of long preparation, and we can trace the same preparation at work beyond the record. We see how the gift of Law, which ancient Rome brought to the world, and the peace which she imposed, provided an arena for the proclamation of the divine act. We see how the gift of Philosophy, which ancient Greece had brought, provided a means of formulating and so handing on the

significance of the divine act. We read in the record
how by special experiences, both spiritual and external,
a people had been prepared to witness the divine act.
But the act in which all this finds its pivot is the
Incarnation.

We see One who was born by no activity of human
will, but only by the acquiescence of the Virgin-Mother
in the divine Will; who called men to such a dependence on and fellowship with God as had never been
conceived, yet lived always as one who Himself
experienced what He taught; who died at the hands
of those He called to share His blessedness, and in the
very hour of His anguish prayed for their forgiveness;
who rose bodily from the grave, and closed His
appearances to His disciples by the enacted parable
of His Ascension from the mountain whereon they
stood till He was enveloped in the cloud of the divine
glory.

He was not understood all at once even by those
who became His most intimate disciples. If our
faith in the revelation of God thus given and in the
God thus revealed is to be a reasonable faith, we must
trace the process whereby they reached that degree
of understanding which made it possible to formulate,
to propagate, and to trust the convictions embodied
in the Christian Creed. From this we may expect
to learn both the empirical basis of our faith, and also
the process by which God leads men to the understanding of His supremely characteristic act and
therein of Himself.

The first disciples inevitably began by thinking of
their Master as a man; yet from the first there was
in Him something mysterious which was the starting-
point for a fuller apprehension. There were strange
sayings uttered by John the Baptist which had attributed to Him such powers as a man could hardly
exercise. His teaching had both a graciousness and
an authority that seemed hard to reconcile with His

supposed origin. His wonderful works exceeded what was known of contemporaries or recorded of any in past times except the greatest. After a period of specially close intercourse with Him they were ready to follow St. Peter in acknowledging Him as the promised Messiah. But this is still far short of a confession of His Deity. In our day many people identify the terms superhuman and divine. They think that if in our Lord besides humanity there was something more than humanity, that something must be divinity. But this is quite a baseless assumption, and the Jews did not make it. What from the scene at Caesarea Philippi onwards the Apostles certainly believed is that their Master was more than human in the sense in which we are human. The Messiah was at that date conceived as a superhuman and celestial Being, who might properly be spoken of as in a peculiar sense the Son of God; but he was not conceived as divine in such a fashion as would lead to His being spoken of as God the Son. The Fourth Gospel, which I believe to be the work of John the son of Zebedee, and quite certainly to rest at least on the memory of the " beloved disciple " who was an eye-witness of what he narrated, records an exclamation of devotion by St. Thomas after the Resurrection which contains the whole Christian doctrine, but this remains an isolated utterance, and the theology implied by it was not yet intellectually grasped. If the Apostles reflected at the time on the saying " I and the Father are one " they would remember that He justified that saying by a reference to the Psalm where those to whom the word of the Lord came are dignified with the divine title. He claimed to be the revelation of God, but the disciples who heard Him say " He that hath seen me hath seen the Father " only reached, before the Passion at any rate, the confession that He was one sent by God.[1] Our Lord's language did

---

[1] St. John xvi. 30.

not necessarily imply that He claimed to be Himself Jehovah. And if it had, we can see that it could only have baffled and perplexed their minds. They were Jews with all the Old Testament behind them; it needed more than a verbal claim to persuade them to ascribe to a man divine honours.

This is still the doctrinal situation in the first days after Pentecost. In the speeches of St. Peter in Acts ii.-v. there is still no suggestion that Jesus, the prophet of Nazareth, is identified in the speaker's mind with the God of Israel. He is the anointed— the Christ—of God; He is exalted to be a Prince and a Saviour; but He is not presented as Himself God.

This is still true of St. Stephen; but here we see a change beginning. St. Stephen is not only the first martyr, but the first Christian of whose death we have any record. The vision of Jesus at the right hand of God does not necessarily carry us beyond the celestial Messiah of contemporary apocalyptic literature. But the words which follow imply something more than that: " Lord Jesus, receive my spirit." Every Jew knew the words of Psalm xxxi. which our Lord Himself had uttered on the Cross, though by adding the word " Father " He had given them a new note of intimacy: " Father, into thy hands I commend my spirit." But here the first Christian to die commends his spirit to Jesus. It is a devotional, not a dogmatic utterance; but its implications will need a whole theology to state them. It is a devotional equation of Jesus with the God of the spirits of all flesh. It is characteristic of the growth of Christian theology that religious experience should precede dogmatic formula. Indeed it is just because of this that Christian theology is a veritable science.[1]

It was St. Stephen, and the movement with which

---

[1] Cf. Rackham on *The Acts of the Apostles* (one of the Westminster Commentaries), pp. lxxi.-lxxiv. The priority of life to doctrine is here very emphatically set forth, and the list of passages of p. lxxii. where our Lord's Deity is plainly implied but as plainly *not* stated is most impressive.

he was associated, who freed Christianity from the limitations of Judaism. It is scarcely possible to doubt that St. Stephen was the chief human agent in the conversion of St. Paul. Certainly the form of Christianity to which St. Paul was converted was that for preaching which St. Stephen had been stoned. But at first his doctrinal position is not distinguishable from that of St. Peter's early sermons. We must remember, however, that the spiritual antecedents are different. St. Peter had been with the Lord in His earthly ministry; he had walked with Him in the corn-fields; he had sat with Him in the boat upon the lake; he had supped with Him among His friends. For him the risen and ascended Christ is chiefly the Man whom God exalted to be a Prince and a Saviour. St. Paul had probably never seen the Lord till on the Damascus road his eyes were blinded by the dazzling light and he heard the voice which said: " I am Jesus whom thou persecutest." For him the Christ who died upon the Cross is first and foremost the celestial Messiah, who even in the earliest epistles is associated with God in the opening greetings as a source of grace and peace.

Here, too, experience comes first. There is the experience of the conversion itself; following on that comes the realisation of reconciliation to God by fellowship with Christ; resultant from that comes the apprehension that in Christ is found the explanation of history because He is the revelation of the Father's will and the agent of its fulfilment. It would be impossible to construct a theological system which should do justice to all the elements in St. Paul's religious experience without affirming the Deity of Christ. But St. Paul, though a man of supreme intellectual penetration and grasp, was not in his Epistles writing systematic theology. It was never his primary concern to give an intellectually satisfying account of his whole religious experience and conviction; and it is not quite certain that he ever used the word " God " as a title of Jesus Christ. But he often comes so near to it that it is only for purposes of almost pedantic accuracy that we can distinguish between what he does say and such an explicit confession. He says that " in Christ dwelleth all the fullness of the Godhead bodily "; he says that Christ existed before the Incarnation " in the form of God "; he says that Christ is " the image of the invisible God "; he says that " God was in Christ reconciling the world unto Himself." Only the Trinitarian position can theologically do justice to such expressions. But it is true that he seldom, and perhaps never, said in so many words that Jesus Christ is God. The punctuation of Romans ix. 5 is doubtful; the reading (as well as the authorship) is doubtful in 1 Timothy iii. 16; and the doubt affects the very question at issue.

Personally I am quite convinced that on some occasions at least the word " Lord "—Κύριος—as applied by St. Paul to Jesus Christ is to be interpreted as meaning an identification with Jehovah. It is only possible to escape from this interpretation, and from the Trinitarian implications of the phrases already quoted, by a series of unnatural interpretations. But those interpretations are not absolutely impossible, and if we are being scrupulously exact we cannot say that beyond all doubt St. Paul identified Jesus of Nazareth with the God of Israel, though we are entitled to say that the alternative view, involving a frequent strain upon language, can hardly be correct. After all, the familiar words with which 11 Corinthians closes—" The grace of our Lord . . .," etc., especially when we pay attention to the order of the phrases, cannot be accounted for by any theory which does not attribute to Jesus Christ the dignity of God Himself. In short, I am entirely convinced that St. Paul fully believed in the Deity of our Lord; it is certain that, even if he had not formulated this belief to himself, his faith can only be articulated by Trinitarian theology; but this faith is usually expressed by him in the language of spiritual function and experience, not usually, and just possibly never, in a specific theological declaration.

The Epistle to the Hebrews exalts Christ above the angels, and attributes His pre-eminence to His inheritance as Son of God. Possibly the quotation from Psalm xlv. in chapter i. verse 8 is intended as an attribution of Deity to the Son, but here too there is a doubt about the interpretation. St. Paul and this author hold a religious position which absolutely necessitates the doctrine of the Deity of Jesus Christ, and far the most natural interpretation of their language maintains that they themselves accepted and affirmed this doctrine. But it is not possible to say with absolute certainty that they did so. And indeed if the doctrine of our Lord's Godhead had been specifically affirmed in very many of the New Testament scriptures, the Arian controversy could never have arisen within the Church. The phrase " Athanasius contra mundum " reminds us that the great upholder of what we now rightly regard as the central and fundamental article of the Christian faith was for a time in a minority even among his brother bishops; and this would not have been possible at all if many of the Apostolic writings had been fully explicit.

And yet some of them are surely explicit. It is impossible to doubt the doctrine of the Johannine books. In the Apocalypse the association of the heavenly Christ with the Eternal and Almighty Father is so close that no doctrine short of the affirmation of His Deity can be said to express it; and in xxii. 13 the Christ is represented as claiming in His own Person the most supremely distinctive title of Almighty God, which the Almighty had used of Himself in i. 8. But the whole book intervenes. Christ is revealed as God through the seer's experience of His exercise of divine functions, and only then is He presented as Himself the Almighty God.

In the Johannine Gospel and General Epistle the position is at last explicit and is stated from the outset. He who tabernacled among men under the name of Jesus is the eternal Word of God, Himself God, the Agent of creation. To be " in Him that is true " is the same thing as to be " in His Son, Jesus Christ." [1] And of this God, who is one with Jesus Christ, it is said: " This is the true God and eternal life." Every supposed god except this God is an idol.

What is the upshot of this rapid survey of the New Testament scriptures? It is that our faith in the Godhead of Jesus Christ does not rest chiefly on any single text or group of texts; it is a faith to which men found themselves irresistibly impelled by their growing spiritual experience as in the fellowship of the Holy Ghost they more and more deeply apprehended the grace of our Lord Jesus Christ and the love of God. We have not here a perplexing dogma imposed by authority upon men's reluctant minds; what we have is a triumphant discovery based on experience as all scientific truth must be based. They use religious and devotional language which completely implies the doctrine of the Godhead of Jesus Christ before they state that doctrine in set terms. The experience comes first; the formulation comes later. That is a spiritual law, and our Lord always observed it. If He had made a claim of Deity in absolutely unmistakable terms, He would have fallen under His own saying, " If I honour myself, my honour is nothing," and He would have put mere intellectual apprehension before spiritual realisation. And even so He would have hindered, not helped, intellectual apprehension. If standing before them in the flesh He had said to those devout Jews " I am God," He would have reduced them to mere bewilderment.

[1] 1 John v. 20.

Therefore, though the claim is there, as we shall see later, its verbal expression is always so interwoven with the spiritual activity that it did not at first challenge the critical or merely intellectual understanding of the disciples.[1] To this topic we must return. For the moment it is enough to say that an unquestionable declaration by our Lord would have largely robbed faith of its spiritual value. If St. Peter had proclaimed his Master as God directly after Pentecost, his authority would no doubt have weighed greatly with later disciples of the same Master. But far more weighty and cogent than any such impulsive declaration is the process that we actually see going on in the experience of the Apostles and of the infant Church. At every stage the same principle is at work. Men trust and find themselves " justified " (to use St. Paul's favourite word) in trusting; as they trust more deeply the vindication becomes more complete. They become aware that Jesus Christ does what only God can do. The functions which He discharges are functions of God.[2]

Now functions, that is actions and reactions, are all we know. If Jesus Christ performs the acts of God, then Jesus Christ is God in the only sense in which any name can justifiably be attributed to any object. The method by which in the New Testament the supreme affirmation is reached is the only method by which any such affirmation could be scientifically justified.

There are some who feel that, if the full and conscious belief in our Lord's Deity was reached by such a process lasting through half a century or more, it may have been the product of a sort of

[1] Cf. Gore, *Belief in Christ*, p. 68. " We can conceive nothing further from the method of Jesus than that He should have startled and shocked their consciences by proclaiming Himself as God. But He had done something which in the long run would make any other estimate of Him hardly possible."

[2] This comes near to the familiar notion that Christ has the value of God, which is often contrasted with the doctrine that Christ *is* God. This contrast is indefensible. He cannot really have the value of God unless He *is* God.

I

self-hypnotism. The early believers would tend to exalt their Lord, and the process continued until they had set Him on the throne of the universe. But this objection ignores the actual conditions. Greeks might deify Heracles; Romans might deify the Caesars; because for them deification only meant admission to a Pantheon which contained a large number of other deities, each of them quite finite, with certain known interests and even with certain known defects. But the Apostles were Jews. For them to acclaim their Master as God was to recognise in their Friend the One Eternal and Almighty God. They did not say that He was one among other gods, as each of us is one among other men. They learnt to see in their Friend and Master the One Almighty, the One Eternal, the One Uncreated, the One Incomprehensible. There was not, and there could not be, the smallest natural tendency to such a result. The recognition of Him as Messiah would make the result itself not easier, but more difficult, for Jehovah and the Messiah were in Jewish thought two Beings and not one. Therefore long before the doctrine is actually affirmed we find the experience on which it rests. Before the last journey to Jerusalem the Apostles already regarded their Lord as super-human. From St. Stephen's martyrdom onwards we find a realisation of His relation to men's souls, which involves His Deity. St. Paul uses phrases which are only just short of the formal assertion of His Deity, and probably did formally assert it on one occasion at least,[1] while on others he identifies Jesus Christ with Jehovah by his use of the title " Lord." When St. John proclaims the doctrine in explicit language, he has added nothing of substance to what was already there; he has only formulated it. It is of supreme importance to notice that St. Paul's exalted Christology aroused no opposition. There were many who were

[1] Romans ix. 5.

ready to oppose him, but none chose this point for their attack. This means quite plainly that his doctrine was recognised as only giving form to what was already implicit in the faith of the first Christians.[1] The doctrine is truly a formulation of experience.

But it is also inevitably more than that. The belief in the Godhead of Jesus Christ is not the mere identification of Jesus with Jehovah as known to the writers of the Old Testament. Rather it is the enlargement and enrichment of the thought of God by the necessity of making room within it for what men had learnt concerning God through the teaching, and still more through the Life, Death, and Resurrection of Jesus Christ. To this modification of the thought of God we must now turn, though the fuller treatment of it must be reserved to a later stage in the argument.[2]

The fundamental note in the Jewish conception of God was Unity. The dogma " The Lord our God, the Lord is One," does not mean merely that as a matter of fact there is no other Being who may fitly be called God. It rests on the fact that the divine attributes are such as to exclude plurality. There cannot be two All-rulers. Polytheism has always to allocate different spheres or departments to its various deities. When once God has been conceived as the Almighty or All-ruler, the bare notion of a multiplicity of gods becomes impossible. It was natural and even necessary that this unity should at first be apprehended in its pure simplicity, free from any thought of distinctions within it. But as soon as men had learnt to see God in Jesus Christ problems arose to which the doctrine of the Trinity offers, not indeed a solution, but a formula of elucidation.

God is known as All-ruler; Jesus was limited in His action by the response that He could evoke. God is known as the All-knowing; Jesus experienced

---

[1] Cf. Gore, *Belief in Christ*, p. 91.
[2] See Chapters X. and XIII.

disappointment. If Jesus is God, then there are in the very Being of God elements which could not be combined in the experience of any one person conceived by the analogy of our personality. The men who were confronted with this problem had also the experience which led to the doctrine of the Holy Spirit as a Third Person in the divine Trinity; but with this we are not now concerned except so far as it explains why the distinctions within the Unity are three and not only two.

The Being and Life of God surpass our powers of comprehension. Christian theology is, in this sense, emphatically agnostic. It constantly declares that God is above and beyond our knowledge. But it does not on that account admit that any one proposition is as true about Him as any other. As has already often been said, the world exists in grades; and it is the destiny of each to be controlled by what is higher than itself; indeed only as this happens does each grade reveal its own latent capacities. Highest of all these grades is Personality. As known to us this may not be the last term. But it affords the best analogy we have for the Most High. We shall think of Him more accurately when we think of Him in terms of Personality than in any other way.

Now this Divine Personality cannot (as we saw) be the Personality of one Person only, if it is true that God is seen in Jesus Christ. Yet there is assuredly one God and no more. The simple Christian need not go beyond this affirmation: "The Father is God, the Son is God, and the Holy Ghost is God. And yet there are not three Gods, but one God." But our task at present is to understand this so far as we may.

What is it that constitutes the distinction of one Person from another? And how far is this distinctness compatible with real unity of Being, or (to use the technical term) of Substance? It seems to me that we are distinguished from one another by two principles. One of these is essential; it is the mere numerical difference in the centres of consciousness themselves. I, being myself, am not you; you, in being yourself, are not I. We are distinct selves. We may hold the same opinions, share the same experience, aim at the same goal; but we do it together and remain distinct. The other principle is accidental. I am the child of my parents, a native of my country, a member of my school and university; these things are not mere external appendages to my personality, but actually make it what it is. And any two finite persons living under the conditions of space and time will be distinguished for ever by the variety in the circumstances of their history. Even two twins can never have quite the same experience. They may stand side by side as they look at a mountain; yet they see it from slightly different angles. Even if they change places, the order in which they see it from the two angles of vision will be different.

Clearly these differences, which I have called accidental, are due to the conditions of our finitude. If we conceive centres of consciousness capable of envisaging the totality of things and themselves immune from the conditions of time and space, differences of this kind would vanish. But the other differences would remain. What we should then have would be three centres of one consciousness. Any further treatment of this theme must be postponed; but so much needed to be said in elucidation of the fundamental Christian conviction that Jesus is God. In Him God is incarnate; and inasmuch as God is one it is not part of God, but God in His fullness who is incarnate thus. Yet it is God in one of the three Persons or centres of His one spiritual Being who is incarnate, and that one which though co-equal in glory is derivative and not primary.

We have now to see how far the interpretation

which the Apostles achieved and the Church formulated finds support in the recorded words and deeds
of Jesus Himself. When above we attempted a
survey of the Gospels it was to gauge the understanding of Jesus Christ which His disciples had reached at
various stages. Now we turn back to the Historic
Figure portrayed in the Gospels and ask how far we
find there a basis for the faith which sprang up in the
infant Church, and what light the record throws on
the problem which that faith creates, the problem
how Jesus Christ is God.

The first point to which I would call attention is
the fact that the Synoptic evangelists are obviously
concerned with history and not with theology. No
doubt they tell the story with a religious aim in view;
no doubt they tell it, each according to the spiritual
needs of those readers whom he has chiefly in view.
But their concern is with history. So, to take the
most signal instance for illustration, the facts of our
Lord's Passion are minutely told, but there is no
attempt to indicate a doctrine of the Atonement.
The Synoptists are concerned to tell a story; what light
does the story throw on our enquiry?

The earliest of the Gospels—St. Mark's—is plainly
designed to suggest that with John the Baptist, and
still more with our Lord, divine power came into the
world. His first words are: " The beginning of the
Gospel of Jesus Christ, the Son of God." The words
" Son of God " do not, as we have seen, necessarily
imply Deity, though, of course, they are compatible
with it. But they certainly imply something more
than mere humanity. Our Lord never relies on His
miracles as evidence for men's faith in Him to rest
upon, but this only makes the more impressive the
picture of power proceeding from Him in works of
love as He moves about among men.

Again, there is that perfection of intercourse with
the Father which every careful reader of the story

notices. A man in the midst of the sinful world who is never separated from perfect communion with God is a miracle quite as great as any of the recorded wondrous works.

Further, we note the explicit claim to be the Judge of all men and of all nations—surely a divine function. And we recall the untroubled confidence with which He substitutes for the Mosaic Law His own legislation as its fulfilment, though He not only admits but even insists upon the divine authority of the Mosaic Law. He calls the law Divine, and alters it. In this He does not state a doctrinal theory of His own Person nor give any indication that such a theory is in His mind. But He does without either arrogance or incongruity what only God can fitly do. But besides this there are words of direct claim to be the Mediator between God and men. " All things have been delivered unto me of my Father; and no one knoweth the Son save the Father; neither doth any know the Father, save the Son, and he to whomsoever the Son willeth to reveal him."[1] Those words, with their markedly Johannine ring, belong to what the critics tell us is the very oldest and safest strand of evidence— the non-Marcan matter which is common to St. Matthew and St. Luke. But they are associated, as such utterances always are, with spiritual experience. Both evangelists associate them with the words about revelation unto babes, and St. Matthew further associates them with the invitation " Come unto Me," which is virtually their translation from the language of theology into the language of practical religion. No one can say " Come unto me and I will give you rest " except one who can say " I and the Father are one," for it is only in the Eternal God that the souls of men find rest. The claim is not made as a claim, but rather in exposition of a spiritual experience, and it is so phrased as to be intelligible to those who recall

[1] St. Matthew xi. 27; St. Luke x. 22.

it in the light of a fuller insight, but hardly intelligible to the Apostles as they first heard the words. We note this feature again when we turn to St. John's Gospel.

Did He ever make use of powers that are altogether outside the reach of ordinary men? The question is hard to answer, because we simply do not know what power would be possessed by a man who was, and always had been, in perfect fellowship with God. It is narrated that St. Peter was able to walk on the water until his faith gave way to fear. But perhaps at the stilling of the storm and perhaps at the Transfiguration, and certainly (as I should say) at the feeding of the multitude, He displayed powers beyond those of men however inspired. It is noticeable that when He stilled the storm He did not pray to His Father or invoke the Divine Name; He spoke as the Lord of the elements, and we recall the bewilderment of the disciples at His doing so.

We turn to St. John's Gospel. It has long been my conviction that the supposed contrast between the teaching of the Synoptists and of St. John does not really exist. The two pictures are to some extent supplementary, but they represent a Figure recognisably identical. In St. John there are more frequent references to the unbroken fellowship with the Father, but nothing that in principle goes further than the passage already quoted, "All things have been delivered unto me of my Father," unless it be the words, "I and the Father are one." And even these words are uttered, not primarily for their theological significance, but in justification of an equation in spiritual experience already implied: "No one shall snatch them out of my hand," "no one is able to snatch them out of the Father's hand." The claim, moreover, is itself justified by the reference to Psalm lxxxii., which, as we saw, prevents it from being a dogmatic assertion of absolute Deity.

The total impression, strong in the Synoptists and permanently vivid in St. John, is that which St. John expresses in his Prologue. " We beheld his glory, glory as of an only-begotten from a Father." Through the human life there worked a power which was felt as coming from beyond, from God Himself, who here had·found His uniquely perfect self-expression.

Can we then penetrate at all the consciousness of Jesus Christ in the days of His earthly ministry? Let us make the attempt, reminding ourselves that just in the degree in which we accept the Church's account of Him we shall expect to find ourselves unable to reach any clear understanding of His Person; man, who is not yet God-possessed, cannot comprehend the perfect union of God and Man.

Christian theologians have tried in various ways to represent the Incarnation in the language appropriate to the thought of their day. As we set out upon the same attempt let us remember that no one theory has or can have the stamp of orthodoxy; and no theory is heretical or heterodox unless it denies that Jesus Christ is both Perfect God and Perfect Man.

First then let us be sure that the Incarnation was a reality and not a sham. He who lived among men and died on the Cross was the Second Person of the Eternal Trinity. But the life He lived on earth was a real human life, subject to all limitations that are the lot of humanity, and subject also to all temptations, save only such as arise from sin committed in the past.[1] He grew in knowledge as He grew in stature, and learnt by the same processes by which other men learn. But He was aware of an intimacy with God which He found that other men had not experienced. He interpreted this as a call to fulfil the promise of the Messiah who should come. The Voice that hailed Him at His Baptism called Him to begin the Messianic work. He comes among men healing and teaching, calling to

---

[1] This, I am sure, is the true meaning of Hebrews iv. 15.

repentance and proclaiming the divine Kingdom which it was the function of the Messiah to found. The divine is working through the human, and normally at least within its limitations. His prayers are real prayers. The Agony in Gethsemane is a real Agony, and the prayer then uttered is a real cry of humanity to its Creator. But all the while through the human channel comes flooding the divine Love and Power and Knowledge of the souls of men. He is conscious that He is something more than one sent by God. He is aware of such union with God, and of commission for such divine functions, that He stands for God before men. He knows that He is in the Father and the Father in Him. As He approaches the glory of the uttermost sacrifice, He remembers a like glory which had been His, before the world was.[1] Most markedly as the human personality [2] reaches its complete development—being made perfect by suffering—it reveals itself as having never been the ultimate fact about this human life. Behind it, working through it, utterly expressed by it so far as human nature allowed, but transcending it as Godhead transcends humanity, is found the Divine Word Himself. In order to live and die and rise again as Man he had subjected Himself to all the conditions of our life. He had, as St. Paul said, "emptied Himself." We shall be wrong if we infer that during those years the Second Person of the Trinity was denuded of those divine attributes for which there is no room in a human life. We have no data enabling us to draw inferences of that kind. What we may justly say is that from that moment there is in God not only a sympathetic understanding of our state and of death itself, but a real experience. He Himself hath suffered, being

[1] St. John xvii. 5.
[2] For those who think of Person or Personality as equivalents of Hypostasis this will have a heretical (Nestorian) sound. But St. Cyril and Nestorius did not mean by Hypostasis what I mean by Personality; nor did either apparently mean by it what the other meant.

tempted. This, I submit, is the impression left on the open-minded reader of the Gospels. They tell the story of a human life; but humanity is not the last word about it. He who so lived is not self-occupied or concerned with doctrines of His own Person. But He spontaneously and with conscious appropriateness does what only God can do. At times, as spiritual occasion arises, the implications of this come vividly before His mind. He is not self-analytical but He is self-revealing: and the self that He reveals is more than human, more than super-human; it is specifically divine.

CHAPTER VIII

THE PERSON OF CHRIST

That the Great Angell-blinding light should shrinke
His blaze, to shine in a poore shepherd's eye;
That the unmeasur'd God so low should sinke
As Pris'ner in a few poore Rags to lye;
That from his Mother's Brest he milke should drinke,
Who feeds with Nectar Heav'ns faire family;
    That a vile Manger his low Bed should prove
    Who in a Throne of stars Thunders above ;

That he whom the Sun serves, should faintly peepe
Through clouds of Infant flesh; that he the old
Eternal Word should be a Child, and weepe;
That he who made the fire should feare the cold;
That Heav'ns high Majesty his Court should keepe
In a clay cottage, by each blast conrol'd;
    That Glories self should serve our Griefs and feares,
    And free Eternity submit to yeares.

CRASHAW.

WE have seen that every grade in Reality finds its own fulfilment only when it is possessed by a higher grade, and that each higher grade uses those which are lower than itself for its expression. From this it follows that humanity only reveals its true nature when it is indwelt by what is higher than itself—and supremely when it is indwelt by the Highest; and that the Highest uses what is lower to express Himself and does this the more adequately as this lower approximates to likeness with Himself, so that of all things known to us human nature will express Him most perfectly. But if this is so, and if in Jesus Christ God lived on earth a human life, then it must be true that in Jesus Christ we shall find two things. In

Jesus Christ we shall find the one adequate presentation of God—not adequate, of course, to the infinite glory of God in all His attributes, but adequate to every human need, for it shows us God in terms of our own experience.   But in Jesus Christ we shall find also the one adequate presentation of Man—not man as he is apart from the indwelling of God, but Man as he is in his truest nature, which is only made actual when man becomes the means to the self-expression of God.

Part of the difficulty which a great teacher finds in conveying the new truth arises from the necessity of using words of which the meaning is already fixed. So the Lord Jesus was compelled to accept the title and office of the expected Messiah, because that came nearer than any other that existed to the truth about Himself.   The central core of meaning attached to this title was that the Messiah would inaugurate the Kingdom of God; and this indeed He did; but all the existing conceptions of the Kingdom and of the mode of its inauguration were so inadequate as to be misleading and productive of great difficulties in the minds of His hearers.   He had to transform the meaning of the terms " Messiah " and " Kingdom " by the use which He made of them.   So, later on, St. John spoke of Him as the Logos, though this word too in current use had many shades of meaning that were irrelevant or misleading.

This difficulty is nowhere more apparent than in the efforts of the early Church to reach some understanding of the Person of Jesus Christ.   Somehow, all Christians were agreed, He is rightly called God and Man.   But when men began to enquire How? and became involved thereby in controversy, they were hampered by the notions of Godhead and Humanity which already existed.   That the same being should be both God and Man in the sense in which those terms were commonly understood in the period of the Church's early history was not an un-

intelligible mystery but a demonstrable impossibility.
And yet nothing else was adequate to the fact. The
Church at Chalcedon virtually gave up the attempt to
understand, while refusing to sacrifice either part of
its apparently contradictory belief. All through the
age of the Councils the whole conception of both God
and Man was undergoing modification, partly through
the influence of the Incarnation itself, partly also
through the clarifying and hardening of the Greek
and (in origin) heathen terminology which was alone
available. The process of modification is still con-
tinuing, and presumably will continue until "the
consummation of the ages." But it is at least a gain
to recognise it; for as soon as we recognise it we are
delivered from the futile endeavour to fit into a coherent
theory of the Person of Christ conceptions of God and
Man which are derived wholly from elsewhere. Certainly we do not approach the problem with minds
nearly blank. The conceptions of God and Man derived from elsewhere—from ordinary experience, from
human religion, from pre-Christian revelation — are
not merely false or irrelevant.[1] They are provisionally
true, if they are adequate to the facts which give rise
to them, and the truth which they contain cannot be
obliterated by further revelation. But their truth is
of this provisional kind; and we shall not be dismayed
to find that if they are to become adequate to a fuller
reality they require modification. On the contrary,
we shall expect this, and deliberately assist it. Our
sacramental philosophy leads at once to the supposition
that nothing is fully known till it is possessed by a
higher. An observer on another planet watching the
nebula out of which our solar system grew might have
formed a theory of matter which would have been
adequate to the facts before him; but he could not
have constructed the sciences of zoology, biology, or

---

[1] In *Foundations*, pp. 213, 214, I wrote so as unwittingly to suggest that
they are.

physiology; and when the data were offered on which those sciences are based, he would have had to revise his theory. Similarly, no observer knowing only animal life could anticipate human nature and human history.

Now if in Jesus Christ God lived a human life for the purpose of inaugurating His Kingdom, that is an event which marks a new stage as truly as the first appearance of life or the first appearance of Man. Therefore the theory or doctrine of the Person of Christ will not be found by merely stating His nature and works in terms of God and Man, but will involve re-stating God and Man in terms of the revelation given in Him. It will help us in this task if we recall in outline the problems that confronted the Church when it attempted this task in the formative period of its doctrine.

One of the earliest of the failures to interpret the Person of Christ to human thought is to us one of the most interesting. Paul of Samosata had attempted to state the union of human and divine in Christ in terms of Will. The grounds for this and for his failure are equally important. He was concerned to safeguard the " Monarchy " of God, and to this end he felt bound to regard Christ's " self " as something other than Deity:[1] but also he considered that a union of " Natures " was unspiritual and unmoral; there was no virtue in it; if it was a fact, then fact it was, to be admired, perhaps, but not to be praised.[2] He thus drew a sharp distinction between Will and Nature, or rather accepted a sharp distinction which he found commonly drawn. And the result was twofold. (1) Will, being conceived as something other than Nature, became a specific faculty which

---

[1] Cf. Raven, *Apollinarianism*, pp. 49 ff. I regret that this most stimulating study was published after the present essay was already written.

[2] τὰ κρατούμενα τῷ λόγῳ τῆς φύσεως οὐκ ἔχει ἔπαινον, τὰ δὲ σχέσει φιλίας κρατούμενα ὑπεραινεῖται (Paul of Samosata in Λόγοι πρὸς Σαβῖνον, quoted by Harnack, *History of Dogma*, iii. p. 42).

showed itself in acts of choice and was purest when least determined. It is impossible to avoid this result if once the fatal contrast between Will and Nature is accepted. Nature is fixed, Will indeterminate; Nature is stable, Will unstable.[1] The Deity of Christ was made to consist in a union constituted by a continuous choice or series of choices—which He might, if he pleased, have varied *while still remaining unchanged in His Nature or in Himself*. Thus His *self* becomes something other than Deity and is only externally related to Deity. This was rightly felt to be insufficient, and Paul was condemned.[2]

(2) There is another and supplementary result of the separation of Will from Nature. As it makes Will capricious, so it makes Nature unspiritual. It was exactly this consideration that prompted Paul's attempt to frame a Christology in terms of Will. The theologians who used the terms Nature, Essence, and their cognates had no intention of being materialistic. But in fact they could not, and did not, escape from the materialistic suggestions of their terminology. The essential marks of matter as distinguished from spirit are not extension in space or motion through it. The essential distinction is that spirit (in the form of life) is self-moving, while matter only moves as it is impelled, and that spirit loves and hates, thinks and desires, while matter does none of these things. The distinction between Will and Nature, which both prompted the attempt and necessitated the failure of Paul of Samosata, was also destined to lead to the failure alike of the heretical and of the " orthodox " attempts to form an intelligible Christology, which arose out of the failure of Paul of Samosata.

The history of those attempts can be sketched here very briefly. The condemnation of Paul involved

---

[1] Hence the later complaint that Areius presented a Χρίστος τρεπτός—a variable Christ.

[2] At Antioch in A.D. 268. Incidentally it is worthy of record that this Council censured the use of the term ὁμοούσιος (of one substance).

the necessity of discussing the problem in terms of
Person, Nature, Essence, Substance.   In those terms
men set themselves to answer the question, How can
the one Lord Jesus Christ be both God and Man?
Contemporary thought assumed a divine imperishable
and perfect nature over against a perishable and
imperfect nature of which human nature was one
form.

The question then arises, How can God, the Perfect
and imperishable, be the Creator or immediate cause of
the imperfect and perishable world?   An intermediary
is needed.   This is a recognised function of the Logos
in the scheme of Philo, and Christ is by St. John
proclaimed as the Logos.   It is partly from this group
of considerations that Arianism arises.[1]   According to
Areius, Christ is begotten before all worlds but is not
eternal; there was a time when the Son was not; He
is a creature, though the first of creatures.   By Him
as an intermediary the rest of the creation was brought
into existence.   At the Incarnation the Son, who is
a creature as distinct from God, but is divine in comparison with all other created things, assumed a human
body but not a human soul.   Thus the Incarnate Son
is neither perfect God nor perfect Man; he mediates,
not by uniting the two Natures, but by standing
mid-way between them.

In the intellectual terms then commonly employed
this was some alleviation of the purely intellectual
aspects of the problem of evil, but plainly it was no
solution even of this.   The transition from the perfect
Creator to the faulty creation is obscured but not
explained by this sort of mediation.   Even on its
strong side Arianism is very weak.   It derived its
attractiveness no doubt from two prejudices, one
Hebrew and one Greek, which the Church had not
yet overcome.   The prejudice derived from Hebrew

---

[1] Arianism is historically a compromise between Adoptionism and the Logos-
Christology.

K

sources is that of the sheer transcendence of God, unbalanced by any doctrine of immanence; the prejudice derived from Greek sources is that of the divine " apathy " or remoteness from all suffering. The Christian revelation was destined to be destructive of those prejudices; but they were deeply rooted, and we are not yet free from their influence, which appears both where they actually persist and in extreme reactions against them.

There could, however, be no doubt that the Arian construction was incompatible with Christian experience. At the Council of Nicaea in A.D. 325 it was decisively rejected, and the triumphant doctrine found its champion in St. Athanasius. But the implications of the teaching of Athanasius had still to do battle with the two great prejudices. A semi-Arianism became prevalent, and though Athanasius became Bishop of Alexandria, his episcopate was largely spent in exile.[1]

The Council of Nicaea had made affirmations—especially that Christ is " not made, being of one substance with the Father "—which could only be gradually assimilated. At first these affirmations were regarded as merely repudiations of Arianism. Thus became possible the compromise put forward by those who wished to say that Christ is " of like substance " with the Father. Plainly this " semi-Arianism " is essentially Arianism, and it is difficult now to see how this fact could pass unnoticed; probably the devotional temper explains the matter. The Arians were concerned to insist that Christ is *not* " of one substance " with the Father; the semi-Arians were concerned to insist that He *is* " of like substance." Intellectually this is really Arian; devotionally its tendency is towards orthodoxy; it encourages rather than discourages the adoration of

---

[1] Banished 335; recalled 338; banished 341; recalled 349; fled 355; returned 361; fled and died after brief return, 373.

Christ. The semi-Arians may easily have been good Christians in their personal devotions and conduct, for spiritual life can persist in full strength with a very inadequate intellectual apparatus, but the doctrine of semi-Arianism would have destroyed Christianity in the course of the centuries.[1]

For St. Athanasius the issue had been quite simple. Areius was trying to account intellectually for the presence of evil in the creation—in itself a harmless but at best a rather unimportant enterprise. His suggested explanation cut the ground away from the supremely important hope of Christians—the hope of deliverance from evil. For both of them the evil is there; for Areius it is an intellectual problem, while for Athanasius it is a spiritual enemy. It is true that the Arian solution of the intellectual problem is a sham; but it is not on this that Athanasius insists. The sin of Arianism is that it shifts the centre of interest from the hope of salvation to the hope of explanation. If Areius had triumphed, the Church would have become a society of persons holding certain highly disputable opinions. What Athanasius preserved is the ground of the hope of salvation.

Until Christianity itself had led to the formation of a tolerably adequate conception of personality, it was inevitable that the problem should be set in terms of Substance or Nature. The failure of Paul of Samosata proved this. But *in terms of Nature* there is no means whereby the faulty and perishable Nature can be delivered from its evils and made perfect and imperishable except by the communication to it in some manner of the Nature which is perfect and imperishable. If Christ is to be the Redeemer, the Mediator of Salvation, He must Himself have this perfect and imperishable Nature to impart; He

---

[1] No doubt the source of the trouble was the terminology. ὁμοούσιος to many of the Easterns suggested Sabellianism. But ὁμοιούσιος is only a compromise, for " likeness " is partial identity, and this phrase leaves entirely open the question what identity lies at the root of the " likeness " of substance.

must be " of one substance with the Father," and this is no merely pragmatist determination to believe what will prove consoling. Experience testifies that Christ is in fact the Saviour; Christians are speaking of what they know when they bear witness to the reality of redemption; a theory of Christ which fails to account for this will be a bad theory, because it will be false to the facts, as well as because it will fail to indicate to those who do not know where the power of salvation can be found.

The question is not yet raised how the Incarnation of the Divine Son in one human life can impart the Divine Nature to other human beings; in the Eucharist, regarded as an extension of the Incarnation, one means of accomplishing this was found. And the prevalent Platonic doctrine of " real universals " was found to help, for, according to this doctrine, if Christ assumed Human Nature, He united with the Godhead something in which each man participates, and the very act of Incarnation is itself the deification of the whole human race and of every man and woman belonging to it. Yet it is only the Church, to which men are admitted by Baptism, which is the Body of Christ—not humanity as a whole. This and kindred problems were bound to arise later, as they did. For the moment Athanasius secured what was most fundamental—that, in Christ, One who is Very God had for us and for our salvation become Man.

In quarters where the authority of the Nicene Council was recognised there could no longer be denial of the full Deity of Christ. But it was still possible without flat contradiction of the Council to deny His complete humanity. This was done by Apollinaris, in whose doctrine the divine Logos is represented as taking the place of the human " spirit " in Jesus Christ. In the Incarnate Person there is a human body, a human soul, and a divine spirit. But this is no less disastrous than Arianism, though it is compatible with a more Christian attitude. If salvation takes place by a communication of essence, not only must the essence communicated be truly Divine, but the nature receiving must be complete; otherwise what is omitted will not be redeemed. Apollinaris was condemned at Constantinople in 381.

This led to yet another attempt. There had long been at Antioch a school of theology which was especially devoted to Biblical exegesis and the study of our Lord's Human Life. This study lay, for the most part, outside the range of the earlier controversies, though it would of course produce resistance to any denial of the Lord's real humanity. After the condemnation of Apollinarianism (which was developed partly in opposition to the Antiochene theology) it was natural that the school of Antioch should offer its solution. It did so in the doctrine of Nestorius, a priest of Antioch who had become Patriarch of Constantinople. This doctrine affirmed, or was held to affirm, that in Christ a Divine Person and a Human Person exist side by side. It proclaims Him perfect God and perfect Man; but in the terminology of that period it provides no real principle of unity. Christ is offered rather as our Example than our Redeemer, and immense emphasis is laid on man's free-will, whereby he can, if he chooses, imitate the ideal displayed to him in Christ. But again the solution destroys just what is most important. Free-will is an insufficient ground of hope. If the free-will freely chooses evil (or in so far as it freely chooses evil) what is to cure it? Certainly it cannot cure itself, because it does not will to do so. If it did, it would be already cured. St. Augustine was urging these arguments against Pelagianism, while St. Cyril was attacking Nestorianism on more metaphysical lines. Both heresies were condemned together at Ephesus in 431.

Once more the pendulum swung back. If Christ is perfect God and perfect Man, yet is not two Persons, must there not be some fusion so that humanity is absorbed into Deity? This was the doctrine of Eutyches, whose formula was: Before the Incarnation, two Natures; after the Incarnation, one Nature. This doctrine was pronounced orthodox by Dioscurus, who had succeeded St. Cyril in the throne of St. Athanasius as Patriarch of Alexandria. But it also destroyed the grounds of hope, for it offers, not a redeemed humanity, but a humanity lost in Deity. Eutyches was condemned at Chalcedon in 451, and the Council drew up what still remains the authoritative declaration of Christian belief.

The formula of Chalcedon was hailed by Nestorius as the affirmation of what he had maintained. It may be that he was not himself a " Nestorian " and never intended what he was condemned for teaching. But the formula of Chalcedon certainly does not affirm two Persons in Christ. The truth is that this great formula derives part of its value from the clearness with which it refuses to explain. It does in one sense represent " the bankruptcy of Greek patristic theology ";[1] it marks the definite failure of all attempts to explain the Incarnation in terms of Essence, Substance, Nature, and the like. It is content to reaffirm the fact. But that is all that an authoritative formula ought to do. Interpretations will vary from age to age, according to the concepts supplied to the interpreters by current thought. It would be disastrous if there were an official Church explanation of the Incarnation. Every explanation is bound to be inadequate; it will be rare that any explanation is other than positively misleading. What the Church must safeguard is the fact; individual Christians may offer explanations, provided that in doing so they do not deny or explain away any part of the fact. The

---

[1] As I said in *Foundations*, p. 230. It is really not the formula, but the history of the whole controversy, that leaves the impression of bankruptcy. The formula did exactly what an authoritative formula ought to do: it stated the fact.

statement of fact achieved by the first four Councils may be set out as follows: [1]

A.D. 325. The Council of Nicaea declares that Jesus Christ is truly God.

A.D. 381. The Council of Constantinople declares that Jesus Christ is truly Man.

A.D. 431. The Council of Ephesus declares that Jesus Christ, both God and Man, is One Person.

A.D. 451. The Council of Chalcedon declares that the One Lord, Jesus Christ, is *both* God *and* Man.

One other ancient controversy requires our attention for a moment. Since the condemnation of Paul of Samosata there had been little discussion of the Lord's Will. But the problems which had been worked out in terms of Nature awaited treatment in relation to the Will. There arose a belief, somewhat akin to Apollinarianism, that in the Incarnate Word there is only one Will—the divine Will. But this involves an imperfect humanity. Consequently the Sixth General Council, held at Constantinople in 680, condemned the " Monothelite " heresy and affirmed that in Jesus Christ there are two Wills—the divine and the human. And there could be no escape from this in the terms in which the problem was stated. If Christ has no human Will, His human nature is imperfect. Yet we are thus brought very near Nestorianism; for if there is a divine Will side by side with a human Will, how is this to be distinguished

---

[1] The unwary reader is warned against the supposition that the significance of the Councils can be really represented in such a tabulation. The summary is bound to be superficial, and can only be true so far as it is commonplace. The formulae of the Councils gather up and focus great movements of living thought, and are only really understood when related to those movements. Moreover, the successive affirmations do not represent discoveries but progressive articulation of what was known all along. But this whole sketch is not an attempt to make a contribution to the study of the period, for which I am quite incompetent, having never in any real sense studied it myself. But it may help our own reconstruction to recall the focussing points of classical theology.

from a divine Person side by side with a human
Person? By this time, however, the life was out of
the controversy, and the decision arrived at was merely
a logical deduction from the earlier affirmations.

The repudiation of Nestorianism involved the
denial of any human " Person " in the Incarnate
Christ. There are two Natures—human and divine;
but there is only one " Person "—the divine Logos.
Hence our Lord's humanity is described as " impersonal." St. Cyril was especially insistent on this
point. Our Lord is 'Man; but He is not *a* man.
There is no element in traditional orthodoxy which
causes to the mind of the twentieth century so great
difficulty as this. But the difficulty arises from the
whole context of thought in the two periods. The
word " Person " is by no means an exact equivalent
even for its own Latin original " Persona "; it is also
a most misleading equivalent for Hypostasis, the
Greek term here in question, though perhaps nearer to
this than to " Persona." The Hypostasis does not
include any of the qualities or activities of the being
concerned; the Council which affirmed two Wills in
Christ still affirmed one Hypostasis. Verbally this
is the Greek form of Substantia, which again is most
misleadingly represented by Substance. The Hypostasis or Persona [1] is the point of reference whereby
attributes are determined as belonging to that being
and not another. It is in any object the point of
reference whereby it is distinguished from all other
objects, even though they share the same attributes.
Two things are green; and the greenness in both is
one; but there are two green things because the one
greenness is an attribute of two Hypostases. Perhaps
the nearest term to Hypostasis in any modern treatment
of the mind is Kant's " analytic unity of apperception "
—though the parallel is far from complete. The plain
fact is that we have ceased to believe in the thing of
which Hypostasis is the name. It would be interesting

---

[1] Or Substantia when this is contrasted not with Persona but with Accidentia.

and instructive to trace the treatment of this term in theology down to the doctrine of Enhypostasia elaborated by Leontius of Byzantium, in which the controversies it had occasioned finally came to rest.[1] It is important to note the spiritual values involved and to conserve them. It may be useful to refer to the old disputes by way of steadying our own speculations. But there is really so little of common meaning between the terms " Hypostasis " and " Person," and there is so little in our thinking that corresponds to " Hypostasis " at all, that discussions about it had better be left to specialists in antiquities. In any case we should not be deterred from using the terms Personality or Person, when they seem to be appropriate, by the fact that the similar use of Hypostasis would be heretical.

The point for which St. Cyril was contending was the universal efficacy of the Incarnation. Christian experience leaves no doubt that " in Christ " (to use St. Paul's great phrase) we are delivered from sin and united to God; Christian devotion constantly pleads the sacrifice of Christ as availing for the worshipper. In the language of Substance and Nature this can only be accounted for if Christ is not a man among men but is Human Nature itself (including yours and mine and every one else's) united to the Divine Word. By the method of thought then in use, to regard Him as *a* man was to make Him an example only—an individual for other individuals to copy. If His union of Deity and Humanity is to avail for me, He must have taken to Himself not a human personality but Human Nature itself, this being conceived as something existing independently, in which individual " persons " shared.[2]

---

[1] Cf. *A Study in Christology*, by Relton; an extremely valuable contribution to the subject.

[2] Christology is mainly a concern of the Eastern Church, for which the Atonement is an implication of the Incarnation. In the West, Roman law took the place of Greek metaphysics as the controlling influence. St. Anselm in the *Cur Deus homo*

We have made no attempt to study in detail the formative controversies through which the Church reached its formulated doctrine; we have only reviewed the outline of those controversies in order to note what will be of value in our own attempt to offer an interpretation by the help of the terms and concepts familiar in the thought of our own time.

When Life supervenes upon Matter, it does not indeed lead to any contradiction of the " laws " of physical chemistry, but it takes direction of the physico-chemical system; it asserts priority in the sense that the explanation of the action of the living thing is sought in the requirements of its life. The physical system supplies the conditions *sine quibus non*; the life supplies the efficient causation. So when Mind supervenes upon the living organism, it takes direction and becomes the cause of the agent's conduct. We shall expect, therefore, to find that when God supervenes upon humanity, we do not find a human being taken into fellowship with God, but God acting through the conditions supplied by humanity. And this is the Christian experience of Jesus Christ; He is spoken of as a Mediator, but that expression is used, not to signify one who is raised above humanity by an infusion of deity, but one in whom deity and humanity are perfectly united. This is the first point which the early theologians were concerned about in their insistence that in Christ there is only one Hypostasis and that this is not human but divine. The root of this belief is, however, the testimony of Christian experience, that fellowship with Christ is in itself fellowship with God. This testimony coincides with what we are led to expect by the analogy of the whole Creation. We may say, then, without any hesitation that Christ is not a man exalted to perfect

---

certainly does not regard Christ as including me in His sacrifice. " Take my beloved Son and offer Him for thyself." For the Greeks the centre of interest is the Incarnation of God; for the Latins it is the Death of God incarnate.

participation in the Divine Nature or Life; He is God, manifest under the conditions of humanity. The first disciples had to approach by gradual stages the realisation of what lay behind the human life and was finding expression in and through it; that was the order of discovery; but it is not the order of reality. We see a man's bodily movements first and from them infer his purpose and character; but the purpose is prior and directs the movements. So we see the human life and infer the divine Person; but the Person controls and directs the life. What we find in Christian experience is witness, not to a Man uniquely inspired, but to God living a human life.

Now this is exactly the culmination of that stratification which is the structure of Reality; far therefore from being incredible, it is to be expected, it is antecedently probable. Even had there been no evil in the world to be overcome, no sin to be abolished and forgiven, still the Incarnation would be the natural inauguration of the final stage of evolution. In this sense the Incarnation is perfectly intelligible; that is to say, we can see that its occurrence is all of a piece with the scheme of Reality as traced elsewhere.

But in another sense it is and must remain beyond our understanding; we can understand the grades of Reality subordinate to our own; we can in some degree, though perhaps not completely, understand our own. For the understanding of those above our own, or of our own as completed by the indwelling of the higher, we have not the necessary data. Our effort, therefore, to deal with the problems that arise from belief in the Incarnation must start with the confession, or rather with the claim, that from the nature of the case their solution cannot be found by us. If any man says that he understands the relation of Deity to Humanity in Christ, he only makes it clear that he does not understand at all what is meant by an Incarnation.

First there is the Nestorian difficulty: can we call a child three months old by the name of God? Or, to put the question in a modern shape, are we to say that the Infant Jesus directed from His manger at Bethlehem the affairs of Mars? This kind of difficulty has an honourable origin in so far as it is based on a determination to think things through, but it also arises from following the speculative enquiry into regions where we have no data, and forgetting the purpose of the divine act which is being considered. That purpose would seem to be twofold—Revelation and Atonement. For the former, what is necessary is that Jesus Christ should be truly God and truly Man; for the latter what seems to be necessary is that human experience as conditioned by the sin of men should become the personal experience of God the Son—not an object of external observation but of inward feeling (to use the language of human consciousness). Neither of these requires that God the Son should be active only in Jesus of Nazareth during the days of the Incarnation. " The light that lighteneth every man " did not cease to do so when He shone in full brilliance in one human Life. Jesus did not control affairs in Mars, or in China. But God the Son, who is the Word of God by whom, as agent, all things came to be and apart from whom no single thing has come to be, without ceasing His creative and sustaining work, added this to it that He became flesh and dwelt as in a tabernacle among us, so that as in the old Tabernacle there dwelt the cloud of the divine glory, so in Him we saw a glory that shone through Him but found in Him its perfect and unique expression—" glory as of an only-begotten Son from a Father." He who is always God became also Man— not ceasing to be God the while. For the Incarnation was effected " not by Conversion of the Godhead into flesh, but by taking of Manhood into God."

No doubt this position involves a difficulty with

regard to the mode of the consciousness of the Eternal Son; but that is exactly where the difficulty ought most clearly to arise, for about the mode of His consciousness we can have simply no knowledge whatever. Meanwhile, if it is admissible at all it brings an immense alleviation of the problem which theologians have sought to solve by pressing to its furthest implications St. Paul's language about the self-emptying of Himself by the pre-existent Christ in the act of His Incarnation. I confess to an uneasy feeling that when this vigorous expression of a great spiritual truth is taken as precise and scientific theology, we are involved in something dangerously close to mythology. To say that God the Eternal Son at a moment of time divested Himself of Omniscience and Omnipotence in order to live a human life, re-assuming these attributes at the Ascension, seems to me just the kind of thing that no event occurring on this planet could ever justify. It is not of course a view that can be condemned as impossible; but it involves an assertion about the Infinite and Eternal which reverence should make us slow to make, and the evidence on which it rests is such as, in my judgement, neither is nor could be sufficient to warrant it.

The position outlined above offers an alternative solution of the problem. The constituent elements of the problem may be stated in the words of Professor Mackintosh:

(1) Christ is now Divine, as being the object of faith and worship, with whom believing men have immediate, though not unmediated, fellowship.

(2) In some personal sense His Divinity is eternal, not the fruit of time, since by definition Godhead cannot have come to be *ex nihilo*; His pre-mundane being therefore is real, not ideal merely.

(3) His life on earth was unequivocally human. Jesus was a man, a Jew of the first century, with a life localised in and restricted by a body organic to His self-consciousness; of limited power, which could be, and was, thwarted by persistent unbelief; of

limited knowledge, which, being gradually built by experience, made Him liable to surprise and disappointment; of a moral nature susceptible of growth, and exposed to lifelong temptation; of a piety and personal religion characterised at each point by dependence on God. In short, He moved always within the lines of an experience humanly normal in constitution, ev n if abnormal in its sinless quality. The life Divine in Him found expression through human faculty, with a self-consciousness and activity mediated by His human *milieu*.[1]

The Professor then continues as follows: " It is impossible to think these positions together save as we proceed to infer that a real surrender of the glory and prerogatives of deity, ' a moral act in the heavenly sphere,' must have preceded the advent of God in Christ. We are faced by a Divine self-reduction which entailed obedience, temptation, and death. So that religion has a vast stake in the *Kenosis* as a fact, whatever the difficulties as to its method must be. No human life of God is possible without a prior self-adjustment of deity. The Son must empty Himself in order that from within mankind He may declare the Father's name, offer the great sacrifice, triumph over death; and the reality with which to reach this end He laid aside the form and privilege of deity is the measure of that love which had throbbed in the Divine heart from all eternity."

So Dr. Mackintosh sets out the religious interest in the *Kenosis*. But the difficulties are intolerable. What was happening to the rest of the universe during the period of our Lord's earthly life? To say that the Infant Jesus was from His cradle exercising providential

---

[1] H. R. Mackintosh, *The Person of Jesus Christ*, pp. 469, 470. The Professor adds a fourth paragraph: " (4) We cannot predicate of Him two consciousnesses or two wills; the New Testament indicates nothing of the kind, nor indeed is it congruous with an intelligible psychology. The unity of His personal life is axiomatic." I omit this paragraph, not because I disagree with it as it stands, but because (1) I think that in the terms which were alone available for the early Church the phrases censured were the best that could be reached ; (2) because in that language there is contained a fundamental truth which must be expressed somehow.

care over it all is certainly monstrous; but to deny this, and yet to say that the Creative Word was so self-emptied as to have no being except in the Infant Jesus, is to assert that for a certain period the history of the world was let loose from the control of the Creative Word, and "apart from Him" very nearly everything happened that happened at all during thirty odd years, both on this planet and throughout the immensities of space.

All these difficulties are avoided if we suppose that God the Son did indeed most truly live the life recorded in the Gospel, but added this to the other work of God. There are indications that this is the Johannine view.[1] We are then able to see how Jesus Christ may be truly human, subject to all the conditions of His human life, "a Jew of the first century," and yet be very God, without any such self-emptying of God as has a mythological appearance and involves stupendous difficulties in general philosophy or theology. The only objection to it that I can see is that it appears to make the Incarnation a mere episode in the Life of the Eternal Son, so that a man may say, "Yes; He accepted humiliation and suffering as a wealthy man may go and join the unemployed; he will suffer some discomfort, but he has his riches all the while, and has never really shared the bitterness of their experience; he has not become one of them." But this objection rests on a misunderstanding. If God the Son lived the Life recorded in the Gospels, then in that Life we see, set forth in terms of human experience, the very reality of God the Son. The limitations of knowledge and power are conditions of the revelation, without which there would be no revelation *to us* at all; but the Person who lives under those limitations is the Eternal Son in whom the life of the Eternal Father goes forth in

---

[1] Cf. St. John i. 9, 15, 18; iii. 13. It may be thought that this theory imports into the doctrine of the Incarnate Son just such a differentiation of "Persons" as we found (pp. 115, 116) that the Incarnation itself involves in the Godhead. This problem is dealt with later. See pp. 280, 281.

creative activity and returns in filial love. The Incarnation is an episode in the Life or Being of God the Son; but it is not a *mere* episode, it is a *revealing* episode. There we see what He who is God's wisdom always is, even more completely than any Kenotic theory allows. This view makes the humiliation and death of Christ " the measure of that love which has throbbed in the divine heart from all eternity." Certain attributes or functions incompatible with humanity are, in this activity of the Eternal Son, not exercised; but what we see is not any mere parable of the Life of God, not an interval of humiliation between two eternities of glory. It is the divine glory itself.

As we watch that human Life we do not say: " Ah —but soon He will return to the painless joy of the glory which was His and will be His again." As we watch that Life and, above all, that Death we say, "We behold His glory." For if God is most truly known as Love, then the glory of God is chiefly seen in the activity of Love.

Indeed, it is the Kenotic theory which makes the Incarnation episodic; it too makes it a revealing episode, but it makes its very substance an episode. Our view regards the mode as episodic—the acceptance of conditions necessary for the very occurrence of a revelation; but the substance is eternal. The limitations are the means whereby the Eternal Son, remaining always in the bosom of the Father, lays bare to us the very heart of Godhead.

In doing this, moreover, the Son of God has made our condition matter of His own experience. To the sympathy and insight of omniscient love no limit can be set, and we dare not say that after the Incarnation He understood us better than before. But it is mere matter of historic fact that before the Incarnation men could not say, and after the Incarnation we thankfully can say, concerning the Eternal Son Himself: " in that He Himself hath suffered being tempted, He is able to succour them that are tempted."

That leads us at once to the next subject of our enquiry. We have spoken of the relation of the Eternal Son to the Incarnate Life; we have now to speak of the relation of that human experience to the Eternal Son. As the problem is now set, the difficulties are not baffling, though it is still true that anything like a complete analysis is for ever out of our reach. First we say without further hesitation that on all matters of mere information He shared the views of His time. Bishop Knox has expressed this point so admirably that I will state my position in his words:

"The human reason in Jesus, if it was not to be merged and lost in the Divine, must have its real state of nescience, of growth in knowledge through docility, through experience, through meditation. If we deny this, we do in fact deny the Manhood of Jesus Christ, and also His knowledge of, and sympathy with, our infirmities. For how large a portion of our troubles, and even of our sins, is due to our mistakes! The infallibility of Jesus—we say it with all reverence and consciousness of our fallibility—was not due to the superseding of human fallibility by Divine Omniscience. It was due to the intimate relation between the Divine and human in one Personality, and was consistent with the full experience of His Humanity. No one supposes, for instance, that the Son of Man used His Omniscience to concern Himself with modern scientific discoveries, such as the use of steam, electricity, or radium. The self-limitation of His Omniscience is not to be ascertained by *a priori* guesses or pronouncements. We are soon out of our depths in fathoming such an ocean. All that we can do is to turn to the records and ascertain the facts."

"It is possible, no doubt, to dismiss all reflexion concerning our Lord's use and teaching of the Law by summary reference to the Divine in His Personality. He interpreted the Law, because He was the author of the Law. He modified or rescinded it by the same power by which He imposed it. But this reasoning does, in fact, merge the human in the divine. At the most important point, His attitude to the Old Testament, His humanity disappears. We are at once on the road to the

L

Docetic, the unreal, phantom Christ, who never was truly Man. The Incarnation, which is the foundation of all our faith, disappears.

" This point deserves more attention than it commonly receives from many of those for whose use this book is specially intended. With the deepest respect for their sincere piety, and for their regard for the Word of God, which called their spiritual life into being, and has sustained it, a very earnest entreaty is addressed to them to consider all that is involved in too hasty recourse to our Lord's Divinity for solution of all Old Testament problems. Especially this loss is involved; that we no longer have the companionship of our Lord in our study of the Divine Word—the problems which occurred to Him in His boyhood, with which He confronted the doctors, disappear: the lessons of His mother's lap, the teaching of Joseph, the lessons at School, the readings and expositions in the Synagogue, His own private meditations—all these became unreal, for He, as Divine, had nothing to learn. It would seem that Bible study is robbed of more than half its joy if the Child Jesus, the Boy Jesus, the Man Jesus, is no longer a fellow-learner with ourselves. It is true that we cannot too jealously guard the Divinity of Jesus. Nor can we too jealously guard His true humanity."

" Incarnation involved self-limitation, but in relation to all that made for communion with God, our Blessed Lord, in relation to the Old Testament, did in fact transcend external conditions, did raise Manhood to its most godlike capacities, did fulfil the Messianic rôle of unfolding the true meaning of the Scriptures. But it was not inconsistent with this that He should have accepted the conditions of a devout Israelite in reference to the Old Testament on its purely intellectual side. It was but repeating in another form His preference of Bethlehem and Nazareth to Rome and Alexandria." [1]

We may sum up this matter by citing a writer of very different ecclesiastical colour from Bishop Knox. Dr. Weston, the Bishop of Zanzibar, holds that the Incarnation " made it both possible and necessary that He should have no consciousness that His assumed human soul could not mediate." [2] How far this principle extends is matter for detailed discussion.

[1] Knox, *On What Authority*, pp. 125-26, 132-33, 145.
[2] *The One Christ*, p. 184.

Some would say that it includes the possibility and prob-ability of actual error as regards matter of fact; others deny this.   In any case it is clear that the doctrine of our Lord's Deity is in no way bound up with the correctness of His opinion concerning the authorship of certain Psalms or any such matter.   There can be absolute goodness of character in spite of incorrect opinions on such matters—indeed on all matters where " fact " and " value " are not identical.[1]

Further, there is on our theory no difficulty about the reality of growth or the reality of temptation in the Incarnate life.   The revelation is in the whole. Had Herod succeeded in killing the Infant Jesus, there would have been an Incarnation, but the revela-tion given through it would have been next to nothing alike in extent and in significance.   At each stage Jesus was the perfection of that stage of human life. The temptations that came to Him were perfectly real, and so was His resistance.   He overcame them exactly as every man who does so overcomes a tempta-tion—by the constancy of the Will, which is the whole being of a man organised for conduct.   That Will always shows its strength chiefly in certain splendid incapacities—as when we say of a good man charged with some mean offence, he simply could not do it. But in Christ this incapacity towards evil was absolute; His perfect freedom showed itself, as perfect freedom always does, in an inability to sin—the *non posse peccare* of St. Augustine. . This is nothing contrary to human nature; rather it is exactly what human nature is always aiming at; indeed it is the effort towards this

---

[1] This seems as good a place as any other for a parenthetic appeal that no one will state the problem in the form of the question, " Does Christ differ from us in kind or in degree? "   This question has an appearance of precision which is utterly illusory, and so it starts the enquirer on a hopeless quest.   The distinction of kind and degree is far from clear, as is shown by the difficulty of answering the familiar conundrum, " Is the difference between differences of kind and differences of degree a difference of kind or a difference of degree? "

But if the question means, " Is Perfect Man *eo ipso* God? " the answer is, " No.   Nothing that happens to a creature could possibly turn him into his own Creator.   At that point the gulf between God and Man is plainly impassable."

that distinguishes human nature as personal. One difference there is between the temptations of Jesus Christ and those of other men; His Will was at each stage undamaged by the previous admission of sin. Pain to Him was as painful as it is to us; the desire to avoid it was in itself as strong; but in us that desire is fortified by the incompleteness of our dedication, the partial formation of our Will. In Him the whole being was always set to do God's Will; so though there was real struggle and real cost, there was no enemy of self-will within, and therefore no danger of defeat. There is nothing to puzzle us here. Every man of moral purpose is conscious of some temptations which he knows that he can overcome, though he has to make effort and suffer pain in the doing of it. But in us there are also temptations which we are doubtful if we can overcome; and there are some against which in the strength of our own wills alone we are powerless. From such Christ was free, for the doubt and the impotence come from the presence of sin within the will itself. As we read the record two certainties emerge: He certainly had real struggles with temptation, and He certainly had no anxiety lest He should yield to them and betray His mission by falling into sin. This is even more impressive than the total absence of any consciousness of sin committed in the past.

With each temptation and victory He grew. At all stages He was obedient to the Father; but the obedience, always perfect at each stage, yet deepened as He advanced from the Boy's subjection in His home at Nazareth to the point where He " became obedient unto death,"[1] so, " though he was a son, yet learned he obedience by the things which he suffered."[2]

As the obedience deepened, so did the Love. The sacrifice in which love finds expression enters

[1] Philippians ii. 8.   [2] Hebrews v. 8.

into the very fibre of the love; so that by expressing itself love becomes more perfect. It was in the Passion, and at the Last Supper, where He symbolically represented it and explained it by anticipation, that the Lord " having (always) loved his own which were in the world, loved them to the uttermost." [1]

This human life is the very life of God. It is both human and divine in every detail. If we know what we are about we may rightly say that the unity of God and Man in Christ is a unity of Will, for Will is the whole being of a person organised for action. But the phrase is liable to mislead, because we have to think by the analogy of our own experience, and in us Will does not in fact cover the whole of our personal being, because we have not attained that perfection of personal unity which is the completeness of Will.[2] Therefore in us Will is still departmental; and to say that the unity of God and Man in Christ is a unity of will consequently *suggests* that this unity is not complete, and concerns something only adjectival. It is better then to say that in Christ God and Man are *personally* one; the Person of the Man Christ Jesus is God the Son.

Then is the humanity impersonal? or does it find its personality only in God the Son? Plainly the position indicated is that which was formulated by Leontius of Byzantium with the terms adjusted to modern usage. Indeed, the actual adjustment of terms is so slight that it may conceal the very real modification in the thought expressed. By Person we do not understand an ultimate point of reference, but the entirety of the spiritual being. As Person Jesus is both Man and God.

---

[1] St. John xiii. 1.

[2] We know that we live on a volcano; even when we have formed the habits of a serviceable life, we know that from the hidden recesses of our being impulses may arise which will sweep us off our feet. They are not yet organised into our will. But Christ is troubled by no such anxiety. His Will and His whole Being are one. Perhaps this is the basis of Dr. Sanday's suggestion that the *locus* of His Divinity was His sub-consciousness.

But we must not lose what was precious in the older way of thinking, especially what was involved in the doctrine of the Two Wills. We cannot predicate moral progress of God the Son; we must predicate such progress, as shown above, of Jesus Christ. Therefore the Will in Him, while always one with, because expressive of, the Will of God, is not merely identical with it. In the struggle with temptation the human will or person is at once manifesting and approximating to the Will of God, until as the Passion approaches and Love is about to be exhibited in the perfection of sacrifice, He prays to be glorified with the eternal glory—which is the perfect sacrifice of perfect love.[1]

Consequently, though there is only one Person, one living and energising Being, I should not hesitate to speak of the human personality of Christ. But that personality does not exist side by side with the divine personality; it is subsumed in it. Will and personality are ideally interchangeable terms; there are two wills in the Incarnate in the sense that His human nature comes through struggle and effort to an ever deeper union with the Divine in completeness of self-sacrifice. And it is only because there is this real human will or personality that there is here any revelation to humanity of the divine Will. Thus I do not speak of His humanity as impersonal. If we imagine the divine Word withdrawn from Jesus of Nazareth, as the Gnostics believed to have occurred before the Passion, I think that there would be left, not nothing at all, but a man.[2] Yet this human personality is actually the self-expression of the Eternal Son, so that as we watch the human life we become aware that it is the vehicle of a divine life, and that the human personality [3] of Jesus Christ

---

[1] St. John xvii. 5.

[2] The question is so unreal that even to ask it is to make false suggestions; but I leave the illustration as an expression of my meaning, which is deliberately crude for the sake of pointedness.

[3] I avoid the phrase " human person," which seems to connote a complete individual more definitely than the phrase " human personality " which I have used.

is subsumed in the Divine Person of the Creative
Word.[1]

The doctrine of the impersonal humanity of Christ
had, however, another and more practical significance
than that of preserving a theoretic union of two natures
in one Person; it was associated with the notion of
" real universals," and implied that when Christ
assumed human nature He assumed the nature of all
of us, so that by His Incarnation we are united, in
Him, to God. That is profoundly important, but it
makes difficulties when so stated; for it ought to
involve that all men, whether believers or not, are
forthwith united to God; and experience tells us
that this union is at best incomplete, while the same
theologians, who state a doctrine logically involving
the union of all men with God, actually limit this to
members of the Christian Church, who have still,
moreover, to renew and deepen that unity by sacraments and lives of service.

We still believe in " real universals," but they are
concrete, not abstract, universals.[2]   There is no such
thing as human nature apart from all individual
human beings. But there is a perfectly real thing
called Mankind or Humanity which is a unit and not
a mere agglomeration. As each man is a focussing
point for Reality as seen from the place within it
which he occupies, he is very largely constituted what
he is by the character of his fellow-men. Influence
is not an affair of external impact but of inward constitution of the person influenced. Therefore Mankind or Humanity is a close-knit system of mutually
influencing units. In this sense the humanity of
every one of us is " impersonal "; and the greater
the man, the less merely " personal " is his humanity.

---

[1] Mr. Grensted writes to me: " I usually try to solve this problem by using the
term ἐνέργεια. Clearly there are in Christ two ἐνέργειαι, of which the human
progressively expresses the divine. And as Will can only be defined intelligibly in
terms of conation, the orthodox result follows. Any other definition of Will gives
one or other of the great heresies, besides breaking down inherently."

[2] Cf. *Mens Creatrix*, pp. 7-23.

He is more, not less, individual than others; but he is individual by the uniqueness of his focus for the universe, not by his exclusion of all that is not himself. He more than others is Humanity focussed in one centre. Into this system of mutually influencing units Christ has come; but here is a unit perfectly capable, as others are only imperfectly capable, both of personal union with all other persons and of refusing to be influenced by the evil of His environment. It is this more than anything else which proves Him to be more and other than His fellow-men. But thus He inaugurates a new system of influence; and as this corresponds to God's Will for mankind, its appeal is to the true nature of men. So He is a Second Adam; what occurred at the Incarnation was not merely the addition of another unit to the system of mutually influencing units, it was the inauguration of a new system of mutual influence, destined to become, here or elsewhere, universally dominant. "By His Incarnation," therefore, the Lord did indeed "raise our humanity to an entirely higher level, to a level with His own";[1] but this was not accomplished by the unspiritual process of an infusion of an alien "nature" but by the spiritual process of mutual influence and love that calls forth love. If this seems less than the other, it is only because we have let our pride teach us to emphasise separateness as the funda- mental characteristic of our personality, so that in- fluence only shapes but does not constitute us; this we have seen to be false. I *am* mankind—England —my school—my family—focussed in a point of its own history. Mankind—" Adam "—has made me what I am. If similarly Christ makes me something else—the participator in His own divine freedom [2]— then indeed " there is a new creation; the old things are passed away; behold, they are become new." [3]

---

[1] Archbishop Temple.   [2] St. John viii. 36.
[3] 2 Corinthians v. 17.

Thus in a most real sense Christ is not only a man; He is Man.   In Dr. Moberly's phrase, " Christ is Man not generically but inclusively," just as He is " God not generically but identically."   All the significance and destiny of the human race is summed up in Him.   He is the Head of the Body.   But this is by no mechanical identification; it is by a spiritual transformation, wrought out, as is the self-manifestation of God in the Incarnation, through the process of time and the course of history.

CHAPTER IX

THE HOLY SPIRIT AND THE CHURCH

"The fellowship of the Holy Spirit."—ST. PAUL.

IN the midst of human history the Universal Spirit had appeared at a particular time and a particular place, had lived as Man a completely human life, had been rejected by His own creatures, had suffered and died, had risen in the body in which He suffered, and had signified by the enacted parable of the Ascension both His liberation from the limiting conditions characteristic of His earthly ministry and also the taking of Manhood, in His Person, into God.

Such an occurrence must be beyond all comparison the most important in history. Indeed, it may fairly be said that history, in its full meaning, dates from that event. Through all the ages God creates, for at all times the universe depends for its existence on His sustaining will; but if any division at all is to be drawn between a date or period of Creation and a period of History subsequent to Creation, it is best drawn, so far as this planet is concerned, at the Ascension and Pentecost, which are two phases of one thing, the taking of Manhood to the throne of God and the indwelling of God in the hearts of men. Creation and Redemption are, indeed, different; but they are different aspects of one spiritual fact, which is the activity of the Divine Will, manifesting itself in love through the Creation, and winning from the Creation an answering love. The act whereby this purpose should be accomplished was complete at the Ascension; all human history from that time onwards is the process of eliciting man's answer. This is still the work of God, but that work is thenceforth within the souls of men rather than on the objective stage. There are still events and occurrences to come; but they come now by the working of causes already present rather than by any such introduction of a new causative force as we find in the Incarnation.

When the physical presence of the Lord was withdrawn at the Ascension, there remained on earth as fruit of His ministry no defined body of doctrine, no fully constituted society with declared aims and methods, but a group of men and women who had loved and trusted Him, and who by their love and trust and conviction of His Resurrection were united to one another. It was in this society that there came the experience of spiritual power, certainly a gift of God, and of inner compulsion to proclaim alike this gift of power and its source in the Life and Death and Resurrection of Jesus their Master. This society is a veritable Fellowship of the Holy Spirit. It is definable in terms of the Spirit; and the Spirit is definable in terms of it. To be a Christian is to confess Jesus as Lord, to have the Spirit, to be a member of the Church; it is all of these or any of them, for no distinction had arisen between them in experience, and none or scarcely any had yet been drawn in thought. Here, in the company of the personal disciples of Jesus, is found an activity of the Divine Spirit so plainly identical with the activity of the same Spirit in Jesus of Nazareth, that St. Paul, who, not having shared the initial training of the others, comes into the society from outside, finds it natural to speak of it as His body and of its constituent individuals as His limbs or members.

Thus the fact of the Christian Church and men's experience of the Holy Spirit appear not only together but inextricably intertwined. Of course, the Spirit of whom the first Christians had experience was recognised by them as one with the Spirit who had taught the old prophets; but the mode of His activity (or, which is really the same thing, of their awareness of Him) was so novel that it marked a new era. St. Peter claims the experience of Pentecost as a fulfilment of the prophetic anticipation of the Day of the Lord;[1] St. John intimates that the Spirit, as Christians know Him, could only come after the full revelation of God in Christ: " There was not yet Spirit, because Jesus was not yet glorified."[2]

It is not difficult to see why this should be so. The control that is exercised over a human being by one who loves him and, revealing that love intelligibly and unmistakably, calls out from him answering love, is far more complete than that exercised by an authority which gives orders and then punishes or rewards in accordance with the obedience rendered. That is spoken of in the New Testament as the status of slavery, whereas by the revelation of the love of God in Christ we have been raised to the status of friends or children.[3] The sway of God over men is thus both compatible with their freedom, since it elicits a free obedience, and also complete as no other can be, since it operates through and not against the will.

We are not at the moment concerned with the Theological implications of our experience of the Spirit. Plainly the term is very near in its significance to the Logos. Before the Incarnation, indeed, there were no grounds for drawing any distinction. But for Christians there is the very clear distinction that the Person of Jesus Christ is external to the disciple—an objective fact of perfect holiness objectively achieved

---

[1] Acts ii. 14-21.   [2] St. John vii. 39.
[3] St. John xv 15; Romans viii. 15.

—while the Spirit is known to him as an inner impetus, often struggling and inarticulate, pointing him to the perfect Life of Jesus, urging correspondence therewith, and supplying the power for accomplishing that otherwise impossible demand. We need not at present say more than this: as God must be such that we can stand to Him in the two relations which we occupy to the Eternal Father, Almighty, Omniscient, and to the Redeeming Son, suffering and disappointed, so also must He be such that we can stand to Him in the relation which we occupy to the indwelling Spirit, prompting and empowering.

At present we are concerned with the Spirit in manifestation. The presence of the Spirit is proved by the appearance of new powers, specially that capacity for fellowship which is called love. These manifestations appear, of course, in the lives of individuals; but only, in the first ages, in the lives of those individuals who are members of the Christian society. In that the Spirit is so potent that all divisions of mankind disappear. " There is neither Jew nor Gentile "—the deepest of divisions based on religious tradition has disappeared; " there is neither Greek nor Scythian "—the deepest of divisions based on culture has disappeared; " there is neither bond nor free "—the deepest of social and economic divisions has disappeared; " there is neither male nor female " —even the division of the sexes has disappeared. In place of all of them there is " one man in Christ Jesus." [1] All are so dominated by His Will that for practical purposes there is only one personality, and that is Christ's.

So St. Paul sees the meaning of human history to be the fulfilment of God's purpose to " sum up all things in Christ," in whom alone already " all things cohere." [2] And he sees the corporate personality of

---

[1] Galatians iii. 28, with Colossians iii. 10, 11.
[2] Ephesians i. 10, and Colossians i. 17.

Christ, which is the Church, gathering into itself all persons and all nations, welding them into unity by relating them to the true principle of their being; thus the " one man in Christ Jesus " comes to his full growth, " the measure of the stature of the completeness of the Christ." [1]

We have already seen that the task of man is to achieve inner and outer unity—the inner unity of complete personality and the outer unity of a perfected fellowship as wide as humanity.[2] For this human nature is plainly destined by the qualities inherent in it, that is to say, by the qualities originally bestowed on it by the Creator. Towards this human nature is impelled by the Creator's act at the Incarnation, and the consequent activity of His Spirit at work upon humanity from within.

Thus the Church's task is defined for it. It is the herald and foretaste of the Kingdom of God. For that it exists, and for service to that end it must be organised and equipped. In the first days organisation was comparatively unimportant. No one belonged to the Church who was not utterly in earnest. To say " Jesus is Lord " was so great a self-committal that only the activity of the Divine Spirit could be held to account for such an utterance.[3] No one then passively acquiesced in Christian doctrine. To believe was to have faith; to be baptized was to experience spiritual re-birth; to be a Church member and to be filled with the Spirit were one and the same.

The very success of the Church brought the seeds of its later difficulties. The world saw in the Church a power which did for men what they needed. Even when Constantine saw in the Church a power of coherence nowhere else to be discovered in the decay of the ancient world, he was recognising a real mani-

---

[1] Ephesians iv. 13.   [2] Chapters IV. and V.
[3] 1 Corinthians xii. 3.

festation of the true Spirit. But already men were in the Church because they had been so brought up, or because it was becoming fashionable, without any deliberate surrender to the Spirit in the Church. Thus in place of the sharp contrast of Church and World there emerged the mutual interaction of a partly Christianised World and a partly secularised Church. That the World should be partly Christianised was good; it was the beginning of the achievement of the Church's task. But that the Church should be partly secularised was disastrous, for it destroyed the Church's power to carry forward its task to fulfilment. But the Spirit was not quenched, and out of the very midst of the Church in its decay was able to raise up men who recalled it in some measure to its first vision and aspiration—Augustine, Hildebrand, Francis, Wycliffe, Luther, Wesley, Keble, Maurice. Moreover, by the diffusion of Christian influence in the world, the list increases rapidly of those who, sometimes as professed Christians, sometimes as aliens from the Church, recall men to the meaning of their Christian faith.

But this secularisation of the Church gave an altogether new importance to its outward order. We tend to be impatient at serious discussion of such matters. It seems that if the Church is indeed the nucleus of that order of life whose attainment is the fulfilment of man's destiny, such problems as those of regular or irregular ministries must be irrelevant.[1] Certainly they ought, if the Church were healthy, to occupy a very small amount of attention; but they are not irrelevant or unimportant. A healthy man pays little attention to his digestive or respiratory processes; but these are not unimportant even to the loftiest endeavours or the most heroic enter-

---

[1] In the New Jerusalem the City, which stands for Life, is 1500 *miles* high ; its wall, which stands for boundaries of membership and order generally, is 216 *feet* high (Revelation xxi. 6, 17).

prises; and if health fails, they may call for close attention.

The Church early began to suffer from one form of ill-health; it ought to be a society of people wholly surrendered to the Spirit of Christ. But many are members of it who are not thus surrendered. In view of the impossibility of estimating spiritual devotion, the Church must retain as members all who persist in claiming membership, unless they disqualify themselves by flagrant defiance of the Church's requirements. It is not compatible with elementary Christian charity to exclude from the society which is the Spirit's normal channel any who wish to be included and conform to the necessary requirements. But this involves a serious dilution of the primitive zeal, and there is urgent need for some firmly established means of keeping alive the knowledge of the end which the Church exists to serve. The Church has, in fact, established four such means: the Canon of Scripture; the Creeds; the Sacraments; the Ministry.

Of these the first is incalculably the most important, and no considerable group of Christians has proposed to dispense with it. The selection of the Canonical Scriptures did not and does not imply any judgement by the Church on other writings; there may be others in which the Spirit as truly speaks or there may not; but He speaks here; and only those in which the experience of the Church has proved the presence and power of the Spirit shall be stamped as authoritative for the faith and hope and activity of the Church. In the Scriptures so ranked as authoritative the most conspicuous and pervasive characteristic is the unvarying proclamation of God's absolute and universal sovereignty, covering the whole range of national policy, of social and economic order, and of personal life. Here is recorded the Gospel which Incarnate God proclaimed, the Gospel of the Kingdom or

Sovereignty of God. Here is portrayed the life of the society which after the Ascension took the place of His Body, as that society appeared while none but sincere believers were drawn into it, striving for the universal fellowship, waiting for the perfected civilisation which comes down out of Heaven from God. It is in the constant study of these writings, and especially those of the New Testament, that the Church has its chief means of keeping alive in the minds of its members what it is to which they are called, and of enabling them to recover forgotten parts of their mission in the world.

The Creeds are summaries of the teaching of the Canonical Scriptures, drawn up originally, for the most part, to avert error rather than to define truth, but used in the experience of the Church as a means of proclaiming the pivotal points of its teaching. It is clear that formulae agreed upon in the fourth and fifth centuries will not be exactly what theologians would compile in the twentieth. But the Church which formulated and accepted them was perfectly aware of the difference between experience and the rationalised account of it; the experience was what mattered; and with a marvellous completeness the temporary forms of thought and speculation were excluded. Unthinking persons sometimes ask how members of the Church to-day can consent to express their faith in the terms of Greek metaphysic; the answer is " We don't; and we never did." Apart from the single phrase " of one substance " there is no Greek philosophy in the Creeds, and that phrase is so general that it binds no one to any particular scheme of philosophy. The great value of the Creeds is that they keep steadily before the mind of the Church and its members the whole articulated body of essential Christian doctrine; thus they tend to prevent an undue concentration of interest on any one point of doctrine or type of experience, and supply (like the Scriptures)

M

a means of recovering lost or forgotten elements of Christian thought and life, and of restoring true balance and proportion.[1]

Of sacraments there will be more to say later on. But it is here in place to speak of the Eucharist, wherein the members of the Body of Christ receive, under a form appointed by Himself, His Life, to unite them to each other in Him, and to impel them to the fulfilment of His purpose. Plainly in a world of many languages the unity of the Church is better expressed and fostered by a common act than it could ever be by forms of words. In Baptism and Holy Communion all can join with true unity of mind and will, realising their oneness. But what most concerns us here is the emphasis which the act of reception at the Eucharist gives to the fundamental truth that the life of men as members of the Church, Christ's Body, is not their achievement but God's gift. No form could be devised which would more eloquently proclaim God's priority and man's dependence. He gives; we receive. As the Nativity was in no way due to the active causation of man's will, though it was conditioned by the self-surrender of the Blessed Virgin to receive for mankind God's gift of Himself, so here and always the Christian life is a supernatural life; we neither make it nor discover it; God gives it, we receive it. And this is the truth of chief importance to the whole life and purpose of the Church. The most seductive and the deadliest of all temptations that come to man is the temptation to suppose that by himself he can achieve his destiny. It is false. Man can only be all that he is destined to be when God indwells him. Of this truth the Incarnation is the expression, and Holy Communion the perpetual reassertion.

[1] I cannot hold the Creeds exempt from criticism. It is not utterly impossible that error may have crept into them ; I cannot attribute to them or to the Church any such authority as to rule out such a question in principle. But the authority behind them is so immense that I must regard such questions as academic only.

Closely connected with the Eucharist so conceived is the regular Ministry of the Church. The Church reserves to ministers duly ordained the right to "celebrate" the Eucharist. This seems to me to be a most wise and important disciplinary provision.[1] The divine life offered in the Eucharist is the life of the divine Love (expressed in uttermost self-sacrifice— Body broken, Blood shed) of which the human counterpart is universal fellowship. What is secured by a universally recognised ministry is that at every "celebration" the act is that of the whole Church through its accredited minister. The Bishop, in ordaining, acts in the name of the whole Church; the very meaning of his office is that he represents the Church Universal in one area—his diocese—and represents that area in the Church Universal. When, therefore, the episcopally ordained priest celebrates Holy Communion he does it by the commission of the whole Church; the worship is that of the whole Church, of all times and all places; it is indeed the service of the Holy Communion, the Communion of Saints. The worshipping congregation is not the individuals, few or many, who are assembled in the same building, but all faithful souls of every age and nation. We lift up our hearts to the Lord, and forthwith it is with Angels and Archangels and all the company of Heaven that we laud and magnify God's glorious Name.

No doubt this may be experienced by Christians who have dispensed with the historic Ministry. But in fact it is at least less prominent among them. The symbolism of a historic succession is a potent force in leading attention, often almost unconsciously, to this aspect of the Christian life; thus it fosters an

---

[1] I do not think it is more than that. I think that if a layman "celebrates" with devout intention, he effects a real consecration, and any who receive devoutly at his hands receive the divine gift. None the less he acts wrongly, not only because he offends against an actual rule of the Church, but because the principle of his act is destructive of the values which the ordered ministry exists to conserve, and which are an important element in a complete Christian experience.

expectation which facilitates the actual experiences. And this is achieved in a manner harmonious with the central feature of Eucharistic worship—the God-givenness of the life in Christ.   For the fact that no man may take upon himself to consecrate the Bread and Wine,[1] which become the vehicles of the Christ-life to those who receive them, is an added reminder that man does not achieve or find that life, but God gives it to him in His own way.

It is apparent that each of these four means to the end for which the Church exists helps to secure one or other, or both, of two great principles—Transcend-ence and Catholicity.   These two go closely together. Experience gives no ground for hope that any religion emanating from human needs or aspirations or specula-tive enquiry can become a uniting power capable of binding all men and nations together in fellowship. If that is to be done at all, it must be by something which is similarly related to all, as only the act of a transcendent Power can be.   It is the fact that in Christ God Himself intervened in human history, and that in the Church the Spirit of God and Christ is actively imparting the life of God to man, which gives any hope that mankind may be actually drawn together, whether on this planet or elsewhere, in realised and universal fellowship.   The first duty of the Church is therefore to maintain and insist upon the Transcend-ence of God and the gift of His life to men through Christ and the Spirit.

But this must never be separated from the duty of the Church to labour, as it has been taught to pray, that God's Name may be hallowed, His Kingdom come, and His Will be done, in earth as it is in Heaven. In the power of God it is to win this world for the Kingdom of God.   The attainment by the Church

---

[1] Lest this be misunderstood, let it be said that most Free Churchmen assert this as strongly as any "Catholic," but their order does not so fully express it or so forcibly call attention to it.

of an established position in the world not only led to a dilution of its spiritual power, but also, and consequently, to something like abandonment of its God-given mission.

The Church of the fifteenth century, when the secularisation of the Church reached its climax, was not apparently doing much to bring about the fulfilment of the Lord's Prayer. The chief witness to the spiritual deadness of the Church of that era is the fact that, when great spiritual power broke forth, it led (as later in Wesley) to a rending of the body that was designed to be its vehicle. And schisms tend to perpetuate themselves; for they encourage disproportionate developments on both sides of the dividing line. Instead of the one fellowship of all types, where each contributes and each is held in check, the types are segregated and develop their own tendencies without the correction or modifying influence that others might afford. Thus the Church loses the opportunity of manifesting before the world the spirit of fellowship; but thus also the Church is prevented from delivering its whole message in the power and sanity of perfect balance. Before the Church can fully discharge its mission, it must recover its own organic unity.

The secularisation of the Church was mainly due, as we saw, to its increasing success. So long as it was persecuted it was relatively pure; none joined it then except in true sincerity. The very power of fellowship that thus arose in it gradually drew in others, who were members of it, not with insincerity, but without the passion of sincerity which had alone been willing to face the persecution while persecution lasted. Thus the spiritual life was weakened, and the power of fellowship declined with it. But meanwhile the Spirit who works upon the world through the Church was beginning to permeate society even outside the Church. To-day the Holy Spirit speaks through many who stand aloof from the Church as truly as in the Church itself. But it remains true that the Church is His normal channel, and by the reading of the Scriptures, by the recital of the Creeds, by the maintenance of an historic ministry as a living symbol of God's transcendence and man's fellowship, by the witness to the same truths in the sacraments, the Church supplies the chief instruments of the Spirit's age-long activity.

The Church, then, is the direct outcome of the divine act of the Incarnation and the continuance of its principle. It is not constituted by separate individuals deciding to come together. It consists of their actual union in response to the divine act. But, of course, this does not exclude the reality of a psychological process in the matter. On the contrary, the emergence of the Church is the supreme example of a well-known psychological process. " The little Christian community believed that Jesus had appeared to certain of their number and had bidden them assemble in Jerusalem and wait together until some mysterious token of His presence and power should come. Just what this should be they probably did not picture—it was quite vague; but the feeling was strong that some strange, supernatural event was to occur. As the days went by in mutual influence, the feeling increased by geometrical progression. Each one made the suggestion to his neighbour and received it back two-fold. They held constant meetings in which they talked the matter over with each other, prayed over it, and thus induced a state of like-mindedness and mutual suggestibility which transformed them (in all reverence be it said) from a collection of individuals into a ' psychological crowd.' ' And when the day of Pentecost was fully come they were all with one accord in one place.' Notice the distinct assertion of like-mindedness. And then came the expected. The clouds burst, the old inhibitions which may have bound them to their own lives were gone, everything was surrendered to the will of God, and a tide of emotion and devoted loyalty swept over them which they had never known before, the results of which will end only with human history." [1] But the power which drew them together, and held them together, and increased its authority over them through their mutual influence was the life of Jesus. Here, as elsewhere in the Christian religion, what we find is not a complete novelty, but the revelation (in virtue of the divine indwelling) of the true significance of a familiar characteristic of human nature. The " crowd " is not the mere sum of its component individuals; its temper is not the average of theirs. It is a collective unit, made one by the elimination for the moment of all in its members which is alien from its concern, and possessed of an eagerness in that concern greater than the individuals in isolation would feel. The concern may be loyalty, or patriotism, or revenge, or hatred; in the crowd it eliminates all else that might restrain or inhibit its expression. If the animating power is Christ, evoking loyalty as a means to the achievement of His purpose, then the " crowd " becomes the Church, and is fitly called His Body.

The ideal Church does not exist and never has existed; some day, here or elsewhere, it will exist; meanwhile its " members " are members also of " the world." The Church only exists perfectly when all its " members " are utterly surrendered to Christ and united to Him. Some such there have been and are. Mostly the members of the Church are still in process of reaching that consummation and have by no means reached it yet. So the Church appears under the guise of a compromising institution; but the true Church is the Body of Christ, and consists of men *so far as* they are members of that Body. For this reason we ought not in strictness ever to speak

---

[1] Pratt *The Religious Consciousness*, pp. 174, 175.

of the failure of the Church; we should speak of the failure of Christians. The failure, which is conspicuous enough in history, is a failure of Christian people to be thoroughly Christian; in so far as they thus fail, the Church does not exist on the historic plane; where it exists, it triumphs, though its triumph, like the triumph of its Head, often appears to the world as failure till the passing of ages brings a true perspective. The true Church does not fail; but the true Church is still coming slowly into historic existence; that process is the meaning of History from the Incarnation onwards; it consists both in the drawing of men and nations into the fellowship of the Holy Spirit, and in the completion of His work upon them in perfecting their surrender to Christ and their union with Him.

It is clear that this experience of the Divine Spirit who pervades the fellowship, involves an extension of the conception of God similar to that involved by the Incarnation. God is known not only as before and above us—our Creator and King; not only as beside us and suffering for us—our Friend and Saviour; but also as amongst us and within us—Life of our life, and energy of our love. We may " quench the Spirit "; but if we have not by persistent self-will utterly extinguished it, then there is always within us a spark of the Divine Fire, a principle of Holiness that never consents to sin. So the school-boy poet had already learnt: [1]

> From morn to midnight, all day through,
> I laugh and play as others do;
> I sin and chatter just the same
> As others with a different name;
>
> And all year long upon the stage
> I dance and tumble and do rage
> So furiously, I scarcely see
> The inner and eternal Me.

[1] " Expectans Expectavi " in *Marlborough and Other Poems*, by C. H. Sorley.

I have a temple I do not
Visit, a heart I have forgot,
A self that I have never met,
A secret shrine—and yet, and yet—

This sanctuary of my soul
Unwitting I keep white and whole,
Unlatched and lit, if Thou should'st care
To enter or to tarry there.

With parted lips and outstretched hands
And listening ears Thy servant stands,
Call Thou early, call Thou late,
To Thy great service dedicate.

This is indeed no discovery of distinctively Christian experience. The mystics have always known it. The discovery is that, when fully known, this " God within my breast " is a source of true fellowship with others. The deepest experience of the Christian is no " flight of the alone to the alone," but a union in God, now known as Love, with Angels and Archangels and all the company of Heaven. The religious soul finds God within itself in all ages. But when God is revealed as Love, this can no longer be a solitary experience; it becomes an incorporation into the fellowship of all those whom God loves and who in answer are beginning to love Him.

It is sometimes said that men easily believe in the First and Second Persons of the Trinity, but cannot understand what is meant by the Third. If so, it only shows how deep is the gulf between their religion and their habitual thought. For the Third Person is the God with whom we are all in daily intercourse, and in whom almost every one to-day believes as a matter of experience, apart from all deliberate teaching. Our sense of right and wrong is already a fellowship with Him; our belief in a tendency of the world to improve is belief in the Holy Ghost. Democracy and Evolution have together made the thought of the Indwelling Spirit, urging us onward and upward, so natural that in fact many people accept it in a manner much too facile. When States were monarchical, and political authority imposed itself on men from above, this aspect of the Divine Life was more difficult to grasp; but now that Democracy has taken possession and authority operates through men from within, all citizens joining to make the law which each must obey, the thought of God as working within men to conform them to the divine intention is easy, and is, in fact, familiar. It has been often emphasised in such a way as to set it in apparent opposition to the thought of the transcendent Creator, and this has given it an appearance of heterodoxy. But it is part of the traditional and necessary faith of Christendom. God is above; He is also within.

As Jesus reveals the Father, so, too, He reveals the Spirit. The power that religious men have found within them, and that the unquenchable hope of man seeks in the movement of the world, is known, by those to whom the knowledge of Jesus Christ has come, as *His* power at work in their souls, in the fellowship of His disciples, and in the world.

PART IV

INNER CIRCLE

CHAPTER X

GOD IN THE LIGHT OF THE INCARNATION

" Does God love,
And will ye hold that truth against the world? "
BROWNING.

OUR thought of God has been so revolutionised by
the Life and teaching of Jesus of Nazareth, that we
are inclined very often to suppose that to Him we owe
the whole of it. It is true enough that we cannot
overstate our debt to Him; but we may mis-state
it, and we do this if we omit from our completed
thought of God those elements which have their origin
elsewhere and which He took for granted.[1] When
He taught men about God, they already meant something by that Name. It will therefore be worth while
before we consider the illumination brought by Christ
to recapitulate what we know or believe concerning
God apart from Him. This might be attempted in
many ways; it will be appropriate to follow one that
is germane to the general argument that is being
worked out.

As we rise in the scale of being from Thing through
Brute to Person, we inevitably find suggested to our
mind a perfection of Personality, which would be
completely self-determining, completely " good " as
wholly realising the absolute values, and completely
unified inwardly and outwardly.[2] Moreover, we find

---

[1] I made this mistake in some measure in *Foundations*, pp. 213, 214.
[2] Cf. Chapter VI.

that such a Personal Being, if He exists, would supply what otherwise is desired but not forthcoming—an explanation of the universe as a whole.[1]   To assume the reality of such a Being is therefore scientifically sound; and this assumption (justifiable on purely intellectual grounds) finds confirmation in certain forms of experience which have just as good *prima facie* claims as any others to be regarded as veridical.[2] If theism were philosophically improbable, religious experience would have to be explained away by whatever processes the psychology of any epoch might prefer.   If there were no such thing as religious experience, Theism, though probable as a philosophy, would be at once too nebulous and too precarious to become the basis of a way of life.   But religious experience, far from being non-existent, is almost universal; and Theism, far from being demonstrably false, is philosophically probable.   The two together give us a reasonable and very practical assurance of the Being of God, that is of the reality of a Personal Being who is completely self-determined or " free," who is completely at one with Himself, who is in complete apprehension and enjoyment of absolute value, and who is the source of all existence other than Himself. These qualities can be expressed in familiar terms; God is known as Spirit, constant, holy, and almighty. To these attributes yet another must be added, as we reflect that in His creative will all time and all temporal process finds its source and unifying principle; He is Spirit, constant, holy, almighty, and eternal.

Greek philosophers came near to such a conception by the way of thought; but the Supreme Being was for them but doubtfully personal.   Plato indeed exclaims, with reference perhaps to his own earlier exposition of the Idea of Good, " Are we to believe that the most Real is deprived of motion and life and soul and mind? "[3]   And Aristotle uses personal

---

[1] Cf. Chapter I. pp. 7-9.   [2] Cf. Chapter III.   [3] *Sophist*, 249 a.

terms of God. But a Being whose activity consists, even if His very self does not consist, of a "thinking of thought "[1] has a personality of a rather attenuated type. Philosophy never in fact goes beyond apprehension of the formal principle of Deity; it never reaches, and from its own nature never can reach, intercourse with the living God. That is no matter for surprise; philosophy never reaches intercourse with living men either. Intercourse with God or with men is not the conclusion of an argument, but a mode of experience. Knowledge of the living God comes not from Greece or from philosophy but from Palestine and from religious experience.

The classical instances of such experience are the Hebrew prophets and Psalmists; [2] among the prophets we must include the historians who wrote the story of their nation with a constant eye to the question— not " What here or there was the purpose of man? " but " What here or there was the purpose of God? " There is no need now to trace out the process of development in their understanding of the God with whom they were in communion; the result may be not unfairly expressed in the words already used: God is Spirit, constant, holy, almighty, and eternal, a Being of Majesty unapproachable, awful alike in greatness and in holiness, to fear whom is the beginning of wisdom. Such a belief Christ found in the world and took for granted. But the precise content of those terms He profoundly modified.

In studying the difference which Christ has made in the conception of God, we have to attend to three points: first, His teaching about the Father; secondly, His manifestation of the Divine Nature in His own

---

[1] *Metaphysics*, 1072 b, 14-30 ; 1074 b, 33-35.

[2] I am sure the Prophets cannot, in isolation, support the immense metaphysical and theological edifice which Bishop Gore, in his *Belief in God*, builds upon them. But such an edifice can (I think) be safely based on the religious experience of mankind, taken in conjunction with the philosophic grounds of Theism, and of that experience the Prophets are the most conspicuous examples.

Life and Death; thirdly, the resultant power of God experienced by His disciples from Pentecost till now. The last we have already, to some extent, considered,[1] and we shall only need to glance at it briefly in this connexion.

We begin then with our Lord's explicit teaching about God. He assumes, as has been said, the Hebrew faith in a living God, who is not only perfect in Himself, but makes a difference to men and " takes sides." [2]   The God of Israel was a God of righteousness; He did indeed long for the filial obedience of His people with a yearning love, as Hosea and some of the Psalmists had tenderly depicted; but the culmination of His activity in History was usually conceived to be the establishment of righteousness by the punishment or even annihilation of the rebellious. We do well to distinguish the faith of the Old Testament as ethical Monotheism.   Its God is chiefly King and Judge; He is the Moral Law personified and so made inescapably effective.

Christ accepts at its full sublime height the righteousness of God, but represents His method of vindicating it differently.   It is as true for Him as for Amos that only by righteousness can we serve or please Him.   Indeed, the righteousness that He demands is even more than the most punctilious observance of the old Law; [3] it permeates all life, and extends beyond conduct to desire.[4]   But His method of bringing us to that righteousness is not that of Jehovah; or, if it be true that the various elements of the new method are also parts of the old, the change may be expressed as a change of relative emphasis so complete as to make the whole character of the method new.   The change is most apparent in the fact that King and Judge are titles never used, while the title Father becomes almost invariable.   The application of this

---

[1] Cf. Chapter VIII.   [2] Balfour, *Theism and Humanism*, p. 21.
[3] St. Matthew v. 20.   [4] St. Matthew v. 27, 28.

to God was, of course, no novelty;[1] but its prominence was a novelty, and still more so, clearly, was the emotional tone imparted to it. The very way in which the Lord uttered the word filled it with such significance that the actual Aramaic term was retained in a Greek narrative and a Greek letter; nothing else explains its presence there. Christ had spoken of, and to, God as Father in such a way as to open up an altogether new relationship on the part of men towards Him—a relationship which we may express by using the Lord's own word, Abba, Father.[2]

The outstanding feature in the character of the Heavenly Father is an unlimited and undiscriminating love. His lavish bounty to all, whatever their attitude towards Him, is both the supreme mark of His perfection and the element in His perfection which we are especially bidden to reproduce in ourselves.[3] About the novelty of this there can be no question; and this picture of God, with the ethical teaching based on it, is by the Lord Himself contrasted with the teaching given to the ancients; it is indeed its completion, not its destruction,[4] but, in completing, it also inverts the emphasis of the earlier teaching. Moreover, it gives rise to questions of special difficulty with regard to the righteousness of God, to which we must return when we have completed our survey of the elements specially characteristic of the Christian conception of God. The chief of these, as has been seen, is the thought of God as the all-loving Father.

But while this love is undiscriminating in its bounty it is far from being weakly amiable. This same Father who makes His sun to rise on the evil and on the good is one who is able to destroy both body and soul in hell.[5] Nothing, not even the fall of a sparrow,

---

[1] Cf. (e.g.) Isaiah ix. 6 ; lxiii. 16.
[2] Cf. St. Mark xiv. 36 ; Galatians iv. 6 ; and especially Romans viii. 15.
[3] St. Matthew v. 43-48.
[4] St. Matthew v. 17.
[5] St. Matthew x. 28; St. Luke xii. 5.

happens apart from Him—a doctrine of comfort if we are living in accordance with His will, but not otherwise. Moreover, the emphasis on the reality of men's choice between the way of life and the way of death implies a conception of God as moral Lawgiver and Judge. There is certainly severity in Christ's doctrine of God. It is the severity of Love, but the Love is very severe. Indeed, it is all the more terrible because of its total freedom from personal ill-will; that might be placated; but the antagonism of utter Love against selfishness can never be placated. If a man is selfish, and to the degree in which a man is selfish, God is his antagonist. The Father does not desire his suffering or his destruction; He desires only to win him out of his selfishness. But for very love, knowing that love is life and selfishness is death, He shows relentless sternness towards those that are unloving. " His lord delivered him to the tormentors . . . so also shall my heavenly Father do unto you if ye forgive not each one his brother from your hearts." [1]

It is noticeable, however, that, with the exception of the words just quoted, which occur in connexion with a parable, our Lord does not speak of the Father as inflicting punishment by His own action. Judgement, indeed, is expressly stated to be a function of the Son, not of the Father; [2] and, even so, it is not the purpose of the Son or His deliberate act; [3] rather it is the inevitable consequence of His coming among men with the offer of true life. [4] To reject that offer is to be condemned. The Son is the Word or Self-expression of God, so that judgement appears to be not the purpose or deliberate act of God, but the inevitable issue of the act in which He reveals Himself. In this way we see how His activity in judgement is compatible with His undiscriminating Love. [5]

---

[1] St. Matthew xviii. 34, 35.   [2] St. John v. 22.
[3] St. John iii. 17; viii. 15.   [4] St. John iii. 19.
[5] The whole subject of Judgement receives fuller treatment in the next chapter.

St. John penetrated to the very heart of His Master's teaching about God when he summed it up in the reiterated phrase, " God is love." [1] That is the fundamental nature of the Being, already known as Spirit, constant, holy, almighty, and eternal, who is Himself the ground of the existence of all things and the explanation of the whole course of History.

The teaching about God which is given by the Life and Death of Christ—His conduct as distinguished from His words—carries this further but makes no change in principle. " He that hath seen Me hath seen the Father ": [2] and what we see is Love in action. The outstanding feature of His miracles is not the supernatural power displayed, but the fact that this power is used only for works of love and never for service of self. His call is to all men; by it they are sifted, and on those who cannot respond are directed denunciations made more terrible by their freedom from personal vindictiveness and ill-will. The love which He displays is holy, and is severe to the point of relentlessness against self-concern and self-complacency; but it is sheer unalloyed love. When the self-spirit in its various forms—religious, financial, political—at last decides to destroy Him, His action still shows only love: " When He was reviled, He reviled not again; when He suffered, He threatened not." [3] God, as Christ reveals Him, acts as Christ taught us in the Sermon on the Mount to act; the Father in heaven is perfect in the way that we are bidden to be perfect.[4]

But what becomes of that belief in God as the personification and vindicator of the Moral Law, the counterpart of that sense of absolute obligation which we found to be the root element in man's religious experience? [5] If God loves the sinner as much as the

[1] 1 John iv. 8, 16.   [2] St. John xiv. 9.
[3] 1 Peter ii. 23.
[4] For a further discussion of the significance of the Passion see Chapter XIV
[5] Chapter III.

saint, why should we trouble to be saints, if it is easier, as it often seems pleasanter, to be sinners? The questions irresistibly arise, as they arose in the minds of those who heard or read St. Paul.[1] St. Paul's answer is in effect that the question is purely academic and represents no reality. If the power of the knowledge of the love of God has taken possession of a man he cannot continue in sin, however forcibly a purely dialectical argument might recommend this course.[2] And that takes us to the root solution; but it does not make everything simple. It is the mere truth that the Christian doctrine of God is liable to appear immoral to any man for whom it is a mere notion and has not become an experience. But even so, it only *appears* immoral; it is, in fact, the most highly moral and the most effectively moralising of all actual or possible conceptions of God, as we shall now see.

At the specifically moral level of thought and life, men think of themselves as distinct and separate individuals standing over against both God and each other; it is the level of " rights " and " duties," of claims and counter-claims. At this level the goal of life appears to be a rendering of what is due to God and men. The Moral Law is the principle which regulates this process. So far as God is the personification and vindicator of the Moral Law, He may be expected to approve and reward those who render their dues, to condemn and to punish thos who refuse. He is thus a postulate of the ethical consciousness, necessary to secure the actuality of the supreme ethical principle. But, in fact, He doe not and cannot by this method succeed in that aim Human conduct is rooted in motives; and the motive derive their power from the desires and emotior actually felt. If the aim is to make man, who i naturally selfish, truly just in his dealings, or, in othe

---

[1] Romans iii. 7, 8; vi. 1.   [2] Romans vi. 2-11.

words, to convince him that he is only one among others of equal worth with himself, the method of rewards and punishments can never succeed; for it is an appeal to self-interest, which by that appeal is confirmed and strengthened. No; if selfish man is to be raised from self-concern to true justice it must be by something which makes no appeal to his self-interest, but calls him out altogether from his self-concern; it must be by the stimulation of his generosity; it must be by self-sacrifice calling for self-sacrifice in answer.

Prophets and philosophers have indeed combined to establish the thought of God as primarily moral Law-giver and Judge. "Wilt thou not slay the wicked, O God?"[1] expresses exactly the mental attitude of Kant's *Critique of Practical Reason*. And the resultant notion of God has a high disciplinary value. Fear of God's wrath and punishment may keep wild impulses in check, though it can never really cleanse the character. But we cannot help noticing that both prophets and philosophers are mainly concerned with the punishment so richly deserved by some one else. This is, in fact, the root fallacy of much moral philosophy; it looks at legislation, divine or human, from outside, as designed to hold in check wicked persons other than the author and his readers. It may be true that those who vote for a law sentencing murderers to death are thinking to themselves, " I vote that any one who kills me shall be hanged "; but the real meaning of the legislation is that through it every citizen says, " I will that if I ever kill a man I may be hanged." The effectiveness of Law and its machinery of enforcement can only be appreciated by those who consider its application to themselves. It is natural, but very misleading, to think that there must be a God that those who injure or disgust us by their crimes may be punished or destroyed; the only thing

[1] Psalm cxxxix. 19.

that is profitable is for each man to consider the relation of God's righteousness to himself.

Now there is no clamour ringing down the ages from the souls of men that God will visit upon themselves the due punishment of their own sins. The clamour for a God who is first and foremost the vindicator of righteousness by punishment of the guilty is for one who will punish not the clamourers but their enemies—the enemies of Israel, of the Church, of Great Britain (or Germany), as the case may be. That none the less this notion of God may be in its measure beneficial to those who hold it has been already said; but it can never do what it exists to do, for it cannot lift men out of themselves.

It not only fails to reach its goal, but it creates new obstacles. Men tend to imitate the God in whom they believe. If they think of God as blessed in His boundless opportunity for enjoyment, their religion degrades them. It is a step forwards of infinite importance when men learn that God is righteous— " of purer eyes than to behold iniquity," and " that will by no means clear the guilty." [1] Such a belief may raise men to the stage of honest dealing and trustworthiness; but as the God that it presents is in the last resort uncompassionate towards sinners, so will the character that it tends to form be hard and uncompassionate. The man who holds this belief and lets it mould him will control his appetites and be honourable in conduct; but he will exact remorselessly the like conduct from others, and be ready to crush them at the dictate of his conscience if they disappoint him. He is confirmed in his self-centredness by the very type of righteousness at which he aims; by his very faith in God he is shut out from eternal life. [2]

Now the God revealed in Christ meets all the needs

---

[1] Habakkuk i. 13; Exodus xxxiv. 7.
[2] Cf. St. John xvii. 3; also Chapter XII. of this book.

indicated. If the God we worship is one who loves all men equally and indiscriminately, then every remembrance of Him must rebuke our selfish character and all its works. I realise (a little) His love for me; but therein I realise his equal love for others. How can I injure those whom He loves? It is precisely the undiscriminating and apparently immoral universality of His love which most of all lifts those who believe in Him out of the selfishness, which leads to crimes and injuries, up to the justice of action whose law is, " Do unto all men as you would that they should do unto you," and to the justice of emotion and purpose whose law is, " Thou shalt love thy neighbour as thyself." [1] The morality of claims and counter-claims represents only a phase of men's growth to that godlike love which is eternal life; in itself it is self-destructive, for it postulates the self-centredness which its whole business is to overcome. The " fulfilment " of the law of claims and counter-claims is the law of love; the full truth and reality of the Jehovah of the Old Testament is the Father revealed by Jesus Christ.[2]

The " non-resistance to evil " which is enjoined upon us that we may be true children of the heavenly Father is no mere amiability which accepts an injury rather than face unpleasantness. It is the method of active love. " The method of love may be identified with non-resistance. The first object of this policy is to make the other individual accept one's judgement of his ultimate quality. If I meet wrath with a soft answer, it is because I know that the angry man has momentarily forgotten himself, and I propose to recall him to his senses. If I meet persistent misinterpretation of my motives with an equally steady refusal to take offence, it is because I discern some seed of fair judgement in my critic, and I propose to give it

---

[1] Hocking makes this point most effectively: cf. *The Meaning of God in Human Experience*, pp. 205, 482-83.
[2] St. Matthew v. 17.

a favourable climate to grow in. My non-resistance, when it is valid, is never mere generosity and kindness: it is the attempt to make my opponent see in himself what I see in him, to lift him in sight of his own ultimate integrity." [1] So, too, the love of God, who makes His sun to rise on the evil and on the good and sends rain on the just and on the unjust, is not that merely amiable quality which shirks the responsibility of action and is properly called sentimentality; it is love active in redemption.

The revelation gives us not only a doctrinal affirmation of the divine love, but its very image. It is always by imagery that principles become powerful over conduct.[2] We are not left to conceive the all-embracing love of God as a general idea; we can call to mind the Agony and the Cross. There we see what selfishness in us means to God; and if evil means that to God, then God is not indifferent to evil. He displays His utter alienation from evil by showing us the pain that it inflicts on Him. So more than in any other way He rouses us from acquiescence in our own selfishness. By His refusal to discriminate in His love, and by His surrender of Himself for men's evil passions to torment, He wins us to deserve His love and kills the evil passions in a degree that would be impossible by any activity of righteous force.

If, however, we are too hardened in self-complacency to let the appeal of His love penetrate to our hearts (as may happen to respectable people though scarcely to notorious sinners), we cannot take selfish comfort in the thought that He loves us still. Because He loves us, and because that self-complacency is shutting us out from eternal life, He will let our selfishness bring upon us its own fruit of disaster. Incarnate Love, on the very threshold of the Passion wherein that Love is supremely manifest, speaks of Himself

---

[1] C. A. Bennett, *A Philosophical Study of Mysticism*, p. 141.
[2] Cf. *Mens Creatrix*, chap. xii.

as the stone which the builders rejected and is become
the head of the corner: " whosoever shall fall on this
stone shall be broken, but on whomsoever it shall fall,
it will scatter him like dust." [1] He will smash and
crush the hard shell of the self-contented soul, at any
cost of mere pain and suffering; for though it is no
pleasure to Him to see us suffer, however much we
may deserve it, He also knows that any volume or
poignancy of pain may be worth while if it gives the
opportunity for love at last to penetrate and call forth
love. The Gospel of God's undiscriminating love
has no syllable of consolation for the self-complacent,
except in so far as it assures them that the aim of
whatever judgement may befall them is to afford a
new opportunity for living as they have no desire to
live.

For fellowship with God is the goal to which God
calls us; it is fellowship with Love—utter, self-
forgetful, and self-giving Love. The selfish cannot
reach it, except they be first changed into what they
are not; and if they could, they would detest it. The
Christian Heaven is no selfish reward for sufferings
regretfully endured; it is fellowship with God. To
go to Heaven means to be used up utterly in service;
but that is also Hell for those in whom love has not
yet conquered self. In either case it is the truth of
all life, for it is the Life of God. If God has not won
us by His love into spiritual fellowship with Himself,
we are on the way to Hell; if He never does so win
us, we must arrive there; [2] if He do so win us we are in
Heaven. All turns on our knowledge of and response
to God who is Love. He is what He is and His
world is what it is; we know or do not know. It is

---

[1] St. Matthew xxi. 44; St. Luke xx. 18.

[2] The Catholic and Evangelical doctrine of Original Sin, which teaches that we
are " lost " unless we be redeemed, is thus simply and exactly true, though its supposed
historical basis is mythical. I use the word Heaven for final and assured fellowship
with God, Hell for final and irrevocable alienation from Him. What the latter
involves is further considered in the next chapter.

not scientific or doctrinal knowledge (εἰδέναι) that is here in question, but the knowledge of personal acquaintance (γνῶναι). " This is eternal life, to know thee the only true God, and Him whom thou sendedst, Jesus Christ." [1] " This is the true God and eternal life; little children, keep yourselves from idols." [2]

---

[1] St. John xvii. 3.   [2] 1 John v. 20, 21.

CHAPTER XI

ETERNITY AND HISTORY

> " I saw Eternity the other night
> Like a great ring of pure and endless light,
>   All calm as it was bright:—
> And round beneath it, Time, in hours, days, years,
>   Driven by the spheres,
> Like a vast shadow moved; in which the world
> And all her train were hurl'd."
>
> HENRY VAUGHAN.

In a former chapter [1] we found that History must be capable of apprehension as a single whole, and that such an apprehension would be an experience deserving the name Eternal. This word does not mean mere everlastingness; it means a unitary synthetic apprehension of the whole process of Time and all that happens in it. What other conditions must be fulfilled to make such an apprehension possible we have no means of completely knowing; we can rise to such an apprehension of a short span of time, though even for that it seems that a selection of the events is necessary. When we grasp a period of History, it is a period already past, and our apprehension is limited to the outstanding events, or to what is closely connected with outstanding events or outstanding individuals. Art can take us further into the mystery; the tragedian can give us an experience of the present in the light of its own future. But that is only possible because the play is written before we read it or see it acted. Perhaps the poet or dramatist in act of writing comes nearer. He does not know in advance just

[1] Chapter V.

187

what he is going to write.   In finding the expression
of its meaning he also finds that meaning itself; yet
what he finds is his own thought.   Mr. Bernard Shaw
has told us that when he has once launched his
" characters " into the drama he has no longer any
control over their conduct; yet as he watches that
conduct, sometimes apparently with great surprise,
he is only observing the articulation of his own till
then unmastered thought, for the Dramatis Personae
act according to their characters, which originated in
his mind.   Perhaps the relation of the creative artist
to his work in the actual moment of creation is the
closest analogy we have in our experience to the
relation of the eternal Creator to the temporal world
that He creates.   If we conceive a father who is both
the origin of his children's being and a creative artist
working out his purpose through the living and free
wills of his children, we come still nearer in principle
but are further off in actual experience, for no father
has the full control over the living material in which
he works that a poet or musician has over the words
and sounds that he manipulates.   In idea, as distinct
from experience, we come nearest to what we want
if we conceive God as a Father who is a perfect artist
in the art of education.   He remains outside the
process, though it originates in Him and He guides
it; men are free, but through their very freedom he
guides them to the fulfilment of His will.   And still
this is incomplete; for it omits the actual supra-
temporal apprehension of the Time-process and all
its details.   We shall come back later to an enquiry
into precisely this aspect of the matter; [1] our concern
now is with the effect upon our view of History caused
by our knowledge not only that there is an Eternal
Mind or Will but that this Mind or Will is such as
is revealed in Christ.

The theme is so vast that we must content ourselves

[1] Chapter XV.

with a few portions of it. Probably the discussion will be clearer for the insertion here of a list of the portions to be discussed. They are: (1) The scale of values, pp. 189-192; (2) the problem of accident, pp. 192-199; (3) the sovereignty of Love in human history, pp. 199-208; (4) the eschatological problem, pp. 208-211.

1. The most obvious reaction of the eternal upon the temporal concerns the scale of values. On any theory it is plain that if anything exists at all which can be called eternal, and if we have any part or lot in it, it must be incomparably more important than what is only temporal. This would be true if " eternal " meant no more than " everlasting," and we may take it in that sense for the moment to illustrate the point. The spiritual value of all eschatological doctrine—Christian or other—lies just here. Our temporal life is set against a background of the everlasting. The pictures of the end of the world may vary; but it has an end. The elements may " melt with fervent heat "[1] or the earth may become too cold to support life, or at any rate such life as we know. Or, if there are blind stars in space, our planet may collide with one of these and be smashed to pieces. It makes no real difference whether what remains to come in man's history on earth is long or short; it must end; and beyond that end the everlasting continues without end. In the years 1914-1918 many people supposed that nothing mattered more than the issue of the war; but if the earth had in those years collided with a blind star and been smashed, this would suddenly have mattered exactly and precisely not at all; but the spirit of self-devotion in the combatants, of care for justice, of charity towards enemies, would still have mattered exactly as much as before. If there is an eternal realm, then fellowship with the eternal Spirit and partnership in the eternal goods is for every living

[1] 2 Peter iii. 12.

soul more urgently important than any temporal interest can be. The eternal Spirit is love; the eternal goods are love, joy, peace, loyalty, courage, wisdom, beauty, knowledge. These are the true goods; that man is truly successful, that nation is truly great, which has these things in abundance.

Moreover, if History is the manifestation and working out of the eternal purpose, even temporal success must depend in the long run upon conformity with the eternal Mind and Will. If the world is the creation and expression of eternal love, then all selfishness is self-defeating. When we say that God is Love, we proclaim Love as the sovereign power in the universe. If God is Love, then every purpose or policy which is selfish, based on the desire to gain rather than to serve, must end in catastrophe, for it is in opposition to the supreme power in the universe; and every purpose or policy based on love, the desire to serve rather than to gain, is bound to reach success, through whatever sacrifices it may have to pass, because it is in alliance with the supreme power in the universe. Of course this does not mean that if our desire is to serve we shall acquire gain; it means that if our desire is to serve, we shall be enabled to serve, which is to " enter into the joy of the Lord." God is love; the world is God's world; there is no conceivable combination of circumstances in which it is impossible to show love. We may suffer as we do it; but if the real spirit of love is in us that will be no disappointment; we shall rejoice that we are counted worthy to suffer.

All this is more familiar as homiletics than as philosophy; my contention is that it is sound philosophy. Philosophers seek to know the nature of reality and the right way to live; Christianity offers the answer to both enquiries in one word—Love; and if we accept the hypothesis, it works both in theory and in practice, in the sense, not that it makes all clear, but that it progressively, if never completely, reduces chaos to order. That statement can only be proved as regards practice by actual experimenting; how the Christian answer works in theory we must now consider.

The chief intellectual difficulty hindering people from accepting Christianity is the difficulty of tracing divine love in the actual history of the universe as known to us. The history of the animal creation suggests a callous indifference to apparently fruitless suffering in the " Determiner of Destiny." But this first impression is ill-founded. No doubt there is suffering, alike from fear and from injury, in the animal world. But there seems no reason to doubt that the animal world is on the whole thoroughly happy. It is only when we read into the experience of animals our own capacity for memory and anticipation that we think of jungle-life (for example) as mainly unhappy. Even if the animal creation were (as perhaps it is) a final stage of development, to be justified in itself or not at all, it would not afford a valid argument against the goodness of the Creator. Moreover, in the apparently cruel struggle for existence, those kinds which are able to combine and co-operate are more successful than others. Mutual aid rather than naked competition is the law of progress in the animal world; and mutual aid, when it becomes self-conscious, is an expression of love.

From our point of view, however, the animal world is part of one great whole which finds its fullest expression in Man and his history. This does not mean that the other animal species are necessarily or even probably developing towards self-consciousness and intelligence as we know them in Man. For that there is no evidence; Bergson's theory of a bifurcation of evolution, one line leading to a great development of " intelligence," the other to a similar development of " instinct," has, I believe, far more foundation in the facts,[1] though of course it is no more than a speculation. It is not suggested that the problem of animal life can be solved by a consideration of what animal life is going to turn into; what is suggested is that animal life supplies only one part of an indivisible problem, and that if broadly and on the whole it is compatible with a theory which fits the facts of human existence, that, considering how little we know of animal life from the inside, we are bound to accept as enough.

2. As we turn to Man and his History we are at first driven back to a stage logically and chronologically prior to animal life. Man lives in a world which he learns increasingly to control; but there is no expectation that he will ever control it altogether, or that he is likely to become master of earthquakes and eruptions; and even if he should learn the laws governing such events enough to adapt his conduct and avoid catastrophe, he will still be liable to accidents of a thousand kinds; and, anyhow, the knowledge of the future cannot now heal the calamities of the past. From the outset we find that Man lives in a world liable at any moment to devastate his hopes by sheer accident. How can it be said that such a world reveals the eternal Love?

The problem is real enough at the best; but it has been made worse by the superstitious habit of attributing to a special act of divine volition any event which is not easily explained by reference to some human will or by the scientific knowledge available at the time. This superstition, like all others, rests on a true conviction; in this case it is the conviction that Will is the only true cause or explanation of anything. The superstition is to suppose that the Will of God acts more completely in Nature than in Spirit (such as Man). All that exists is the self-utterance of God's Will: His fullest and completest utterance was

---

[1] Bergson, *L'Évolution créatrice*, pp. 146-164, specially 146 and 152.

through Human Nature, which He assumed at His Incarnation. No doubt in mankind generally there is a partial frustration of His purpose through the self-centredness of the individual wills of men. But it remains true that the human will is a more adequate instrument of the Divine Will than any natural force can be. We can trace the activity of God far more truly in the lives of men than in the occurrences of Nature. If that is realised, we shall at least be delivered from the supposition that calamities due to accident, whether small or great, are due to the act of God (as insurance offices say) except in the sense that He has created the universe and all things within it.

What, after all, do we mean by an " accident "? The word seems to stand for an event of which the causes have no connexion with the causes of the human conduct affected by it. A land-slip takes place in an uninhabited region; it is not usually called an accident. A land-slip takes place in a popular watering-place and overwhelms a number of holiday-makers; it is a terrible accident. An event is only an accident if it crosses some human interest or purpose; but also it must be due to non-human action. An explosion in war destroys a number of men; but if it was due to a mine laid by the enemy it is not an accident (though the deaths caused are called " casualties "). An explosion due to volcanic eruption destroys a number of men; no one hesitates to call this an accident. In short an accident is an interference with human purposes due to the action of natural forces, known or unknown, but incalculable in their bearing on the purpose interfered with. An accident therefore is merely a particular illustration of the fact that all human purposes have to be fulfilled in a world which, as a whole, is subject to general laws. There is no reason to attribute any particular accident to a special act of the Divine Will; the explanation lies in the convergence of two independent lines of causal action.

If when I am walking down the street a chimney-pot is blown down, hits me on the head and kills me, that does not prove that God decided to end my terrestrial existence on that day and took this means of doing so.   The wind that knocked down the chimney-pot was due to causes traceable in the last resort to the nebula in which the solar system originated.   The looseness of the chimney-pot was due (perhaps) to neglect on the part of a builder, which had its own moral explanation in his family history.   My presence was due to my pursuit of my ordinary duties.   No special act of God is involved except in so far as He did not work a miracle to save me when these three independent lines of causation converged to the production of the " accident."   If there are to be general laws at all, there must be accidents, unless there is to be a miracle every time an accident would otherwise occur.

Now there can be no doubt about the moral value of general laws.   It is only on the basis of an assumed fixity in Nature that any purpose can be formed at all.   Unless we have reasonable certainty that the sun will rise to-morrow, that the Law of Gravitation will still be valid (or, at least, as valid as it is now), that food will still nourish, and speech still convey thought, we cannot set out to order the present with a view to the future; and this is the basis of all intelligent choice, and therefore of all purpose and morality.   It is not fatal to morality that the world may end to-morrow— perhaps by an astronomical " accident "; but it would be fatal to morality if the world might continue to exist, but react on novel and unpredictable principles. The fixity of the Laws of Nature is no evidence against the Love of God; on the contrary, it is strictly compatible with it, inasmuch as it supplies the only basis on which mankind could set out upon the moral life whereby primarily man's fellowship with God and service to Him is achieved.

But why, if He is Love, does He not intervene to save His children from the occasional evils resulting from the action of those fixed laws? Could He not either divert the chimney-pot or breathe into my subconscious mind a suggestion that would prevent my walking where it was about to fall? People seldom ask these questions with reference to accidents that might befall themselves; but they ask them when their friends are concerned; and they pray that their friends may be preserved from such accidents. Is this reasonable? If not, is it because God cannot, or because He will not, intervene? In any case, what becomes of omnipotent Love?

I would answer first that God certainly can intervene and (moreover) that, in my belief, He often does; this cannot be proved, and it would be unsound to base any general philosophic view upon this conviction. The experience of religious people is, however, decisive to any one who accepts the religious hypothesis. People who take care to keep their devotional life fresh and vigorous find repeatedly that they are " guided " to act or speak in ways the value of which is only afterwards appreciated. To maintain spiritual contact with God produces, it would seem, a sensitiveness to the Divine Will which usually shows itself only in the actions which it prompts.[1] Personally I believe that a similar result may be produced by intercession. When I prayed for the safety of my friends during the Great War, I did not suppose that God would deflect bullets to save them, but I did and do believe that He might see fit to prompt them to some apparently " accidental " movement which would

[1] Personal testimony is the most appropriate support of such a statement. I have found that at times when I have been taking due trouble about my own devotional life I have frequently felt an unreasoned impulse to go and see some one whom (as it turned out) I was able to help considerably. I have also noticed that if I get slack about my prayers, such coincidences cease. Preachers who pray over their sermons often find that some sentence which they doubtfully insert, or utter on the spur of the moment, is exactly calculated to meet the spiritual need of some one in the congregation.

save them. The impulse to pray is justified if such a thing is even possible.

But it remains true that even if there are instances of such intervention, they are rare; and perhaps they increase rather than diminish the difficulty. For if God ever acts so, why does He not act so always? The argument that the Divine Love is compatible with accidents and casualties must follow other lines than these. And it is the reaction of Eternity on History which provides the cogency of the argument.

Of primary importance is the scale of values. We can see this if we trace the scale implied by certain popular difficulties. "If A prays for his boy at the front, and B does not, is A's boy more likely than B's boy to come through safe? If he is not, what was the use of praying? If he is, it is unfair to B's boy that he should suffer for his father's unbelief or neglect." I could not myself say, in round terms, that A's boy is more likely to come through safe; I should say that the father's prayer would win him increased strength for whatever might come to him, and further, that, if it were really best for him and all concerned that he should come home safe, the prayer might be the condition needed for the realisation of this best result.[1] But, anyhow, there is no unfairness to B's boy, unless it is assumed that bodily death is always a great evil to him who dies; and if we once learn to see terrestrial life on the background of eternity this assumption is found to be baseless. The evil of war casualties is not the supposed injury done to those who die, but the loss to those who remain alive—loss of friends and loss of useful citizens. It is worth mentioning, perhaps, that the supposed "unfairness" in the objector's complaint is merely part of the general fact of human influence. If the religious theory of life is right, B's boy must suffer for his father's unbelief or negligence of prayer whether or not he remains

[1] On the general grounds for Prayer and Intercession see Chapter XIII.

physically alive when danger is over. We are all gainers or losers by the quality of our homes in child-hood. Part of the theological difficulty about " acci-dents " is due to the acquiescence in a scale of values which is incompatible with any vivid realisation of the eternal background of our temporal history.

But only part of it can be so accounted for. How can a loving God remain inactive while accidents which He could prevent bring heart-breaking grief to His children? We must now separate accidents in the strict sense from events, like wars, which are due to human wills. Is the Japanese earthquake compatible with the Love of God? Yes, if it is true that the whole purpose of human history is to fashion souls, and a great fellowship of souls, knit together in mutual love through common participation in the Eternal love. That is the goal of human history according to the Christian scheme;[1] and to it we are moving in our process of evolution from our animal ancestry. The crucial problem of human life is to acquire detachment from the present and to become rooted in the Eternal. In the education necessary for this, no influence is so powerful as the discipline of accident. If God in fact intervened on every occasion, or on many occasions, when apart from His action the normal process of events would lead to a calamitous " accident," it may be doubted if the spiritual side of human nature would ever be able to assert itself. For such beings as, in fact, we are, the knowledge that our earthly life is precarious offers an invaluable reminder that the highest values are not bound up with earthly life at all. " Accident," speaking broadly, is one of the most effective forces for the spiritualising of men.

When, therefore, some precious life is cut off by an accident, or when widespread devastation is caused, we should not say "Why does God choose to do this?"

---

[1] Cf., for instance, the first chapter of the Epistle to the Ephesians.

God does not " choose to do this "; what God chooses
is to create a world to which " this " is incidental.
And it is good for us all that He does.   But while He
does not specifically choose that the accident should
occur, He is ready to support both those who die and
those who remain on earth with the experience of
His loving presence: He does not leave them merely
in the grip of a mechanical universe grinding out its
causal sequences, but by means of all that comes gives
His children a new motive to find Himself.   Of
course this argument is peculiarly irritating to the
atheist or agnostic.   The Christian finds confirmation
of his faith whatever happens.   If he has earthly
happiness, he turns to God with thanksgiving; if he
has earthly sorrow, he turns with renewed eagerness
to the Eternal Love, and gives thanks for what impelled
him thither once more.   In all things that happen he
finds God, not because he traces the eternal purpose
in an infinite number of " particular providences,"
but because he has learnt how to make all temporal
experience direct his attention to its eternal background.   Consequently he " gives thanks at all times
for all things," [1] because he has found it literally true
that " all things work together for good to them that
love God." [2]   And that is what must happen if God is
Creator.   " Good " is service and love of God; those
who love and serve Him find in all that happens
occasion to love and serve Him more.   For whatever
comes, comes, either by His specific choice or by
operation of His perpetual purpose, from His hand.

    " But is He to be called Love who lets us suffer so
incredibly that we may learn to love Him?   Is not
this rather a monstrous Egoism set up on the Throne
of the universe?   If a man killed my friend, or let
him die, to make me love him, I should call him cruel,
and certainly he could not in that way make me love
him.   Why is it not so with God?   If he lets my

---

[1] Ephesians v. 20.   [2] Romans viii. 28.

friend die by an accident, is He not cruel? Shall I
not rather defy than love Him, even though He put
forth His omnipotence to destroy me? "

The question is natural enough, and the poets of
revolution, such as Shelley and Byron, have clothed
it in magnificent rhetoric. But it is only natural if
we are thinking of God as another individual Person
standing to us in the same relationship as other people
do. But He is not that. He is Himself the true
Life of our life; the Love which is His Nature is the
true energy of our souls. He is within us as well as
without. We defy ourselves when we defy Him.
The Eternal Love which He calls us to understand
and return is not other than our love for the friend who
dies. The love, wherewith we love, is the Holy
Ghost. The call to a deeper love of God which comes
through the death of a friend is not the call to forget
the friend and to love God instead; it is a call to
realise more deeply what our love for our friend really
was and is—an activity of God in us—and to rise
from the temporal relationship of a " natural " friendship to an apprehension of the Eternal Love in which
that friendship lives on in spite of the friend's death.
In those who are thus able to rise by sorrow to eternal
joy, the familiar words of the Prayer Book Psalter are
fulfilled; they " going through the vale of misery use
it for a well, and the pools are filled with water." [1]
Of entry into the realisation of Eternal Love, wherein
all earthly loves are reaffirmed and consecrated, all
earthly sorrows and all earthly joys can be true
sacraments.

3. We have already spoken of wars, and thus
introduced the problem which arises not from the
impact of natural forces upon human purposes, but

---

[1] Psalm lxxxiv. 6; cf. Inge, *Personal Religion and the Life of Devotion*, pp. 88, 89:
" Bereavement is the deepest initiation into the mysteries of human life, an initiation
more searching and profound than even happy love. Love remembered and consecrated by grief belongs, more clearly than the happy intercourse of friends, to the
eternal world; it has proved itself stronger than death."

from the history which is constituted by those purposes themselves. For the miseries that are due to " historic causes " we have begun already to see the explanation. The Love of God desires for us what is best for us, which is partnership in Itself; it does not desire for us that we should be happy and comfortable while we shut out our own highest good. Therefore persistence in selfishness spells misery. The best thing of all cannot be merely given to us or forced upon us; it is only apprehensible by an act of choice; until we choose we cannot have it; and, being selfish, we do not choose. But in this sphere the Eternal makes His sovereignty over the temporal felt through Judgement. We have seen already that the course of History, quite apart from all theology, points to universal fellowship as its own goal.[1] That is the historic expression of Love, which we learn from Christ is the Sovereign Principle of existence. As we watch the course of History from another point of view we see this Eternal Principle asserting its sovereignty in the catastrophes to which men come by relying on principles at variance with it.

Our Lord spoke of His " Coming "; and His disciples thought of it as a Return or " Second Coming." Their minds were full of the expectation of specific Days of the Lord, when God would vindicate His authority by the punishment or destruction of all who defied it. But God seeks no such triumph. Men may involve themselves in destruction; His act is always for salvation. So Christ spoke of His Coming as something very imminent, and before the High Priest He spoke of it as then and there accomplished: from that moment [2] Daniel's prophecy was fulfilled, and the Son of Man was seated on the right hand of power. To reveal in uttermost perfection the Eternal Love was to clothe it with the only power

---

[1] Cf. Chapter V.
[2] ἀπ' ἄρτι, St. Matthew xxvi. 64; ἀπὸ τοῦ νῦν, St. Luke xxiii. 69.

appropriate to it.   From then till now, God " reigns from the Tree."   The prophecy has been progressively fulfilled.   The writer of the Apocalypse exactly expresses the facts.   " He cometh with the clouds "; that is present; from the moment of the Passion to the consummation of history He works by the sovereign power of love; " and every eye shall see Him "; that is future; for the universal apprehension of His sovereignty is still to come.

But there is Judgement, and it is traceable.   Our Lord plainly spoke of His own coming in Judgement; and He intertwined it, if the records are to be trusted, with predictions of the Fall of Jerusalem.   That was to be the next illustration in history of the divine Judgement which is committed by the Father to the Son.   Jerusalem fell for the same reason that it rejected Christ; it fell through its nationalistic ambition. Called to a unique spiritual destiny as the trustees for the knowledge of the true God, the Jews yet preferred to cling to their secular and worldly ambitions.   That preference led to their rejection of Christ; it also led to their extinction, for it made them a nuisance to imperial Rome, which was not tolerant of nuisances. So Christ read in their rejection of Himself their coming doom.   " If thou hadst known, in this thy day, even thou, the things which belong unto peace. But now they are hid from thine eyes.   For the days shall come upon thee when thine enemies shall cast up a bank about thee and compass thee round, and keep thee in on every side, and shall dash thee to the ground and thy children within thee; and they shall not leave in thee one stone upon another; because thou knewest not the time of thy visitation." [1]   This does not mean that God, offended at an outrage to His dignity, would wipe out the arrogant city in a petulant irritation.   Non-resentment against injuries is the quality by which we are to show that we are His

[1] St. Luke xix. 42-44.

children. But the failure of the Jews at the crisis of their destiny showed how deeply ingrained was the quality that led to it, and so revealed the fate to which that quality must lead. And when Jerusalem fell for a characteristic which involved repudiation of Christ, the Son of Man came in Judgement. So it was when the turn of Rome itself came. Rome fell largely because its social fabric rested increasingly on slavery; slavery is contrary to the truth about human nature as it is revealed in Christ; and when Rome fell because it based its civilisation on a principle alien from the mind of Christ, the Son of Man came in Judgement. So it was when mediaeval Europe broke up, because the Church in its effort to make the world God's Kingdom had surrendered to the world by adopting its methods and some even of its vices. So it was when the French Revolution overthrew an order which persisted in maintaining unjust privileges. So it was in 1914 when a civilisation largely based on greed was wrecked, and that State which had made greed for power an avowed principle of action was stripped of all power. At each one of these great moments the authority of Christ was vindicated by the catastrophe in which its rejection issued. Love is shown to be King by the fact that what offends against love destroys itself. In that sense, and to that extent, the Kingdom of God is now and always has been a present fact. From the authority of the Creator's law there is throughout the creation no escape.

But that is not a full actualisation of the Kingdom or Sovereignty of God. Law is vindicated when those who break it are punished; but it is not the aim of Law or the Legislator that men should suffer punishment; the aim is that men may not commit offences. Consequently we are bidden to pray that God's kingdom may come. Mainly this further coming of His kingdom consists in the establishment of His

authority in men's lives by the surrender of their
hearts and wills to the appeal of His love.   But as
there are ways of life that incur the consequences in
which we read His judgement on those ways of life,
so we naturally seek for principles in accordance with
which we may order life so as to express the Mind
of Christ.   It may suffice here to give four such
principles, with some slight suggestions for their
application.[1]

First and fundamental is that principle which in
politics is called Liberty, but which is better represented by such a phrase as the Sacredness of Personality.   This lies at the root of all our Lord's teaching
about men, and all His dealing with men.   It follows
from the thought that God is the Father of every soul;
it is required by the fact that God is Love, and desires
the love of His children.   The personality of the
child of God whose love God Himself desires is
certainly a sacred thing.   We turn to application.
Does our provision of education at present correspond
with a belief in the sacredness of the personality
of every citizen?[2]   Or we turn to industry and
economics.   The text-books of Political Economy
which held the field in the nineteenth century upheld
what is called the " commodity view of Labour."
This is the doctrine that Labour should be treated
like a commodity, sold as dear as possible and bought
as cheap as possible.   But Labour either is not a
commodity at all, or else it is a unique kind of commodity; for it is not separable from the Labourer.   If
I buy a pair of boots, I do not buy the bootmaker.
But if I want to obtain a man's Labour, I must have the
man; I must have both his body and his mind.   When
I hire (or buy for a specified period) a man's labour, I
hire *him*.   If then I treat Labour as a commodity,

---

[1] For a fuller statement see the Reports presented to the Conference on Christian
Politics, Economics, and Citizenship, Birmingham, 1924 (*Copec Reports*, Longmans).
[2] Cf. the chapter on " Education " in *Mens Creatrix*.

I am, so far, treating the Labourer as a thing, not as a Person. Our industrial system to-day does not rest on the commodity view of Labour; a multitude of factors have come in to modify it. But we have not yet explicitly repudiated it or adopted another principle in its place.

This first principle is balanced by the second, which is the Reality of Membership. If all are children of one Father, all are members of one family. Therefore no individual is entitled to use his liberty for his own advantage only, but should exercise it in the spirit of membership or fellowship. We may apply this also to Industry. It is sometimes urged that industry should be co-operation for public service, as if this were a remote and almost unattainable ideal. But industry never is anything else. Incidentally it is very bad theology to suggest that the Mind of Christ conceives only what is utopian; the conception of anything in the Mind of Christ is the reality of that thing. Consider the English Cotton Industry. It is almost entirely located in Lancashire. But the cotton is not grown in Lancashire. It is grown in America or in Africa by one set of people; it is shipped across the sea by other people; it goes through innumerable processes in the mills and sheds of Lancashire; then the finished product reaches the shops and is sold to the consumer. The whole process goes on simply and solely because the public wants cotton goods; it exists for public service. And it is co-operative in its very nature. All the groups of people who take charge of the processes set out above are co-operating, whether they know it or not. And at every stage there is co-operation of the three factors —Capital, Management, and Labour. On the day that the co-operation stops, the industry stops. Industry *is* co-operation for public service. If, then, the people who are engaged in it work it as if it were competition for private profit, of course it goes wrong. But our thought must be concrete, not abstract. Competition and Co-operation are logical opposites, but they are not incompatibles. Consider a game of football. If it is Rugby football, there will be thirty players; and if it is a real game, all the thirty will be co-operating for the fun of the game. The form of their co-operation is for fifteen to compete against the other fifteen. Each team consists of fifteen players who co-operate to compete effectively against the other team. Inside each team, every player may be competing against all the rest to be the best co-operator in competing against the other team for the co-operative fun of the game. Co-operation and competition may be inextricably intertwined. But it makes all the difference which is uppermost—which exercises a check upon the other. If you have the co-operative spirit uppermost, you have good sportsmen, who would rather be beaten in a good game than win in a bad one; but if the competitive spirit is uppermost, you have men who play only to win, and will do any dirty trick that the referee will let them. So in industry our need is a full and frank recognition that industry is in its own nature fundamentally co-operative, so that all competition within it is kept in check by the co-operative spirit and purpose.

The third principle which follows from these two is the Duty of Service. If I am to use my freedom in the spirit of membership in the community, it follows that I fulfil my own destiny when I make my life an act of service. Here it will suffice for illustration to refer again to the public provision for Education, and the motive which public opinion commonly supposes to be the driving force of Education and the basis of all desire for it. It cannot be denied that the notion of self-advancement—whether to spheres of service or not—plays a larger part here than Christian principle would allow. In particular the rising generation is very inadequately trained to think of the trade or profession whereby daily bread is to be earned as the chief sphere of service; yet if every one exercised his trade or profession in that spirit half our problems would be solved.

This leads us on to the fourth principle, which is the most distinctive of the Christian scheme—the Power of Sacrifice. What is the driving power of progress? The natural man thinks it can be accomplished by force. But force alone achieves nothing positive, because it does not convert heart or will. Force has its place. It is right to use force in order to prevent other force from doing positive harm. Such is the use of force represented by the police.[1] But this function of force is purely negative. It prevents harm from being done, and so leaves the way open for real progress. This comes not by force but by sacrifice. There are in the world two kinds of Victory. One is the Victory of Pride or Self-assertion, which consists in imposing on the conquered the will of the conqueror. In such victory there is no peace; there is the bitterness of defeat, the hope of revenge, the renewal of the conflict when resources permit. And there is the Victory of Love—the only kind of victory with which God is content. Here there is no defeated party, for the victory consists in the conversion of enemies into friends. The means to this victory is not force, but sacrifice. I should be ready to affirm that so far as real progress has been won by means of strikes, it has never been really due to the inconvenience caused to employers or to the public, but to the sympathy called out by the endurance of the strikers, and (still more) to a realisation of the justice of their cause to which their endurance may call attention. We may apply this principle, and the last, to international questions. How far do we think of our national greatness as consisting in the power to dictate to other countries, and how far as consist-

---

[1] And by the British and French armies in 1914.

ing in service rendered to mankind even at loss to ourselves?

For the community which we are freely to serve is, in the last resort, the human race itself. But we cannot set ourselves to serve mankind directly. We must give our service in a narrower community, but use the wider loyalty to check the narrower, never so serving family as to injure country, never so serving country as to injure mankind. It is thus, and by application of such unchanging principles as have been described to the changing conditions of successive generations, that we can bring eternity into history, and work, as we pray, for the coming of God's perfect sovereignty.

For the transformation of life in accordance with such principles the chief requirement is not legislation by the State but a true conversion of individuals. It is at once clear that for this the thought of eternity is a most potent influence. As the great occurrences of history exhibit the operation of the divine Judgement on a national scale, so the opportunities or difficulties that come to individuals exhibit the divine Judgement on the characters that they have been forming. Every opportunity or emergency is in its degree a " crisis " —and " crisis " is the Greek for " judgement "— because by his reaction to it a man is judged. The judgement is not a verdict or sentence pronounced afterwards; it is the verdict of the events themselves as they occur in accordance with the divine ordering of the universe. " This is the judgement, that light is come into the world, and men chose darkness rather than light." Two men may have grown up together under the same influences, following the same interests. A sudden emergency comes, and it is seen that their two characters, which had seemed indistinguishable, were really profoundly different. The Day of the Lord is come suddenly upon them, and " the one is taken and the other left."

So the eternal is present within the process of History, revealing itself in judgements which are not interventions but are the manifestation of what is always there. For the individual, if not for the nation, there is also this impact of the eternal upon the temporal —that so soon as a man has done anything at all, he is to all eternity the man who did that thing. His choice becomes part of the eternal fact. Its value may be affected by later events; its occurrence is fixed.

4. Thus at every point the Eternal impinges on the Temporal and revolutionises its values. There remains the question of finality. Is the judgement which we see at work in History ever completed in a final Judgement wherein the meaning of History for men and for mankind is gathered up? The question is rather of speculative than of practical importance. We may discuss it under three heads.

First, it is clear that judgement on a nation may be final; a nation may be wiped out; or its history may be so broken that no restoration can set that same history again in process. No "restoration of the Jews to Palestine" can now affect the finality of the judgement of which the armies of Titus were the instrument.[1]

Secondly, if it is true that the free response of each individual is necessary to his entry into that fellowship with God which is "salvation"—as it must be if the meaning of this fellowship is revealed in Christ—it must be possible for the individual to persist in refusal, and that persistence may become final. If it does, that is "perdition"; and there is nothing left that Almighty Love can do with such a soul except to bring it to an end. That, no doubt, constitutes a failure in God; and the argument for "universalism" rests on this consideration. But to deny the possibility of failure in God is also to deny the freedom of man to

---

[1] There is a singularly vivid and impressive instance of a national choice involving a final national judgement in Trevelyan's *Manin and the Venetian Revolution*, pp. 198, 199. It is inconceivable that the old Austrian Empire will ever exist again.

repudiate God, and therefore also the freedom of his self-devotion when he offers it.   As we know more about the reality of human responsibility than we do about the mode of Divine Omnipotence, it is wiser to insist on the possibility that men may involve themselves in perdition than on the difficulty of reconciling this with something that anyhow transcends our comprehension.   After all it is the rather abstract notion of Omnipotence that makes us hesitate to affirm the possibility of perdition; it is the concrete and self-manifested quality of Love which leads us to believe that God so longs for a freely offered life that He risks the loss involved in a choice which brings perdition. Because He is love, He made us free; because we are free, we may choose to perish; it is belief in His Love which leads us to believe in the possibility of "eternal loss."

But of course this does not mean "eternal torment." Love cannot inflict that.   The doctrine of the Church has suffered at this point from the introduction of a belief in the inherent indestructibility of every individual soul, which has its origin in Greek rather than in Palestinian sources.[1]   The New Testament certainly implies that all men survive physical death;[2] but it equally implies that not all men attain to eternal life.[3] But whether in the form of "eternal torment" or of "annihilation" the New Testament certainly teaches that on the choice of every will an infinite issue hangs. The question at stake is not one of less or more, nor one of sooner or later; it is one of life or death.   And it is good for us that it should be so.   It is bracing to the will that it should have real responsibility; and of this a dogmatic universalism would deprive it.[4]

---

[1] Cf. Gore, *Belief in God*, pp. 130, 131 footnote.

[2] Cf. 2 Corinthians ii. 10.

[3] Cf. St. Luke xx. 35.   The "fire" is everlasting, but not necessarily or even probably that which is cast into it; and it is not even clear that $\alpha\iota\dot\omega\nu\iota\sigma$ means "everlasting."

[4] I have considerably modified my emphasis in this whole matter since I wrote *Mens Creatrix*—cf. pp. 290, 357.

Thirdly, we have the question whether there is a future event in which all the history of mankind is gathered up—the traditional Day of Judgement. This is simply the religious form of the question whether Time has a temporal end. It is impossible to satisfy the mind or imagination with either answer. What happens *after* the Day of Judgement? Can static perfection or attainment be interesting? Or will there be further tasks for the souls of just men made perfect to essay? No answer can be given. But perhaps the last question suggests the nearest approach that we can make to a solution. There are many relative ends of the world; there was an end of the ancient world, and an end of the mediaeval world, perhaps there will be an end of the " modern " European world—in 1924 it looks as if that end were not far off. Such phrases are not remote from the suggestion of apostolic language, for the phrase in the New Testament is " the end of the age." Moreover, there must be an end to such human life as we know on this planet, either by a dramatic *finale* or by the gradual depopulation of the earth through cold. There may be no end of History, if by History we mean successive events. But there must be an end to *human* History—to the series of events which arises from that struggle or balance of spiritual and animal which is called Human Nature. And the end must be the fully established Kingdom of God, wherein all living souls respond to the Divine Love, and for love's sake are obedient to the Divine Will. Whether at that stage all who have ever lived will so respond, or some will have lost their life through love of it cannot be foretold. But the end of History is the complete coming of the Kingdom.

Whether, or how fully, that Kingdom can come on earth is unimportant. It can come more than it is come yet; and here or elsewhere it will be established in perfection in the souls of men. For it is ready to come now. From the beginning of the Gospel it is at hand. The only condition of its coming is that men should " repent," that is that they should cease to look at or value experience as temporal only, and begin to look at and value it as constitutive of eternity. The Kingdom of God will come when men conduct their History as citizens of Eternity. In the Eternal are the foundations of that outward unity for which all History is the search; but only they can build a civilisation on those foundations who are also building on the same foundations that inward unity which is the goal of every individual soul.

One word must be added. The revelation of the Eternal in Jesus Christ forbids us to find the meaning of man's life only, or even chiefly, within the process of successive events which make up man's terrestrial history. It is to be found in a new creation; not only in a fuller apprehension of the facts of this world-order, but in resurrection to a new order of being and of experience, of which we can only say that so far as we here and now become partakers of the fruits of the Spirit, we are in our degree already realising our citizenship in Heaven.

CHAPTER XII

MAN IN THE LIGHT OF THE INCARNATION

" If a Divine Being chose to become incarnate for the sake of sinners, it is impossible to regard our earthly lives either as an unworthy choice or as a punishment. They are rather the means by which Divine love may be brought down into an imperfect world, as the rest of nature is the means by which the wisdom and beauty of the Divine mind are made manifest."—W. R. INGE.

BEETHOVEN composed his Mass in D major while Napoleon was advancing on Vienna; when he came to the last chorus—" Dona nobis pacem "—he wrote above his score, " Prayer for inward and outward peace." [1] It is seldom that the nature of man's utmost need is presented to him in a manner so vivid; but at all times it is true that the need of man is for inward and outward peace. With the achievement of outward peace or unity we were concerned in the last chapter; but one of the elements in the problem was there omitted. Why is it that nations and societies fail to order their conduct in accordance with the eternal principles? They have no organs of choice or purpose other than the wills of the citizens. It is in the last resort because individual men misunderstand their own nature and their own true good that Politics and Political History present such a dismal spectacle. As Plato saw quite clearly, all political actions and institutions have their origin in the char-

[1] Incidentally, also, he set the words to a fugue on a theme familiar in Handel's *Messiah*, where it goes with the words " He shall reign for ever and ever." Beethoven was far too enthusiastic an admirer of Handel for this to be accidental; just then, at any rate, he knew what is the one condition of human peace.

acters of the general body of citizens, though it is
also true that political institutions tend powerfully to
reproduce in subsequent generations the type of
character which they reflect and from which they grew.
Moreover, as Plato also saw, inasmuch as no nation
is eternal while the soul is (or can be) eternal, the really
important question about any political order is, not
whether it makes the nation strong, but whether it
tends to develop in the citizens the type of character
that best fits them for their eternal destiny. Hildebrand was quite right in principle when he said that
Politics ought to be subordinate to the Church as the
trustee of the Gospel, though he, and still more his
successors, hopelessly compromised this principle
when they tried to make the Church the supreme
political authority instead of a source of spiritual
energy to all political authorities. The root of
that mistake is the belief that the regeneration of
social life can precede the conversion and consecration of individual life. Karl Marx and Lenin are
associated with a very different social outlook from
Hildebrand and Innocent III.; but their distinctive
principles are different expressions of one and the
same fallacy.

In our former consideration of Human Nature [1]
we were led to the notion of Humanity as a Social Fact.
We found that the individual is a group of more or
less competing impulses and interests, with little
discoverable unity at first apart from his physical
organism, but with an inborn tendency and even
straining towards unity; we found, further, that he
and his fellows actually, in large measure, constitute
each others' characters (or growing unifications) by their
mutual influence, but that each system of experience
is also self-determining from a core of original being
which is that individual's own contribution to the
total scheme of things, but of which the peculiar

[1] In Chapter IV.

effects can never be estimated with any approach to accuracy. The net result is that Humanity is a single unit, but that the several persons who compose it are real individuals.

The use of analogy in philosophy is to explain the less known by the help of the more known. But the more known is nearly always the simpler and more elementary, so that the analogy tends to obscure the distinctive features of the subject under investigation. So it is commonly assumed that society must be either a mere collection of individuals, or else that it is an organism; if the former, then its unity is a mere matter of convenience; if the latter, then the individual is only a " limb " (it is St. Paul's metaphor) whose life utterly depends on its union with the whole. The first minimises, the second exaggerates, the principle of cohesion in social unity. Not indeed that the unity of human society is less real or less close than that of an organism, but while the unity is real and intimate, the constituent persons are also real and self-determining.

Our conception of Man therefore contains these elements: men constitute various social units, some side by side (as family and political party), some included in others (as family and nation), but all at last included in the social unity of mankind. Each individual is largely constituted by the influence of other individuals upon him; and each takes his share in constituting others. Thus together they constitute Humanity; this is a real unit because all its constituent members are mutually constitutive of one another; it is not a unity existing independently of, or over against, the individual human beings [1]—there is no " Human Nature " apart from human beings; but the Humanity which consists of human beings is a real unity, wherein each of them is linked to every other in a nexus of mutual determination.

[1] As the early Fathers assumed it to be, fashioning their Christology accordingly.

Further, these partly self-determined and partly mutually determining individuals are centres of appreciation of value, with the result that (knowing the values apprehended by themselves) they are disposed to assert themselves unduly and out of proportion to their place in the scheme of things or the true structure of society. This tendency is Original Sin; and it is present both in every individual and in the whole social influence—these two reinforcing one another. It appears as an exaggeration of the importance of what is one's own—one's self (pride), one's comfort (sloth), one's reputation (vanity), one's property (avarice), one's physical pleasure (greed and lust)— and this may lead to a direct antagonism against those who in any way deny this importance or thwart the enjoyment it is held to justify—envy, contempt, spite, malice, hatred.

The ethical goal for man is an apprehension of Value according to Truth, or, in other words, that a man should set the right store by the various goods of life, irrespective of the question who enjoys them. He must aim not only at justice of conduct but justice of purpose, including as it does emotion and desire, from which conduct springs. " Thou shalt *love* thy neighbour as thyself " is the true form of the categorical imperative; it tells a man to count every one (including himself) as one, and nobody (not even himself) as more than one. If that happened on a large scale the bitterness of life would be gone. But the obstacle is found in precisely that which most marks man's advance beyond the animals—his sense of Value as a principle. For of necessity each man appreciates his own values not only more readily but more fully than the values of others. He is a being particular and finite called to live by a principle universal and infinite; and his particularity distorts his vision. It is only God who is able to see the scheme of life in such a way as to hold the scales of justice even. If man is to rise to the level of true justice, it must be because God indwells and inspires him.

If this is to happen at all, how can it happen? There are two possible ways; one is by God indwelling the various individuals—and this method God has actually followed in all times and places. Nowhere has He left Himself without witness, either in the order of Nature, the course of History, or the conscience of men. In conscience especially He has spoken as men were able to receive His Word— " the light that lighteneth every man." This may be called the method of Divine Immanence. To it we owe the art and philosophy of Greece, the legal achievements of Rome, and, generally, the whole impulse in mankind towards progress. God made man in His own image, capable of apprehending universal principles and absolute values; that capacity is itself a divine potency at work in men, which constantly spurs them on to its further realisation.

But this method of immanent activity is subject to one or other of two limiting conditions. Either the influence implanted within a man's own character is so strong as to make him as a separate being a mere automaton, or else it is one influence among others, to which the character in process of formation must deliberately submit. In the former case, freedom is destroyed, and in place of a truly loving child the Heavenly Father receives only His own activity returned. In the latter case, the free choice of the individual remains, and the reasons which make freedom give birth to pride will prevent the absolute surrender which is needed for the realisation of a complete divine indwelling. It is too much to say that the method of mere immanence must fail; perhaps here and there, in some Buddhist or Moslem saint, it has succeeded, so far as success with an isolated individual is possible at all; but the chances of success on any wide scale are, *a priori*, so small that no reasonable hope of " salvation " can be based on it. The existence of this divine potency in every man is, however, what makes possible the success of the other method.

This is that God should Himself enter the course of human history by taking into Himself the experience of mankind as focussed in some one of its centres. And this is what, in fact, He has done. As we have seen, He submitted to human conditions in all their completeness; yet His life was a divine intrusion into the course of human events—an intrusion vividly represented by the Virgin-Birth. The human Life is truly human, and subject to real temptation; yet it is also true that He could not yield to the temptation. This is not even a paradox to any one who has seriously considered what is involved in the temptation felt by a man of high character to an act contrary to his character: he is attracted by the wrong course; he has to keep a hold on himself; he knows he is making a real choice; yet (being himself) he could not yield.[1] The effort needed to overcome the temptation is a real effort, but it is also a necessary effort because his character, being such as it is, must so react to the situation. Raise this to the ideal limit, and you have a character which still needs effort to resist evil, but (being such as it is) is bound to make the effort and to succeed in it.

The one character which has caused this claim of positive sinlessness to be made on its behalf is the character of One who is realised by those who study Him to be personally one with God.[2] The world to which He came was His own creation; the people to whom He came were His own children, though not able to make good by moral achievement their claim

[1] Cf. p. 64, specially the Note, where it is pointed out that the inability expressed in the words " could not " is objective, and not part of the subjective experience of the agent. In the case of our Lord I believe it to have been subjective also. Cf. p. 148.

[2] Cf. Chapters VII. and VIII.

to that title. They were involved in the nexus of sin. In the social unity of mankind the Divine Spirit was at work; but its predominant feature was the self-assertion of its individual members, constantly renewed as each new-born soul awoke to the realisation of its own group of values, and reinforced by the tone of the social environment. If in such a world there is born and lives One who at all stages acts as a channel of the central and universal Spirit, that is a moral miracle far more wonderful than any Virgin-Birth; for it presents us with a human soul free from the constitutive influence of its social environment so far as this is evil or defective; and that is a breach of an otherwise universal law as complete as would be a total reversal of the Law of Gravitation.

The mode of this divine intrusion we have already considered. There is no general " humanity " in which the Divine Word could be clothed, apart from all particular human centres of experience; but the Divine Word took to Himself human experience in one such centre, so completely subsuming the human personality that God and Man in Jesus Christ are one Person.[1] From Him a new influence goes forth, the attractive power and compelling appeal of perfectly holy love, expressed in the human fashion that calls forth sympathy.[2] This power is not other than the divine potency in men that urges them to progress; but it is its perfect counterpart. In the response of love which the human being makes, he is at once free and enslaved; he is the willing slave, as the lover is the willing slave of his mistress. This was the one way by which God could draw men to Himself without overpowering their freedom. When I direct my

[1] Cf. Chapter VIII.
[2] The possibility of sympathy has never (as far as I know) received sufficient attention either from psychologists or from philosophers. If it is a merely sentimental reaction on the part of a completely separate " self," it is of little consequence; but if it is (as I believe) a real union of personalities through an experience in which both share, it is always a true atonement.

action to please a friend, my conduct is determined by his pleasure, but there is no sort of conduct in which I am so supremely conscious of utter freedom. If I learn to love God in answer to His love for me and for all men, this principle receives its fullest expression; His slavery is perfect freedom.

We have already seen how the manifestation of the Divine Love launches into the world a society of which the distinctive characteristic (in so far as its members are true to its vitalising principle) is a spirit of fellowship that overleaps all divisions. But men come into that society one by one; and the degree of their loyalty depends, at least partly, on their own free choice. The existence of the society—the Church —is the starting-point and constant support of their effort to respond to the Divine Love, but the vitality of the society in actuality depends on the depth of conversion and consecration in the individual members. In fact, the chief choice which any individual makes is the choice of the influences to which he will deliberately submit himself. For the Christian, the choice is broadly between the spirit of Christ, chiefly but not solely active in the Church, and the influences in the world which work upon his lower nature. As it was through one centre of experience that the supreme revelation came, so the response must be made by individuals, one by one, each as he does this, and in the degree in which he does it, making the task easier for others.

For this reason the Church must make respect for freedom its most fundamental principle of action. Persecution strikes at the root of the whole principle of Christianity. Discipleship must be freely chosen and freely maintained. But close behind it comes the principle of fellowship. We are free, in order that we may freely prefer the general good to our own separate good, and every other use of freedom is wrong. A man must be allowed to go wrong if he wants—so far as the Church is concerned; [1] but his conscience should be aroused, and the appeal to his capacity for devotion made, as potently as may be.

What is the difference made for us by the manifestation of the Divine Love in a human life ? We found that the self-centred life cannot attain to the inward and outward unity in which alone it can find joy and peace; and its inability is due to its very constitution as self-centred. But how can any life in fact be anything else? A man must be the centre of his own social relationships. From that centre he appreciates all values, so far as he appreciates them at all.

Now it is, of course, quite true that every man is himself and not some one else; and also that he exists in order to realise the values apprehensible from *his* centre and no other. What is required is not that he should become either some one else or no one in particular, but that he should discharge his particular function in response to the Universal Spirit, the Spirit of the Whole. But until this is genuinely known, he cannot respond to it ; and the impulse within him towards progress and perfection is not, and from its nature and conditions cannot be complete, unless it arises in response to a revelation of the Universal Spirit in that concrete form which alone evokes sympathy and therefore alone can give to emotion that universalised quality which marks it as emotional justice. In other words, if a man is to love his neighbour as himself, he must first love God with all his heart; and if that is to happen, God must reveal His love in such a manner as to claim his heart.

" Salvation " therefore consists in the substitution of the Spirit of the Whole for the spirit of the particular self in the control of all life—conduct, thought, feeling.

---

[1] It may be right for the State to prevent him by coercion, but this is only ideally right when the State's act expresses his own real purpose in the way referred to in Chapter X. p. 181.

If a man can say truly, " I live, yet not I, but Christ liveth in me," he is " saved." And this alone is salvation. Consequently, for the man as yet unsaved the essential need is " conversion "—a change in the direction of his life: and this must take the form of self-sacrifice—the repudiation of all that belongs to the particularity of the self alone and has no part in the universal good. The pain of such self-sacrifice is a necessary cost or price of salvation; but the self-sacrifice itself is not a price of salvation; it *is* salvation, and salvation *is* such self-sacrifice.

Sacrifice is only painful for one or other of two reasons: either there is a clinging to the particular good which has to be abandoned, and that is selfishness in the soul that makes the sacrifice; or else there is indifference or hostility in those for whom the sacrifice is made, and that is selfishness in them. It is always selfishness—or continued exaggeration of the particular interests of Selves—which makes painful the substitution of Love for self as the controlling influence of life. But the essential sacrifice need not be painful at all; it can be the most intense delight. All who have loved know this. Whenever a man chooses to do or to suffer, because of his care for others, what apart from that care he would not choose to do or suffer, that is the essence of self-sacrifice. It may be done conscientiously with pain as an act of duty; but when the care for others amounts to love, and this love is returned, there is no pain; there is no feeling even of conscientiousness; there is, instead, only an intense delight.[1]

Yet even love itself is self-centred, and leads to a group egoism as dangerous as individual selfishness, unless it is either love of God or rooted in love of God. The mother who is utterly devoted to her children may be possessed by an intense family-selfishness. Even for the salvation of love we depend on the power

---

[1] This is repeated in a wider context on p. 273.

of the self-manifested love of God to draw us into
fellowship with itself by eliciting an answering love.
But if in answer to God's love I begin to love Him,
my love for Him must make me, for His sake, love
those whom He loves as He loves me.   To love God,
as He is revealed in Christ, prevents all malice or
envy or contempt, so far as it influences us at all, and
redeems our very love from selfishness.

A searching illustration of the Christian conception
of Man and his destiny is provided by the teaching
of the New Testament about riches.   Plainly they are
regarded as a snare; the reason seems to be that
Heaven is the fellowship of self-sacrifice, and riches,
being an extension of what is one's " own," increase
the area of our selfish attachment.   The poor man who
is even to satisfy his natural impulses of generosity
must make some real sacrifice; the rich man who
wishes to have the satisfaction of kindness to the
needy may " shake the superflux to them," and it is
harder to reach even the initial discipline of real self-
sacrifice.   The sequence of ideas which led to Mon-
asticism was perfectly justified in itself.   It is easier
to win detachment from particular interests if worldly
possessions and ambitions have been once for all
renounced.   But it is a false method none the less; [1]
for it ignores our responsibility to the world and comes
near to commending self-sacrifice for selfish reasons.
A man must take all the responsibilities of his position;
" my station and its duties," which Mr. F. H. Bradley
has taught us to regard the surest guide to ethical
duty, [2] is a thoroughly valid principle, though it does
not help in the most important of all choices—the
choice of " my station."   There may be responsibilities for wife and family, and the education of
children.   To set these aside for the sake of individual

---

[1] This is no denial that some individuals are called to the contemplative life;
they certainly are; but this vocation, though for them the true one, is no " higher "
than any other.

[2] In *Ethical Studies*.

salvation would be self-contradictory, for it would be to enter on a selfish search for unselfishness. A man must fulfil the duties of his station; if these bring " riches," he must have them " as though he had them not." He must use the wider loyalty to check the narrower, never pursuing the interest of his own family at a more than counterbalancing loss to the whole community. To take a concrete case, he must consider a political proposal in the light of its effect on the general well-being, not in the light of its effect on his own financial position; and he must exercise his vote accordingly. Whatever happens he will never make " riches " his aim, or choose a profession only or chiefly because it offers the opportunity to make a fortune. If, however, the course by which he can give the best service brings " riches," he will try to avoid the snares that accompany them and to make the use of them which most benefits the community.

On the other hand, real poverty is also a spiritual hindrance. The modern and certainly non-Christian organisation of society has given rise to a form of poverty almost unknown in the Palestine of Apostolic times. To be in fear for the morrow through the modern nightmare of insecurity roots a man in his own self as effectively as any riches. The destitute man is possessed by his need for the material support of life; the rich man is encumbered with possessions and may be possessed by fear that he will lose them. The " poverty " which is spiritually desirable is that which provides a sufficiency for the needs of a real human life, but not enough to mark a man off from the majority of his fellow-citizens, and so make difficult the widest fellowship. All that stereotypes a man's particularity or encourages a sense of his interests as conflicting with those of others is perilous. For the aim of human life is that it should become so indwelt by God, the Spirit of the Whole, that His universal Purpose expresses itself in complete articulation through the diverse yet harmonising lives of all finite spirits.

Man emerges from Nature and reveals new qualities even in Nature itself. He finds his own destiny when God takes possession of him and controls him. Does this affect his relationship to the Nature from which he emerged? Apparently it does. In the record of the only Life which perfectly illustrates the point, we read of a capacity to heal diseases by an efflux of spiritual power [1] and to walk on the water.[2] Moreover, Christ is reported as saying, " The works that I do shall ye do also; and greater works than these shall ye do, because I go to the Father." [3] The perfect union of Human Nature in the Son with the Father was to make possible an even greater exercise of power than could before that be shown only by the Son Himself in Human Nature. We are still at the very beginning of such discoveries as are to be made in this field, and all that can be said is speculation only. But the suggestion of the New Testament certainly is that when Man is really indwelt by God, Nature will reveal new and entirely unpredictable qualities. " The earnest expectation of the creation waiteth for the revealing of the sons of God." [4] And certainly this is congruous with what on other grounds we have found to be the most probable theory of the universe. As Life revealed in Matter qualities that Physics and Chemistry could not have predicted; as Mind did the same for Life and for living Matter; as Spirit did the same for the thinking living organism—so, we may expect, will God for the spiritual being whom He has, by the operation of His laws, created out of Nature. But we must mark the conditions, for they are clearer

[1] St. Mark v. 30. This shows that cure at least to have been more than a case of " suggestion," though no doubt " suggestion " may have had much to do with it and with the other cures recorded in the Gospels.

[2] St. Mark vi. 48.   [3] St. John xiv. 12.

[4] Romans viii. 19.

than are the results to be hoped for. Christ's " miracles " are works of power; but their chief characteristic is that the power is under the control of love. The contrast of the Apocryphal Gospels reminds us that in the New Testament Christ nowhere used miraculous power in His own interest. If there are powers held in store for men as they enter into closer fellowship with God, they are powers that can only be exercised for the fulfilment of God's purpose of love—never for convenience, or in a " test case," or for display, or for the satisfaction of exercising power. If such powers exist, they are part of the Omnipotence of Love, and are only released when the finite spirit which is to use them is in perfect union with the Almighty Love.

It is clear from what has been said that Heaven (if we accept the traditional name for the home and goal of the human spirit) is not fitly symbolised by the notion of a *place* to which men may travel separately. Heaven is the universal fellowship of all spirits in the Love of the Divine Spirit. . As long as any existing spirit remains outside, rebelling against the fellowship and refusing the self - sacrifice which constitutes membership, so long Heaven does not exist for any one—not even for God.[1] And yet in God the achievement is sure, so that the individual who has really and fully surrendered his heart to God has not only attained the goal of his destiny so far as circumstances permit, but finding in God the assurance of the end and the eternal perfection, he also finds for himself the fruition of perfect joy and peace.

For he knows that if he is seeking God, he has in himself the seed of eternal life. Some Greek philosophers tried to prove that the individual soul is immortal; but they failed. Plato's arguments only lead to the position accepted by Aristotle, that the

---

[1] *I.e.* for God as enduring through Time; the words in the text are true but are not the whole truth; cf. Chapter XV.

spiritual principle is indestructible. Only God is in Himself immortal; but whatever is united with Him shares that immortality. And Christ's Resurrection has proved that human nature, when indwelt by God, conquers death. Our hope of immortality rests on this revelation of what is possible, and on the Love of God to make it actual. For if God loves, He will not let the object of His love be abolished out of existence. Only, then, if a man so repels the love of God as to have nothing left in him but evil, will God allow him to perish.

If, therefore, a man has learnt the true goal of his being and is seeking to open his heart to God so that God may dwell in him and he in God, he knows that he has all Time before him in which to explore the riches of the Divine Love which to all ages he never will exhaust. He is therefore earnest, but quite unhurried. His present limitations do not trouble him. He has the everlasting years before him, and he has God with him all the way.

PART V

OUTER CIRCLE

CHAPTER XIII

WORSHIP AND SACRAMENTS

"Just this, I think, is what worship means: that the Whole must become a separate object of pursuit, taking its turn as if it also were a part, as if it were *another* among the many goods of practical occupation."—W. E. HOCKING.

MAN, we have found, represents that stage in the stratification of Reality where Reason or Spirit—the capacity for apprehending universal principles and absolute obligation—supervenes upon Mind (as calculation of means to ends) and Life; as the lower stages first revealed their full potentialities when Spirit thus came upon them and indwelt them, so, we have found, Man only reveals what it is in him to be when God indwells him. The meaning of such an expression is given by the historic fact of the Incarnation. It is only since the full revelation of human nature was given through the actual indwelling of it by God that the true character of man's spirit has become apparent. We now see it as being already the sphere of operation within man of that same Divine Spirit who is perfectly revealed in Jesus Christ. He reveals both God and Man, and our conception of both has suffered profound modification because of what He was and did. The spiritual character of Man made possible at once the Incarnation and men's response to it. That response consists in a quickening of the inner activity of the Divine Spirit released by man's new devotion to God in answer to His love revealed. Those in whom that One Spirit is active through their responsive love to God are by that Spirit bound together in a Fellowship of which He is the bond of unity and energising power; this is the true (or ideal) Church. But these same people are also members of " the world," and cannot sever themselves from the world without neglect of real responsibilities.   They are therefore under the influence both of a partly un-converted society and also of the Divine Spirit at work in the Church.   To both influences their nature qualifies them to respond.   There is a constant tendency to settle down in some compromise between the two.   Even when that happens there is still an activity of the Divine Spirit, holding selfishness and worldliness in check.   Compromise is not surrender; and total surrender is rare in those who call them-selves Christians at all.   And so long as a man has not utterly quenched the Spirit, there is possibility of revival.   But, plainly, compromise cannot be accepted as really tolerable.   Those who have once heard the call of the Divine Spirit within them to give their lives—St. Paul makes it emphatic by saying their " bodies " [1]—as a reasonable return for the love of God towards them, know that they have no right to contentment until this is done.   Yet the influence of the world still operates; and there is no possibility of increasing our self-dedication until it becomes perfect, unless we deliberately and repeatedly turn our minds towards that Love of God, that God of Love, to whom we would be dedicated.   This is the place of Worship in Christian discipline.   If we already love Him, and in whatsoever degree we already love Him, we shall desire times when we give our hearts and minds to Him alone.   But apart from such a desire, the very obligation to give our lives to God will require a perpetually repeated concentration of attention upon Him in order that we may more and more fulfil our obligation.   Throughout our growth

[1] Romans xii. 1.

as Christians worship is a duty; as we advance it becomes a delight; and at all times a true act of worship is the fulfilment—for a moment—of the true destiny of our being. It is this both in momentary actualisation and in promise of future and permanent attainment. It is the one way to that attainment. The command that we should love our neighbour (which is the practical expression of our search for outward or social unity) cannot be fulfilled except so far as we love God. Our " neighbour " may be for one reason or another the sort of person that we cannot love (so to speak) directly, and the effort to do so will only increase our antagonism. But God, if we once understand Him, we all can love, and so the command to love Him is one that can be obeyed without other conditions being first fulfilled. All can love Him, because for each He is the Life of Life; by Him I live; by Him I came to be; by Him I aspire, so far as I aspire at all, to better things. If I realise Him, I must love Him. So I may fitly be commanded to love Him; and from this I shall go on to love my neighbour, for God's sake if not yet for his own. But as I become more perfectly united to God, I begin to love my neighbour as God loves him, that is for himself, or for the good thing that he at least can be and can bring into being. In the perpetual return of our hearts and minds to God in worship we both enjoy a foretaste of our perfect happiness, and find the renewal of spiritual strength by which we do the work which fits us for it.

The Christian finds his closest approach to God in Jesus Christ, in whom he is also united to his fellow-disciples. Consequently his most normal mode of worship is as a member of the worshipping body which is the Church. This worship may be rendered by corporate silence, or by united utterance, or by symbolic action. Of the first two little need be said, except that in principle they are as " sacramental " as the last. Plainly, speech is a physical fact; if anything in the world is " an outward and visible sign " of something " inward and spiritual " it is vocal utterance. By means of atmospheric vibrations set up in one man's larynx and striking upon another man's ear, the latter apprehends the thought and feeling of the former. Speech is an " efficacious sign " if ever there was one. But it suffers from two limitations: it is too articulate for the deepest feelings, which are best expressed by a gesture which suggests their totality without any analysis of their content— the pressure of the hand, the bowing of the head, or the like; and it is only intelligible to those who know the particular language used, whereas a gesture or symbolic act can be such as to be universally intelligible. It is perhaps less obvious that corporate silence is physical, and the use of it for worship sacramental; but it is true. No one who has sat or knelt in deliberate corporate silence can doubt that it induces a nervous tension which is one of the conditions of its impressiveness; and nerves are physical.

It is important to notice that, as Canon Quick has pointed out,[1] there is in speech a double relation of outward to inward. I speak words with a purpose, of which my speech is the instrument; but the purpose is to convey a meaning, of which my speech is the symbol. An " efficacious sign " is precisely one where these two relations are combined; but though combined they are not confused, and each must be allowed for in our interpretation of the place of " externals " in religion.

The act of worship, then, like all other human acts, must at least have physical expression, and is so far always sacramental. Moreover, it is generally assumed that if the worship is silent, that silence is charged with the power of the Spirit; if forms of words are used, they are words prescribed by the Church which was guided

[1] *Catholic and Protestant Elements in Christianity*, pp. 26-29.

by the Spirit in choosing them; if free prayer is used, the speaker is guided by the Spirit in his utterance; if the sermon is a part of the service, the preacher is taught of the Spirit. So we cannot say that in other worship the outward form expresses and conveys *our* thought or desire, while in a sacramental rite the outward form expresses and conveys the power of God. In fundamental principle there is no difference whatever between specific sacraments and any other mode of worship.

But there is a difference of aspect and emphasis. In preaching, the personality of the human medium counts for most. This does not put preaching on a lower plane, for there is on earth no medium so adequate for the Spirit as a consecrated personality; but it is in life rather than in speech that personality finds its full expression, so that the sermon does not utilise this medium to the full, while the limitations of individual apprehension and loyalty must affect the message delivered through such a channel. In spoken prayer the activity of the worshippers is prominent; it may be guided by the Spirit, but the human limitations are still conspicuously operative. Even in corporate silence the activity of concentrated attention (the most intense of all human activities) is the condition of efficacy. But in the sacraments commonly so called everything combines to insist on the priority of the divine action. We only benefit in so far as we are actively receptive; but the initiative is not only ultimately but manifestly and avowedly with God.

It may conduce to clearness if we attempt some exposition of the two dominical sacraments in accordance with the position taken up in this book.

First, we must remember that they are part of the life of the Church. We put the matter on a false basis if we isolate each particular sacramental act, and ask what happens precisely then and there, or what precise gift is then and there given or received. The sacramental act does not exist in this isolation; it is an act of the Church, and derives at least a part of its significance from this fact. In truth the Church is itself the permanent sacrament; it is an organised society possessed (though not always availing itself) of a supernatural life—the life of God—which united humanity with itself in Jesus Christ. But all of this again was only possible because the universe itself is an organ of God's self-expression. Thus we have the following background of the sacramental worship of the Church: the universe is the fundamental sacrament, and taken in its entirety (when of course it includes the Incarnation and Atonement) is the perfect sacrament extensively; but it only becomes this, so far as our world and human history are concerned, because within it and determining its course is the Incarnation, which is the perfect sacrament intensively—the perfect expression in a moment of what is also perfectly expressed in everlasting Time, the Will of God; resulting from the Incarnation we find the " Spirit-bearing Body," which is not actually a perfect sacrament, because its members are not utterly surrendered to the spirit within it, but none the less lives by the Life which came fully into the world in Christ; as part of the life of this Body we find certain specific sacraments or sacramental acts.

Baptism is the sacrament of regeneration and of incorporation into the Church (or into Christ). These are not two things, but one. It is through the Church that the influence of Christ reaches us; even when we read the Gospels by ourselves, the influence of Christ is reaching us through the Evangelists, who are members of the Church. Now a human being is (as we saw) morally constituted to a great extent by his social environment; if he is left to " the world " he may become a respectable citizen, but he is shut off from the divine Life offered to men in Christ, and cannot escape from the self-centredness which is

" natural " to man.   This is the indisputable fact of
Original Sin.   It is through becoming a member of
the Church that he comes under the constitutive
influence of that divine Life offered to men in Christ.
This is not to say that *formal* membership is indispensable to the operation of that influence; manifestly it
is not; a man who has never become a member of the
Church in the formal sense may surrender his soul to
Christ and be utterly governed by His Spirit.   But
this can only happen if that Spirit is really active in the
world, and this implies a channel for His activity.   It
is because there is a Church so constituted as to keep
alive belief in a gift of Life from the transcendent God
that Christians other than Church members, and some
who do not so call themselves, are brought under the
constitutive and regenerating influence of Christ.
Because there is a Church which practises Baptism
(and other such rites), those who do not receive
Baptism do none the less (as their lives show) receive
in their measure the benefits of Baptism.

The influence of the sacrament is thus twofold;
it acts in two directions; there is not only its effect on
the person baptized, but there is also the effect on the
Church itself in keeping alive the memory of the kind
of society that the Church is, and so in maintaining
its actual life as one which has regenerative power.
The Church itself is the sacrament of human nature
indwelt by God; to become a member of the Church
is to become a participator in human nature so indwelt;
and whatever tends to release in men's souls the divine
energy bestowed on the Church, makes the act of
entrance into it more completely revolutionary.   So
the value of Baptism to its recipient is partly indirect,
and reaches him through the influence of his own and
countless other Baptismal Services upon the Church
which by his Baptism he enters.   The statement tends
to become involved; that is what always happens when
we try to analyse a single and living whole.

But this, of course, is not the only effect of Baptism on its recipient; that effect in its completeness is only seen when the incorporation into the Church is a reality and Christian influences are active in moulding character; and then, of course, the precise effect of Baptism cannot be distinguished from the general effect of those influences. Moreover, no one supposes that Baptism administered in infancy and followed by neglect will produce any spiritual effect that can be traced by human observers. But that there is such an effect cannot really be questioned; it appears in two ways. All spiritual teachers know the effectiveness of an appeal to the fact that the learner was in fact incorporated into Christ and by a historic rite made a member of the historic Church. But beyond this is the effect of the rite itself. Through His Body (the Church) acting by its appropriate organ (the priest) Christ receives the child to Himself. Of course this affects the soul of the child; but the effect is germinal, and only becomes perceptible when favourable conditions have made possible its development into conscious and willing membership of the Body of Christ.

The symbolism might have been other than it is. One sect, I am told, baptizes with flowers instead of water. Christ might have so appointed; but He did not. The little group of His disciples carried on the rite associated with John the Baptist's call to repentance. No doubt the symbol (like all symbols) is to some extent arbitrary, though it seems impossible to conceive one more expressive of its meaning—the cleansing from the effect of worldly influence (which is Original Sin) so that heavenly influence may do its perfect work. But even if another symbol equally good could have been chosen at the outset, no other can be chosen now. The rites of the Church are fixed by that first decision, because the Church is essentially rooted in history; and it is so rooted because history is the arena wherein God's purpose (for men, at least) is to be fulfilled.

The vital importance of the historic background and of real historic continuity with it is evident for all to see when we turn to the other dominical sacrament —the Eucharist.   Here the symbolism consists in an actual repetition of the action of the Lord at the Last Supper on the night of the betrayal.   Whether the Supper was actually the Passover (as the Synoptists say) or was held before the day of the Passover (as St. John says), the Paschal Feast was in all men's minds.   It commemorated the Exodus.   At the Transfiguration, a culminating point in the Lord's human " religious experience," the theme of His colloquy was the new Exodus which He was to accomplish [1]—an Exodus which for Him was death, for His people deliverance.   The Paschal Lamb was the sustenance for the journey away from bondage to freedom.   At that Supper the Lord took bread, gave thanks for it, broke it, and gave it, saying that it was His Body and that what He was doing His disciples must do.   The old covenant which St. Paul later would not hesitate to call bondage was ratified with sacrificial blood.   The Lord now gave the Cup, saying that it was His Blood, and ratified a new Covenant.   The next day His Body was pierced by the nails and the spear; the next day His Blood was shed, and the Life of which it was the symbol was given in perfect completeness of surrender to the Father.

" This is my Body."   " Do this."   What had the words meant?   First they must have meant, " As I treat this Bread, so I treat my Body; and you must do the same."   The sacrificial language, especially as concerns the Blood, stamped the whole episode with a sacrificial character.   And, plainly, it was preparatory for the morrow's event.   It would help the disciples to realise that the Death of Christ was a

[1] St. Luke ix. 31.

sacrifice, even the only true sacrifice.   And what they should learn of that sacrifice would help to interpret the symbolic act by which He had prepared them to understand it.   But the perfect sacrifice of Christ is not limited to His Death; it consists not in any momentary offering but in the perfection of His obedience, which was always complete.[1]   The Death is not other than the Life; it was its inevitable result and appropriate climax.   It is Christ's union of humanity with God in perfect obedience which is the essential sacrifice, of which the Cross is the uttermost expression and essential symbol.[2]

This union was accomplished by Christ in His own Person, but not for Himself alone.   As we saw,[3] by living amongst men the sinless life, the life of perfect obedience, He became the Head of a new society, the pivot of a new moral system, of which perfect obedience to God is the animating principle. This is the Church; and so far as men consent to be raised to the fulfilment of their own destiny, it will at last include all mankind in the unity of obedience to God through their participation in the Spirit of Christ.   Consequently in this service, which is preeminently the Christian's means of access to the Eternal, and wherein he worships not as an individual but as a member of the Church of all times and places,[4] the relevant conception of Christ is not that of the historic Figure but that of the Universal Man.[5]   The sacrifice of Christ is potentially but most really the sacrifice of Humanity.   Our task is, by His Spirit, to take our place in that sacrifice.   In the strict sense there is only one sacrifice—the obedience of the Son to the Father, and of Humanity to the Father in the Son.   This was manifest in actual achievement on Calvary; it is represented in the breaking of the Bread;

---

[1] Hebrews x. 1-14, specially 8, 9.
[2] *I.e.* a symbol which is a perfect instance of what it symbolises: cf. *Mens Creatrix*, pp. 129 ff.
[3] P. 152.   [4] Cf. p. 163.   [5] Cf. p. 153.

it is reproduced in our self-dedication and resultant service; it is consummated in the final coming of the Kingdom. "We do show forth the Lord's death till He come." The Death and the Coming are the initial and crowning moments of the process which exhibits in time the eternal sacrifice and the triumph which Divine Love wins by means of it.

It is essential to the spiritual value of this sacrament that we do what the Lord did. It is all symbol, no doubt, but it is expressive, not arbitrary, symbol; that is to say, the spiritual reality signified is actually conveyed by the symbol. The symbol is emphatically not *mere* symbol; if it were that, we should only receive what our minds could grasp of the meaning symbolised. It is an instrument of the Lord's purpose to give Himself to us, as well as the symbol of what He gives. What we receive is not limited by our capacity to understand the gift. When with the right intention I receive the Bread and the Wine, I actually receive Christ, whether I have any awareness of this at the moment or not, and always more fully than I am aware. We, by repeating and so identifying ourselves with His sacrificial act, become participants in His one sacrifice, which is the perfect dedication to the Father of the Humanity which God in Christ has taken to Himself.

"This is my Body." Here, in this Bread so treated, we see Christ's Body broken for the Kingdom. Because the Eucharist means what has just been set forth, it is a means of access for us to the very Life of Christ, and the consecrated Bread is the medium of that Life to us. By means of that Bread He is present to our souls. He is not locally in the elements. "Corpus Christi non est in hoc sacramento sicut in loco" is the explicit declaration of St. Thomas Aquinas,[1] who gave precise formulation to the doctrine of Transubstantiation. But what is Presence at any

---

[1] *Summa Theologica*, Pt. III. Q. lxxvi. A. 5.

time?   According to one view, the " present," whether
temporal or spatial, is a mere meeting point of various
non-presents—as of Past and Future.   No *stretch* of
time is actually " present ";   what is actually present
is a mere point of intersection in which nothing can
happen.   Another view, more correctly as I think,
takes the " specious present " as the real present, and
defines Past and Future with reference to it.   The
Present is, then, that which is directly apprehensible.
And, in fact, by the word " present " we do in practice
mean what is apprehensible.   Through the consecrated elements we find Christ specially apprehensible
so that though He is not personally localised, He is
accessible by means of what is local.   The elements
come by the act of Consecration to be the vehicle to us
of His Human Nature and Life.   That is now their
value, and therefore their true " substance." [1]   There
is nothing here of magic or even of miracle, if miracle
means a fact for which other experience offers no
analogy.   But there is here something possessed of
as high a dignity as any miracle could ever be—a
clear manifestation of the principle which informs the
whole universe, the utilisation of lower grades of being
for the purpose of the higher, even of the highest.

It is in the whole repetition of Christ's act that
the spiritual value or reality lies.   The consecrated
elements are the permanent witness of that repetition,
and it is as such that they become the means or occasion
of the special accessibility or presence of Christ.
This is only beneficial, of course, to those who approach
in faith.   This value, like all values, is only fully
actual when it is appreciated or appropriated.   For
this reason those were right who said that the Presence
was in the faithful receiver.   But they were wrong
if they held that it was there exclusively; the receiver
finds, and does not make, this Presence.   By means
of the elements Christ is present, that is, accessible;

---

[1] Cf. p. 15 and the note at the end of this chapter.

but the accessibility is spiritual, not material or local, and Christ is only actually present to the soul of those who make right use of the means of access afforded.

No doubt Christ is always and everywhere accessible; and He is always the same. Therefore it is possible to make a "spiritual communion" which is in every way as real as a sacramental communion.[1] But it is far harder. Our minds are greatly affected by our bodies. When with our very bodies we repeat the sacrificial act by which the Lord interpreted His death, we find ourselves empowered to intend with fuller resolve our union with Him in His obedience to God. The consecrated elements are quite truly and certainly a vehicle of Christ's Presence to our souls.

That Presence is given under a form which at once indicates that it is given to be received. Any other use of it seems to me both unauthorised and dangerous. It is dangerous because it suggests that the value of the Sacrament is intended to reside in itself.[2] But this is not so. The Presence is given to be received; when received it incorporates us into the Body of Christ, so that in the power of His eternal sacrifice we may take our allotted share therein, "filling up what is lacking of the sufferings of Christ for His Body's sake, which is the Church."[3] The proof that we have received the Presence is the increase of love in our daily lives.

"Do this." Do what? Do the sign, no doubt; but only as a means to doing the thing signified. The

---

[1] Where Christ is at all, there (I hold) He is altogether. To say that His Divinity is present elsewhere but His Humanity only in the Eucharist seems to me mythology, and nonsense at that. Everywhere and always we can have full communion with Him. But He has provided a way perfectly suited to our needs and capabilities, and if we neglect this our presumption in doing so will hinder our communion by other means.

[2] This is clearly presupposed by (e.g.) discussions of the moment in digestion at which the Presence is withdrawn, or by any view which holds that by receiving the Holy Communion we gain Christ's Presence within us only for a time. See Bishop Gore's strictures on the results involved in such views in The Body of Christ, pp. 121-123.

[3] Colossians, i. 24.

R

Eucharist is a sacrifice; but we do not offer it; Christ offers it; and we, responding to His act, take our parts or shares in His one sacrifice as members of His Body. The Bread which the Church, by the hands of the priest, breaks and gives is the Body of Christ, that is, it is the Church itself.[1] Christ is Priest and Victim in the one eternal sacrifice; on earth His Body is the Church, and what He does, He does through the Church. But the Church is His people. Christ in us presents us with Himself to the Father; we in Him yield ourselves to be so presented; or to put it in other words, Redeeming Love so wins our hearts that we offer ourselves to be presented by the Love that redeems to the Love that created and sustains both us and all the universe.

So the reality of our communion with Christ and in Him with one another is the increase of love in our hearts. If a man goes out from his Communion to love and serve men better he has received the Real Presence. If he feels every thrill and tremor of devotion, but goes out as selfish as before, he has not received it. It was offered, but he did not receive it.

For all worship is representative, not exclusive. We set apart certain places as sacred, not to mark other places as profane, but to represent and remind us of the sanctity of all places. We set apart certain times as sacred, not to mark other times as secular, but to represent and remind us of the sanctity of all Time. We consecrate certain food and drink, not to mark other meals as non-religious, but to represent and remind us of the fact that all our food should build us up as members of the Body of Christ. The energy which I acquire from food and drink I may use for selfishness or for love, for gain or for service; let there then be some food—common in its own type— which by association with the self-sacrifice of Christ

---

[1] Cf. St. Augustine as quoted by Bishop Gore in *The Epistle to the Romans*, vol. ii. pp. 240, 241, and *The Body of Christ*, pp. 204 ff.

reminds me of the only right I have to eat at all, which is that I may live for God.

The Eucharist is the heart of Christian worship. And in it we find the clue to a problem much discussed in our time. Is worship in direction and purpose objective or subjective? Should we take part in worship chiefly in order to give glory to God or chiefly in order to win benefit, specially spiritual benefit, for ourselves, whether we think of this chiefly as our own separate well-being or our greater devotion in service? There is no more practical question than this, for on it the whole spirit, and, in the long run, the whole custom, of worship depends. Professor Pratt, who obviously finds the objective conception of worship very difficult, none the less regards it also as fundamental, for " the subjective value of prayer is chiefly due to the belief that prayer has values which are not subjective." [1] He is chiefly, however, concerned with prayer, and gives less attention to sacraments. In the Eucharist we find the clue, for here the distinction of subjective and objective is plainly a distinction of aspects only. In the experience itself, which is the spiritual reality of the service, there is a gift objectively offered by God and subjectively received by man; the gift is such that man's reception of it is identically his offering himself to God, for it is the very energy of self-sacrifice which is offered and received. Is this act subjective or objective? Plainly, it is neither exclusively; but it is both in combination. It is a supreme instance of actual value, which consists as we saw in a system of valuable object and appreciating mind related to each other in a perfect correspondence.[2]

It is with this in mind as the norm of worship or religious experience that we turn to other forms of worship, where the emphasis is predominantly on one aspect or the other. In meditation the subjective

---

[1] Pratt, *The Religious Consciousness*, p. 236.
[2] Cp. p. 33.

aspect predominates; it is the effort to appropriate individually the truth of God. But there could be no sane meditation unless there were an objective truth of God on which to meditate. In intercession the objective aspect predominates, but there can be no intercession where there is no subjective love and supplication. Perhaps it is because of the objective results aimed at in Intercession that this form of worship is specially attacked by those for whom the aim of worship is merely subjective benefit. The facts are against them, and their theory is very difficult. If we avoid the manifest absurdities of materialism and the equally manifest absurdities of dualism, we must expect to find that very strong will-effort directed upon any human being will affect that human being. The limits of such activity of one soul upon another, just as the limits of the power of spirit over matter, we are learning to regard as far wider than our fathers conceived. If there is a God, we shall expect that our will-effort directed upon another through the divine wisdom and love will have still greater effect. Moreover, since the whole spiritual relationship of man to God is such that God will only release His full energy of beneficence in answer to our trust in Him, that is to say, there are blessings which He will not confer until we ask Him (for otherwise He would either make us self-reliant instead of reliant on God, or else would over-ride our wills and negate our freedom), it follows that by intercession we release an energy of God which takes our will-effort into itself in its beneficent activity. About the results no one who has made a habit of methodical intercession can have any doubt; and the world cannot be so co-incidental as all that!

But while reverent and trusting intercession is a practical force of proved objective efficacy, it is not the completest form of human worship. It is a way of bringing things to pass in the process of time. In our highest worship we are lifted into some apprehension of the Eternal, in such a way that the ethical purposes of Time are not left behind, but are part of the warp and woof of the experience of the " moment eternal." To this we are brought in the Eucharist. It is rooted in past history, for it is essentially a repetition of a historic action; it issues in the life of service for the future coming of the Kingdom of God; but it holds that past and that future together in a present realisation of the eternal, truly given and truly received.

NOTE

ON SOME ASPECTS OF EUCHARISTIC DOCTRINE AND CONTROVERSY

IT seems to be time for a new attempt to define, however provisionally, some of the terms chiefly current in Eucharistic controversy. In the text (p. 240) some reference is made to the difficulties attendant upon the word Present. Perhaps it is really enough to say that Present is the opposite of Absent. Under what circumstances is a person " present "? Plainly, he is " present " if he is in the same room; but would he still be " present " if a thick glass screen were interposed, so that though still visible he ceased to be audible? [1] At least such a circumstance would modify his " presence." We do not usually speak of a friend as " present " if he speaks to us over the telephone, so that we hear his voice but do not see his form. " Present," though primarily a spatial or temporal term, always turns out to mean accessible or apprehensible. The doctrine of the Real Presence is the assertion that by means of the consecrated elements Christ is really and fully accessible to us and apprehensible by us.

[1] I owe the illustration to the Rev. L. W. Grensted.

But what is said to be " present " is the Body and Blood of Christ. In what sense are these words used? Christ said of the Bread, " This is my Body "; and of the Cup, " This is my Blood of the new covenant." Those words as used now must have their meaning determined by their first use when the Lord Himself uttered them. At that time He actually stood before His disciples in the flesh and blood of His Incarnation. This makes it, as I think, utterly impossible to interpret them of that same Body of flesh and blood risen, ascended, and glorified, though such a view has high authority.[1] However much the complete subordination of the Glorified Body to the Spirit released it from all carnality and spatial limitation, so that it can now be given to the faithful in communion, yet this cannot be said of the archetypal Eucharist which the Lord Himself celebrated in the night in which He was betrayed; and what cannot be true of that Eucharist cannot be true of ours.

Yet the profoundly impressive words were spoken and cannot be dismissed as mere metaphor; and there are other recorded words (in St. John vi.) where " flesh " takes the place of " body," and it is declared to be necessary to " eat the flesh of the Son of man and to drink His blood." Plainly this does not imply anything cannibalistic; that is guarded against by the explanation that " flesh and blood " stand for " spirit and life "; yet if they only meant what these latter terms are commonly understood to mean, there was no reason to introduce the earlier and very difficult phrase.

Bishop Gore suggests that " by His flesh we understand the spiritual principle or essence of His manhood as distinguished from its material constituents, and by His blood, according to the deeply-rooted Old Testament idea, the ' life thereof '—the human life of Jesus of Nazareth in His glory." [2] For devotional

---

[1] Cf. Gore, *The Body of Christ*, pp. 61, 62, 98, 126-30.   [2] *Op cit.* p. 25.

purposes (which are here far the most important) this exposition is completely satisfactory; but I confess that it does not help me towards understanding. The meaning given to the words, especially to " flesh," is far from natural.

Of course, Bishop Gore explains most clearly that the objective Presence of Christ in the Eucharist is spiritual and is spiritually received; that is, it is received into the soul by faith, not into the body by the mouth.[1] But this does not remove the difficulties.

The mediaeval Church attempted to overcome them by the doctrine of Transubstantiation. This rests, of course, on the distinction between substance and accident. " Substance " for this theory is wholly imperceptible; all that is perceptible in the Bread remains unchanged, but the Substance of the Body of Christ is substituted for the Substance of the Bread. No one now uses this method of thought; in this book we have seen reason to think that what St. Thomas ought to have meant when he said " substantia " was what we mean when we say " Value "; though, of course, he did not mean this. The only entity in any object distinguishable from the sum-total of the " accidents " is, I submit, its value. If Transubstantiation means Transvaluation the objections to it partly disappear; otherwise they are very formidable. For this doctrine has to deny the continued existence of the Substance of the Bread; and so, as Article XXVIII. accurately says, it " overthroweth the nature of a Sacrament." Later on an attempt was made by Lutherans to escape this difficulty by the notion of Consubstantiation—that is, that the Substance of Bread remains, the Substance of the Body of Christ being added thereto. This has the right devotional value; but, unfortunately, it is nonsense. The Accidents could not inhere in two Substances at once. The doctrine of Consubstantiation was only possible

[1] *Op. cit.* pp. 65, 143-4.

because the categories of Substance and Accident were ceasing to be a part of the furniture of living thought, and the term Substance was beginning to be used with all the vagueness of the modern term Reality, which often turns out on investigation to stand for Meaning or Value. If, however, " Substance " is understood to mean Value the objections to Consubstantiation also disappear. " Convaluation " is, in fact, just what is wanted. The Bread still has the value of Bread; it has also the value of the Body of Christ.[1]

It should be noted that the ordinary connotation of the word " body " has been immensely affected by the science of organic chemistry, which is a very recent science. Most people of to-day, when hearing such a phrase as " the substance of the body," would think at once of chemical " substances "—nitrogen, oxygen, hydrogen, carbon, and the like. Of course, these are among the " accidents " of scholastic terminology; and no theologian would, I imagine, ever have asserted a physico-chemical continuity between the Body of our Lord in His earthly ministry and the Body which is offered to the faithful in the Eucharist. Even if it be held that the Body thus offered is the Glorified Body, it must be remembered that this is conceived as so transmuted as to be no longer a physico-chemical entity at all.

---

[1] The difficulties in which the subject was involved in the sixteenth century are vividly represented by the Black Rubric, even in the form in which it still appears in our Prayer Book. There we read that " the natural Body and Blood of our Saviour Christ are in Heaven and not here; it being against the truth of Christ's natural Body to be at one time in more places than one." In Heaven, and not here! so completely was the mind of that period obsessed by the form of space. Heaven is indeed " not here " so long as " here " is peopled by spirits disobedient to God; but no one, we may suppose, now thinks of Heaven as a place " elsewhere," and exclusive of " here." No doubt if it is to be answered that Christ's Body is still subject to spatial conditions in such a sense that if it is " here " it is " not there," and if it is " there " it is " not here," then to assert its presence on countless altars is to talk nonsense. But this view involves astronomical difficulties; for if Christ's Body exists under that spatial mode, where is it? We mention this controversy, however, only to illustrate the additional perplexities of theologians in the period of the Reformation, for, as has been made clear, we do not hold that the Eucharistic Body of Christ is the Body of His Ascension.

We have admitted that this view has high authority; on the whole it would seem that no other view has anything like the same weight of authority; moreover, it has a great spiritual significance to which we shall attend shortly. Yet it is open to the fatal objection already made; when Christ, in His natural Body, said to the disciples as He administered the Bread, " This is my Body," He cannot have meant " This is my risen, ascended, and glorified Body," nor certainly can He have meant that the Bread was His physical organism, or that the Cup contained the Blood then circulating in His veins. I think it is possible to see how the misconception arose. Jeremy Taylor, in an often quoted passage, gives the clue: " In the explication of this question it is much insisted upon that it be inquired whether, when we say we believe Christ's body to be ' really ' in the sacrament, we mean that body, that flesh, that was born of the Virgin Mary, that was crucified, dead, and buried. I answer, I know none else that He had or hath." [1]

But He has another Body—the Church. And St. Paul in one place speaks of the Church as His Body in so close proximity to his account of the institution of the Eucharist that the two thoughts must have been present together in his mind (1 Cor. xi. 23-25; xii. 27). The fact is that the thought of the Church as the Body of Christ, for all its prominence in Pauline doctrine, never gained a hold upon the general belief of Christians at all comparable to that gained by the thought of the consecrated Bread as His Body. St. Augustine indeed brings them together, but this is recognised as a peculiarity of his teaching. Bishop Gore follows St. Augustine in this, and lays great stress on the fellowship of the Church. But he places the two thoughts in a sequence which, though certainly legitimate, is not inevitable or required by Scripture— " by receiving His body from above we are to become

---

[1] *The Real Presence*, §§ 1, 11. Quoted by Gore, *op. cit.* p. 62.

His body on earth." [1] If by "body" we mean "spirit"—(" the spiritual principle or essence of His manhood) " [2]—no objection can be raised to this ; but that makes the use of language very strange.

It is easy to see why the thought of the Eucharistic Bread as the Lord's Body was, and is, more vivid than that of the Church as His Body. The Church of our experience mediates His Spirit very imperfectly because its "members" are not wholly yielded to His control. In the Eucharist the worshipper experiences an actual fellowship with his Lord such as he does not experience from Church-membership in general. In the Eucharist we find what we ought to find, but as yet do not find, in the Church that celebrates the Eucharist. Here for the mystic moment, perfection is attained; one day, when the Church's task is complete, that perfection will be actualised in the Kingdom of God. Meanwhile our contention is that when St. Paul called the Church the Body of Christ he used the words in just the same sense as when he called the Eucharistic Bread the Body of Christ. And inasmuch as apart from the Resurrection there would have been no perpetual commemoration of the Death (for there would have been no Church to commemorate it), and what we become partakers of is the Life Eternal which has risen out of death, triumphing over it, we see how appropriate devotionally is the association of the Eucharistic Bread with the Glorified Body of the Lord. Perhaps the transposition of an adjective is all that is needed. That Bread is not itself the Glorified Body of the Lord, but it is the Body of the Glorified Lord— the Body of Christ who is known to us as crucified, risen, ascended, glorified.

There are, then, certainly two distinct uses of the term "Body" as regards our Lord. There is His fleshly Body, and there is the Church. Our suggestion

---

[1] *Op. cit.* p. 286.   [2] *Op. cit.* p. 25.

is that there is a third use, as distinct from each of these as they are from one another; there is His fleshly Body, there is the Church, and there is the Eucharistic Bread.

What, after all, is " my body "? It is an organism which moves when I wish it to move. If I will my hand to move, it moves without my thinking how to set it in motion; if I will anything else to move, it remains unmoved unless with my body I lift it. " My body " is that part of the physical world which moves directly in response to my will, and is thus the vehicle and medium whereby I effect my purposes. In precisely this sense the Church is the Body of Christ; in precisely this sense (I suggest) the Eucharistic Bread is the Body of Christ. The identity which justifies the use of one name is an identity of relation to the Spirit of Christ and to His disciples. As through the physical organism which was His Body Christ spoke the words of eternal life, so through the Church which is His Body He speaks them still. As through the physical organism which was His Body He revealed in agony and death that utter obedience of Humanity in His Person to the Father, which is the atoning sacrifice, so through the broken Bread He shows it still and enables us to become participants therein. Thus by means of Bread and Wine, blessed and given as by Himself at the climax of His sacrifice, He offers us His human nature given in sacrifice (Body broken and Blood outpoured) to be the sustenance of our souls.

The objector will say, " This reduces everything to mere symbolism." To symbolism—yes; the word " mere " is question-begging and probably represents a misunderstanding. In the physical universe symbolism is the principle of existence. Each lower stratum of Reality exists to be the vehicle of the higher. The organism which was Christ's Body in His earthly ministry derived the significance entitling it to that name from the fact that it was the instrument and vehicle—the effective symbol—of His Spirit. The Eucharistic Bread is His Body for the purpose for which it is consecrated, which is Communion, in exactly the same sense as that in which a physico-chemical organism was once His Body; it is the vehicle—the effective symbol—of His Personality. The identity which makes it appropriate to speak of our Lord's fleshly organism, the Church, and the Eucharistic Bread by one name—the Body of the Lord—is an identity of relation to His Personality on the one hand and to His disciples on the other.[1] The addition of the outpoured Blood makes it plain that it is the symbol of His Personality as offered in sacrifice. As we receive His sacrificial Personality we become able to take our part in the one sacrifice, which is the self-offering of humanity to God.

---

[1] I have been asked how I should put this before " simple people." It does not seem very difficult. I should say something like this. " When in faith you receive the Bread and the Wine you receive the Lord Jesus Christ into your soul as truly as those who opened their doors to Him in Palestine received Him into their homes."

CHAPTER XIV

THE ATONEMENT

" O Captain of the wars, whence won Ye so great scars?
    In what fight did Ye smite, and what manner was the foe?
Was it on a day of rout they compassed Thee about,
    Or gat Ye these adornings when Ye wrought their overthrow?"

" Twas on a day of rout they girded Me about,
    They wounded all My brow, and they smote Me through the side:
My hand held no sword when I met their armèd horde,
    And the conqueror fell down, and the Conquered bruised his pride."

      *   *   *   *

" What is Thy Name? Oh, show!"—" My Name ye may not know;
'Tis a going forth with banners, and a baring of much swords:
But My titles that are high, are they not upon My thigh?
   ' King of Kings!' are the words, ' Lord of Lords!'
   It is written ' King of Kings, Lord of Lords.'"

FRANCIS THOMPSON.

OUR whole position is threatened with ruin by the fact
of Evil. We have taken value, conceived as a perfect
co-relation of subject and object, as the constitutive
principle or true "substance" of all things. But this
only intensifies the urgency of the problem of Evil,
which always threatens to overwhelm Theism of any
kind. If God is good, and God made the world, why
is there evil in the world? I have attempted some
discussion of the main outlines of the problem elsewhere;[1] here we are concerned with it only from the
point of view of a Value-metaphysic which finds its

---

[1] In *Mens Creatrix*, pp. 261-92. This chapter has been criticised as a very
inadequate statement of the Christian solution. It certainly is; but my critics
failed to notice that it is avowedly a statement of the problem and its solution in
terms of a general philosophy, without regard to Christian revelation, which in that
book is first introduced in the following chapter.

centre in the historic Incarnation of God in Jesus Christ. We shall therefore not repeat the argument which leads to the conclusion that evil, in principle, may be justified by the fact that it affords the occasion for a higher form of good (such as heroism and moral victory) than would be possible without it. It is enough to insist that this argument does not merely claim that the positive value of the resultant good is greater than the negative value of the evil, so that on the balance good predominates; what it claims is that the facts or episodes which are evil in themselves can become constituent elements of the absolute good.[1]

The philosophic treatment of evil often seems to the religious man singularly inept. It appears to take a cold abstraction which it merges in a system that absorbs it, and substitutes this for the washing of the sin-stained soul in the Blood of the Son of God. But there is no real conflict here between religion and philosophy. The interest of religion is mainly practical, to overcome the evil that exists. The interest of philosophy is mainly theoretic, to show that the evil *when overcome* is justified.[2] It is to be noticed that even from the standpoint of philosophy the religious interest is the more important; if evil, when overcome, is justified, the business of primary importance is to overcome it. Part of the disappointment of religious folk with philosophy in this connexion is, however, due to another cause. The religious man is concerned with the problem of evil chiefly as a problem of sin and its forgiveness; but this concern at once assumes the view-point, or level of thought, of a man who is by his sin alienated from God. It is therefore a mockery to speak to such a man from the view-point of the unity of all things in God, unless he

[1] Cf. Bosanquet, *The Principle of Individuality and Value*, Lecture vi., and *The Value and Destiny of the Individual*, Lectures vi. and vii.
[2] How passionate the impulse of philosophy can be even when its form of expression is at its coldest all sympathetic readers of Spinoza are aware.

is first told how he may himself recover that unity with God, and therewith the apprehension of the world and life which it makes possible. For this reason the Atonement is commonly thought of as only a means to the Forgiveness of Sins; it is in fact much more than that; it is the mode of the Deity of God. But for men it is first the means to forgiveness, and must be understood as such before its deeper meaning can be apprehended.

The very notion of forgiveness presupposes an alienation, a severed unity. Man as sinner stands over against his Creator; we are back on the level of "justice"—of claims and counter-claims; God is Other than man, and demands from man his due. And this is sheer fact. No theory of Atonement which merely denies this alienation or otherness between God and man can begin to be satisfactory. The alienation is spiritual fact. The first need is not to deny it, but to end it. The unity of God and man must be reconstituted in me before I can look on God's creation from God's view-point and find it very good; and as I belong partly to "the world," this can never completely happen, at least in "this age"; only by faith, not by actual attainment, can I conceive the world as God sees it, though I may hope hereafter to have "the fruition of the glorious God-head."

Philosophy itself is profoundly concerned about this practical problem. It may proclaim the perfection of the Absolute, and declare that in the temporal conquest of evil the eternal perfection consists. But if so, it assumes that in some way the evil can be conquered. Forgiveness, we shall see, is bound up with this conquest. What is the Christian doctrine of Forgiveness?

We begin with the teaching of our Lord. This need not here be dealt with at length, for no one can read the Synoptic Gospels without noticing its prominence. Many of the miracles of healing are accompanied by declarations of forgiveness of sins; the claim to make such a declaration was one of the first occasions for accusation against our Lord by the religious leaders of the time. The Fourth Gospel does not anywhere use the words " forgiveness " or " forgive "; but, as we have received it, it contains the words spoken to the adulteress: " Neither do I condemn thee; go and sin no more." The classical expression of our Lord's teaching is of course the parable of the Prodigal Son. Its significance is luminously clear. The son is allowed to take his patrimony and go his own way; the father does not in any smallest degree curtail his liberty; when he is gone, the father longs for his return, and shows as soon as his son approaches that he has always been ready to restore him to the old relationship; but he does not send for him or fetch him; he waits until the son comes to himself and makes up his own mind to return as a penitent. Dr. Rashdall is perfectly right when he says that the plain teaching of the parable is that God freely forgives all who repent, and that the rest of the teaching of our Lord accords with this.[1]

But what our Lord said must not be separated from what He did; and what He did supplies an answer to two problems that arise immediately in connexion with the doctrine of free forgiveness conditioned only by repentance. The first of these is the question how forgiveness can be freely given without loss to the majesty of the moral law. The second is the question how, if repentance is the condition of forgiveness, that condition is in fact to be fulfilled. To those two questions the Cross gives the answer.

The great doctrine of the Atonement has suffered more, perhaps, than any fundamental doctrine of the Christian faith from the pendulum-swing of human thought as it sways from one reaction to another.

[1] *The Idea of Atonement in Christian Theology*, pp. 25 ff.

Let us then make a few points clear at the outset. (1) No doctrine can be Christian which starts from a conception of God as moved by any motive alien from holy love. If it is suggested by any doctrine of the Atonement that the wrath of God had quenched or even obscured His love before the atoning sacrifice was offered by Jesus Christ, that doctrine is less than Christian. The starting-point in the New Testament is never the wrath of God but always His love. " God commendeth His own love toward us, in that, while we were yet sinners, Christ died for us." " God so loved the world that He gave His only-begotten Son." [1]

(2) Forgiveness does not consist of remission of penalty. So long as we think of it in that way, we show that we have not reached the Christian relationship to God. When a child who has done wrong says to his father, " Please forgive me," he does not only mean, " Don't punish me "; he also means, " Please let us be to each other as if I had not done it." If I have injured my friend and ask him to forgive me, I am not asking him to refrain from prosecuting me; I am asking him to let our friendship stand unbroken in spite of what I have done. To forgive is to restore to the old relationship. It is because men have pictured God's judgement of souls so much in the likeness of the courts of earthly justice that this has been so often obscured. The prisoner in the dock has never been in any close relationship with the judge on the bench. He is not occupied with anxious thoughts concerning the grief which his misconduct may have caused to that worthy fellow-citizen; his only concern with the judge is to know what the judge is going to inflict upon him. If we think so of our responsibility before God, we have not taken up our position as Christians at all. " You did not receive a spirit of slavery to relapse into fear, but you received a spirit of adoption, in which we cry

[1] Romans v. 8; St. John iii. 16.

S

Abba, Father." [1] The slave has his orders and is punished if he disobeys; his only feeling when he has done wrong is fear. The son knows his father's love, and calls upon him by the name of endearment. So the forgiveness that Christ wins for us is not chiefly a remission of penalty; it is the restoration to the affectionate intimacy of sons with their Father. And it is for this that the Father longs.

(3) None the less, there is a real antagonism of God against the sinner so long as he continues in his sin. It is true, of course, that God loves the sinner while He hates the sin. But that is a shallow psychology which regards the sin as something merely separate from the sinner, which he can lay aside like a suit of clothes. My sin is the wrong direction of my will; and my will is just myself so far as I am active. If God hates the sin, what He hates is not an accretion attached to my real self; it is myself, as that self now exists. He knows I am capable of conversion, and desires not the death of the sinner but rather that he should be converted and live; in that most true sense, He loves me even while I sin; but it cannot be said too strongly that there is a wrath of God against me as sinning; God's Will is set one way and mine is set against it. There is a collision of wills; and God's Will is not passive in that collision. There is an antagonism of God against me—not indeed an ill-will towards me, for what He wills is my good— but most certainly a contrary will actively opposing me. And, therefore, though he longs to forgive, He cannot do so unless either my will is turned from its sinful direction into conformity with His, or else there is at work some power which is capable of effecting that change in me. To forgive is to restore to the old intimacy; there can be no intimacy between God and me in so far as I set my will against His. Moreover, I am only one of His family. He cannot

1 Romans viii. 15.

restore me to the freedom of the family if there is ill-will in me against the other members of it.[1] Our tendency to draw illustrations from the law-courts makes us think of forgiveness concerning each of us singly; but that is false both to fact and to Christian principle. Consequently, so long as there is ill-will in me there is an antagonism on His side to be ended as well as on mine. It is of my making, but it exists in Him and not only in me. It is not anger, if by anger we mean the emotional reaction of an offended self-concern; it is anger, if by anger we mean the resolute and relentless opposition of a will set on righteousness against a will directed elsewhere. God must abolish all sinners; but He seeks to abolish sinners by winning them out of their sin into the loyalty and love of children in their Father's home.

(4) It is congruous with what has just been said that we should remind ourselves that our Lord came to save His people from their sins and not merely from the punishment of their sins. It is only through preoccupation with thoughts of punishment that people have come to invent doctrines of transferred penalty. Of course, it is true that if we are not sinners God will not treat us as if we were; and if by His suffering Christ has won us out of our sin, then by His suffering He has delivered us from the suffering that would have been the result of our continuance in sin. But it would be monstrous to speak of this as a transference of penalty. The Atonement is accomplished by the drawing of sinful souls into conformity with the divine Will.

We can now turn back to the two problems that arise out of our Lord's proclamation of God's free forgiveness on the sole condition of repentance. The first of these was the question, How can forgiveness

---

[1] So a father might say to a son who had quarrelled with both the father and a brother, and after leaving the home in a rage was anxious to return—" I am willing to have you back, but can you be friends with Jack ? " This point is referred to again on p. 265.

be freely given without detriment to the majesty of the moral law? If, as soon as I repent, God welcomes me back to intimacy, does it not seem as though He had not greatly cared about my sin? This is the real root of all the theories of vicarious punishment which have so grievously offended the most sensitive Christian consciences. Those theories represent a wrong way of setting forth what is itself profoundly true. Free forgiveness is immoral if it is lightly given. It is a part of true love that the father should welcome home the returning prodigal; yet the prodigal knew something of what the father had suffered through his selfishness. But men do not universally understand what their selfishness means to the Father in Heaven. The promise of free forgiveness on condition of repentance to men so blind and callous as we are would be demoralising. It could only be safely given by One who was also to lay bare the heart of God and show what sin means to Him, and therefore how righteous as well as deep is the love from which the forgiveness flows.

For if the God who forgives suffers under the impact of sin in a fashion that requires Gethsemane and Calvary for its manifestation, it is impossible to say that He forgives through indifference. No one who hears the word which pronounces his pardon from the lips of the Crucified will be for a moment tempted to say, "He does not mind." Therefore the Cross, by showing what sin costs God, safeguards His righteousness while He forgives. On the Cross God set forth His Son "to be a means of propitiation, through faith, by His life offered in sacrifice, to show Himself as righteous and as making righteous him that has faith in Jesus." [1] St. Paul regards the forbearance of God in the past as having imperilled His righteousness; but that righteousness is now fully vindicated by the Cross, which reveals the antagonism

[1] Romans iii. 25, 26. I have paraphrased the word "Blood."

between God and sin. And this is what is required. There are two ways of expressing antagonism to sin; one is to inflict suffering on the sinner, the other is to endure suffering. Either repels the charge of moral indifference.

In choosing to show His righteousness by enduring pain and manifesting His endurance of it, God acted in the one way by which the other condition of perfectly righteous forgiveness can be fulfilled; that is, that the sinner be won from his sin to righteousness, from selfishness to love. Here experience can guide us. There is no doubt at all that the Cross of Christ has been His chief means of drawing men into fellowship with Himself. For St. Paul union with Christ is something so complete and intimate that whatever may be said to have befallen Him has befallen the disciple also;[1] and this makes it for ever impossible to describe his doctrine fairly as substitutionist. But it is on the moment of Death and Resurrection that this sense of union is concentrated. Whether or not our Lord actually spoke the words in St. Matthew's Gospel at the distribution of the Cup at the Last Supper, experience shows that the shedding of Christ's blood was indeed " for the remission of sins " in the sense that by His Passion they have been drawn to God and have received forgiveness.

All of this does not exactly amount to saying that the Death of Christ was a propitiatory sacrifice; but it does, as I think, prove that the Death of Christ fulfilled the aspirations previously expressed in such sacrifices, and I have no doubt at all that the Lord Himself intended to direct our thoughts to perceive this by the act which He performed at the Last Supper and the words by which He both marked this act as sacrificial and connected it with His Death, which took place on the following day.

We are at present dealing with the Atonement only

---

[1] Romans vi. 1-11; 2 Corinthians v. 14; Colossians iii. 1-3.

in so far as it concerns the forgiveness of the sins of men. There is a wider range to be covered before we appreciate the full depth of that mystery. " It was the good pleasure of the Father that in him should all the fulness dwell, and through him to reconcile all things unto himself, having made peace through the blood of his cross; through him, I say, whether things upon the earth or things in the heavens." [1] The fact that in human history the Atonement takes the form of the Passion is largely due to human sin. But human history is only an episode in the cosmic process, and the Divine Self-sacrifice, wherein is expressed the Love which is the inner heart of the Universe and its supreme Law, has a range of efficacy far beyond human history. What constitutes the problem is not only the sins of men, but also what St. John calls the "sin of the world" (cosmos). The words with which our Lord ended the discourse preparing His disciples for the Passion were, " I have conquered the universe ": ἐγὼ νενίκηκα τὸν κόσμον. What is set before us in the Cross of Christ is not merely the reaction of the Divine Nature to human sin; it is the unveiling of a mystery of the Divine Life itself—the revelation of the cost whereby God wins victory over the evil which He had permitted, and thereby makes more glorious than otherwise was possible the goodness which triumphs. In so far as the term " propitiation " represents something objectively accomplished in and by God Himself, apart from our forgiveness altogether (though that is involved) and even apart from our sins (except in so far as these are part of the cosmic evil)—to that extent it is the term which of all that are open to us carries us furthest into the mystery of the Atonement.

We may, then, summarise our Lord's teaching on forgiveness by saying that He did indeed proclaim God's free forgiveness of sin on condition of repent-

[1] Colossians i. 19, 20.

ance; and He also did what alone could save that proclamation from imperilling belief in the divine righteousness, by showing in His Passion what men's sin means to God. By showing this He further secured that all who believe in Him should fulfil the condition. After all, others have taught that forgiveness follows repentance; what no other could do was to secure that repentance should follow sin. But Christ has done this for all who believe that in Him we see the Father. Fear of punishment might deter me from sinful action, but it could not change my sinful desires; on the contrary, it would be more likely to intensify them by the action of that psychological law described by St. Paul [1] which we have lately learnt to call the Law of Reversed Effort. But to realise what my selfishness means to the Father who loves me with a love such as Christ reveals, fills me with horror of the selfishness and calls out an answering love. The non-Christian may say, " Yes, God will forgive me if I can repent; but what can make me repent? " The Christian answers, " By living in the fellowship of Jesus Christ, by prayer in His Spirit, by receiving His Life in His Sacrament, by practising His companionship, I can assure myself of true penitence for every sin into which I fall."

Thus it is that we plead the sacrifice of Christ. His love, shown pre-eminently in His Death, has transforming power over all those who open their hearts to it. We mean to live in His fellowship; and we know that if we do so we shall be transformed into His likeness. It is because we can say first,

> Look, Father, look on His anointed Face,
> And only look on us as found in Him,

that we can go on to say,

> Lo, between our sins and their reward
> We set the Passion of Thy Son, our Lord.

[1] Romans vii. 7 to end.

We plead His Passion, not as a transferred penalty, but as an act of self-sacrifice which re-makes us in its own likeness.   Its work on us is not yet perfect.   We still misuse God's grace; our prayer is still languid and our faith dim.   But Christ will perfect His work in us, and we ask our heavenly Father to regard us (as He Himself wills to regard us) not as the prodigals we are but as the true brethren of Christ that we are becoming.

There is one feature in our Lord's teaching about forgiveness which we have so far passed over.   It is indeed misleading to say that Christ proclaims forgiveness upon the sole condition of repentance unless we remember how inclusive a term repentance is.   For He does not anywhere state this condition of divine forgiveness, though He does suggest that it may be a condition of human forgiveness.[1]   The condition that He Himself lays down is that the sinner who would be forgiven must himself forgive any who have injured him.   This is reiterated with an insistence which is unmistakable.   The petition for forgiveness in the Lord's Prayer is the only one that has any condition attached to it—" Forgive us our debts, as we also have forgiven our debtors "—and the only one on which a comment is added: " For if ye forgive men their trespasses, your heavenly Father will also forgive you.   But if ye forgive not men their trespasses, neither will your Father forgive your trespasses." [2]   This comment is reinforced by the parable of the unforgiving servant.[3]

We saw earlier that the purpose of forgiveness is to reconstitute the unity of the divine and the human. We now see how it accomplishes this.   God's forgiveness of men and men's forgiveness of their brothers are bound up in each other; and it is not difficult to see how this comes to pass.   God's forgiveness is

---

[1] St. Luke xvii. 3, 4; and even here the emphasis is not on the condition but on the duty to be ready to forgive repeatedly.
[2] St. Matthew vi. 12, 14, 15.
[3] St. Matthew xviii. 21-35.

restoration to intimate fellowship with God; but fellowship with God is fellowship with self-forgetful and self-giving Love, of which forgiveness is a necessary outcome. If we do not forgive, we are not in fellowship with God. The repentance, which is the condition of God's free forgiveness, is a turning away from our selfish outlook and the adoption of God's outlook, from which forgiveness necessarily proceeds. God's forgiveness of us and our forgiveness of our brothers are not related as cause and effect but rather as the obverse and reverse of one spiritual fact. They are in their own nature indissolubly united. It is not by an arbitrary decree that they are associated together; they are one thing. And here especially we have to remember that we are children before our Father. How can the Father take into affectionate intimacy with Himself two children who refuse to be on friendly terms with one another? He *can* only forgive us, as we forgive our brothers.

The forgiveness of sins, as an article of the creed, is the supreme test of practical Christianity. In a world where no injury was ever done, the spirit of Love would show itself in maintaining the perfect harmony; in such a world Love would be more truly supreme than it is in our world as yet; but also in such a world Love would be far less deep and full than it has in our world the opportunity to become. To love those who love us is beautiful and pleasant, but it is also easy; to love those who hate and injure us is very difficult, and may be painful, but it is glorious. This is the supreme manifestation of the Life of God in humanity. Christ exhibited it in the Passion, and He calls us to a like heroic love. We are to be perfect in the way that our heavenly Father is perfect; but His perfection is declared to consist in the indiscriminate love which He offers to friend and enemy alike.[1] If we have received the Life Divine which is offered to us in Christ, we

[1] St. Matthew vi. 43-48.

shall always readily forgive; and in our world this is
the chief test of our reality as Christians. If we bear
malice or feel resentment it is proof that we still think
like men and not like God.[1]

Nothing can exceed our Lord's emphasis on the
duty of forgiveness. " If thy brother sin, rebuke
him; and if he repent, forgive him. And if he sin
against thee seven times in the day, and seven times
turn again to thee saying, I repent; thou shalt forgive
him." [2] And it is not only until seven times, but
" until seventy times seven." [3] In other words, we
are to show an absolute readiness to forgive, which is
undisturbed by any magnitude of the injury done or
any frequency of its repetition.

The Forgiveness of Sins is an article of the Creed;
that is to say, it is one of the constituent parts into
which the whole organic body of Christian faith may
be articulated. All the articles of the creed name
objects of practical trust. When a man says " I
believe in God " he ought not to mean that after a
careful review of the evidence he inclines to the
opinion that there probably exists a Being who may
not improperly be called God; he ought to mean " I
put my trust in God; I am determined to live in
reliance on His love and power." So the Christian
trusts in Jesus Christ, and in the Holy Spirit, and in
the universal Church, and in the fellowship of the
saints, and in the resurrection of the body and the life
everlasting. He is determined to live by confident
reliance on all these. So, too, when he says that he
believes in the forgiveness of Sins, he ought not to
mean that he holds the opinion that God forgives sins,
but that he believes in forgiving sins as a principle of
practical life—God's life and man's. He puts trust in
God's forgiving love; but trusting that as good, he
must needs imitate it; and therefore he trusts also the

---

[1] Cf. St. Mark viii. 33.　　　　[2] St. Luke xvii. 3, 4.
[3] St. Matthew xviii. 22.

excellence and power of forgiveness in human affairs. For as we have seen, and as our Lord has taught us, God's forgiveness of us cannot be separated from our forgiveness of one another. We must forgive even as God forgives.

But what of the condition attached? The words are " If he repent, forgive him." What if he do not repent? " If thy brother sin against thee, go, show him his fault between thee and him alone; if he hear thee, thou has gained thy brother. But if he hear thee not, take with thee one or two more, that at the mouth of two witnesses or three every word may be established. And if he refuse to hear them, tell it unto the Church; and if he refuse to hear the Church also, let him be unto thee as the Gentile and the publican." [1]

These words must not be isolated any more than other words of Christ. It is true that there neither can nor ought to be a perfect renewal of former intimacies with those who have injured us and remain impenitent. Their attitude evokes an antagonism which may be perfectly free from malice. But we have no right as Christians to rest content with that antagonism. Christ promised forgiveness to those who repent, but He also took action to elicit their repentance. His Apostle bids us " If thine enemy hunger, feed him; if he thirst, give him drink." So we shall soften his hard heart as the smith softens the iron by heaping upon it coals of fire. " Be not overcome of evil, but overcome evil with good." [2]

So if our enemy refuses to repent, we are not to fall back on mere retribution. He cannot indeed be received into intimate fellowship; he excludes himself from that. We are to treat him as a Gentile and a publican. And how did Christ treat the Gentile and the publican? We seem to need two words—Forgiving-ness and Forgiven-ness. God is always forgiving,

[1] St. Matthew xviii. 15-17.   [2] Romans xii. 20, 21.

in the sense that he desires to forgive; but we are not always forgiven because we persist in the bad self-will which creates an alienation between us and God.   For real Forgiveness the action of two wills is needed; it cannot be complete till the wrong-doer changes his attitude or, in other words, repents.   But he may be led to do this by the Love shown in his victim's readiness to forgive.   So forgiving-ness is always a duty; but it cannot become true forgiveness unless the injurer is willing to accept the position of forgiven-ness, which always calls for humility, because it involves an admission of wrong-doing.

Really the Christian's duty is quite clear, though it is very hard to fulfil.   We cannot admit the impenitent injurer to our intimate fellowship, but we must long to do so; and we must be ready to go to any lengths of self-sacrifice to soften his heart and win him first to repentance and thereby to fellowship.   We shall treat him as a stranger; but we shall lavish our kindness on him, especially such kindness as costs us dear, in the hope that so we may turn his ill-will into goodwill.   It is the wisdom and effectiveness of such conduct that we proclaim when we say, as part of the Christian creed, that we believe in the Forgiveness of Sins.   The world does not believe in it; it believes in punishing sins, and has no other treatment for them. A Christian world would believe in forgiving sins as a matter of practical politics.   This might or might not include medicinal punishment, but it leaves no room for resentment in feeling or retribution in action. But none will be able to follow in practice this faith in forgiveness except he live in the daily companionship of that divine Lover of souls, who yearns to draw all into perfect fellowship with Himself, and suffers what we see in Gethsemane and on Calvary to draw to Him those whose penitence is not yet complete, that they may be restored to intimate fellowship with Him and in Him with one another.

The Forgiveness of Sins is the practical and human part of the whole doctrine or fact of Atonement. But, as has been seen, that fact is something even bigger than the forgiveness of human sin. The method and cost by which that forgiveness is wrought and made effective reveals new depths in the divine. It was only in hesitating figures that men dared to conceive the suffering of God, until Christ died; and though the heart of man ached for the revelation of the Divine Passion, the philosophers would have none of it. Aristotle's "apathetic" God was enthroned in men's minds, and no idol has been found so hard to destroy. He reappears in the Greek fathers, and in the first of the Anglican Thirty-nine Articles. There is a highly technical sense in which God, as Christ revealed Him, is "without passions"; for He is Creator and supreme, and is never "passive" in the sense of having things happen to Him except with His consent; also He is constant, and free from gusts of feeling carrying Him this way and that. His anger and His compassion are but the aspect of His holy love appropriate to varying circumstances. But the term really meant "incapable of suffering," and in this sense its predication of God is almost [1] wholly false.

The revelation of God's dealing with human sin shows God enduring every depth of anguish for the sake of His children. What is portrayed under the figure of physical suffering and literal blood-shedding is only a part of the pain which sin inflicts on God. We see Him suffering the absolute frustration of His Will. We see Him in the abyss of despair, as perfect adherence to right seems to end in utter failure. We

---

[1] "Almost" because it is truer to say that there is suffering in God than that God suffers. The Greek conception of the impassibility of the Divine wrought fearful havoc in the theology of the patristic period. If Christ is the revelation of God, then God is not impassible. But to say baldly that He is passible is not true either. There is suffering in God, but it is always an element in the joy of the triumphant sacrifice

hear from the Cross the Cry which expresses nothing less than the agonised dread that God has failed Himself, has failed to be God. No further entry of the Supreme God into the tangle and bewilderment of finitude can be conceived. All that we can suffer of physical or mental anguish is within the divine experience; He has known it all Himself. He does not leave this world to suffer while He remains at ease apart; all the suffering of the world is His.

But suffering is not the last word. The Cross leads to the Resurrection. This is not merely a victory which cancels the former defeat; it is a reversal which makes defeat itself into the very stuff of victory. Christ not only made captives of His enemies, but led captivity captive. The Cross, which on the first Easter Eve stood for the failure of good and the triumph of evil, has been from the first Easter Day onwards the point in which all the triumphant power of good is focussed. Evil brought Christ to the Cross; by the Cross Christ abolishes evil.

This is possible, of course, because the failure of good was apparent only. If Christ had ever thought first of self; if He had inverted the prayer in Gethsemane, and asked that whatever the Father's will might be the cup might pass from Him; if He had left the heights of perfect love and defended Himself by force, the force of twelve legions of angels or any other—then no Resurrection could have made the Cross into the defeat of the defeat of Love. The Cross and Resurrection are the perfect triumph of the perfect sacrifice of perfect love; and this is set before us as the Life of God.

If so, then all the evil of the world may find its justification. We do not see this yet; but we see its possibility. God did not will the evil by any specific choice; but He willed a world where evil would have its place; He willed finite centres of consciousness, capable of apprehending value, but not capable (being finite) of grasping the one true Value which is God's whole work as God sees it; such creatures were bound to exaggerate the importance of the finite values they could apprehend, and thus arose self-will which is the Fall of Man and sin. Hence sprang hostility and bitterness and oppression and war. In the midst of the human history largely made of these things came the manifestation of the perfect love, which is the fulfilment of all finite Values, because its purpose is the harmony of them all. That manifestation calls forth the spirit of love in men, by which they can be lifted out of their self-centredness into an answering love.

Would we have it otherwise? Should we prefer a world of perfect but static harmony, with no opening for heroism, no occasion for generous forgiveness, no endurance of pain on the part of love for the sake of those to whom it gives itself? All attempts to conceive a world in which evil plays no part result in a world profoundly unsatisfying to our highest instincts —those instincts which lead us to find in Tragedy the highest achievement of man's creative spirit.[1] If indeed the Cross and Resurrection reveal the nature of the world's totality, then the world answers to our highest aspirations and demands.

This does not mean that the world, as revealed by Christ, is actually Tragic. The total impression of Tragedy is of nobility wasted, of victory spoilt.[2] If there were no Resurrection the revelation in Christ would be tragic. There would still be nobility, but to no purpose; there would still be moral victory, but despoiled of its fruits. Cross and Resurrection together give us Tragedy transmuted into triumph as the key to the interpretation of the world. The analogy of Tragedy recalls the supreme illustration of the alterability of values. In any Drama, and

---

[1] Cf. *Mens Creatrix*, chapter xi., specially pp. 151, 152.
[2] Cf. *Mens Creatrix*, chapter xi., specially p. 145.

pre-eminently in Tragedy, the value of the opening scenes is affected by what follows. The past as fact is fixed; " what is done is done "; but its value is not fixed. A man who commits a sin is to all eternity the man who committed that sin; but the value of the sin is one thing if he remains hard and impenitent, and quite another thing if he repents. In the former case the sin is the occasion of his perdition; in the latter it is the occasion of his forgiveness, with all that joy that only forgiven sinners know. A world into which evil has come can never again be a world innocent of all evil; but it may become a world in which evil has been overcome of good—a nobler world than one always innocent. So the occurrence of evil in the course of history is no obstacle to the eternal perfection; on the contrary, the Love of God makes evil a contributory cause of that perfection; and this is the Atonement.[1]

We must needs base our cosmic conception on the fragment of Reality which our terrestrial experience affords us. If it gives us a clue which may even possibly lead to a complete comprehension we must be satisfied, for that is the utmost that we can expect. What, however, does this tell us concerning the Nature of the Supreme Spirit? It tells us that sacrifice is the root principle of Reality [2] because it is the characteristic activity of God. Plato found Justice as a principle which brought unity into the multiplicity of the soul, and of society, and (under the name of the Idea of Good) of the universe; and Justice for him came near to love, for it meant the rendering by every capacity or citizen or principle of its own function in the economy of the Whole. But it stopped short of

[1] " If there is a God whose omnipotence might be defined as being equal to any emergency, whose insight could interpret and place all evil, and whose passion could consume and transmute it, if further, I can ally myself with Him, so that His power becomes mine, then I can see how the universe's problem and mine can be solved " (C. A. Bennett, A Philosophical Study of Mysticism, pp. 161, 162).

[2] Cf. the passages from Bosanquet's Gifford Lectures cited on p. 254.

Love, because it saw no excellence in sacrifice; and while all else submitted to the Supreme Principle, this merely directed, but never submitted itself to, the good of its subordinates. No one dared to attribute self-sacrifice to Absolute Godhead until Christ died upon the Cross. Yet it is just this that is needed to make sense of all experience, and to set forth God as veritably All-mighty, King not only of conduct but of hearts and wills.

Sacrifice is not always painful; [1] that depends on the response. The form of sacrifice is that one chooses for love's sake to do or to suffer what apart from love one would not have chosen to do or to suffer. This is painful when the choice of love is made in the face of some recalcitrant selfishness that still lingers in the soul; and it is painful when the love that prompts it is ignored or repulsed. Sometimes, too, it is painful by accident, as when a man deliberately faces pain to save some one else from pain. But sacrifice expressing a love that is returned can be such joy as is not otherwise known to men. Sacrifice is, in our experience, the noblest of spiritual qualities and the highest of known joys; and sacrifice is, for Christians, the open secret of the heart of God.

So God vindicates His own Deity. Only such a God can be the God of the world we know. For the Name of God signifies the union of perfect goodness and absolute power. We should have to deny the one or the other if we could not believe in God as revealed in the Cross and Resurrection of Jesus. He reigns from the Tree. Because, and only because, His goodness is so perfect as to include self-sacrifice, His power is known to be supreme and all-controlling.

[1] Cf. p. 221 and footnote there.

T

CHAPTER XV

LOVE DIVINE: THE BLESSED TRINITY

" The Living and True God was from all Eternity, and from all Eternity wanted like a God. He wanted the communication of His divine essence, and persons to enjoy it. He wanted Worlds, He wanted spectators, He wanted Joys, He wanted Treasures. He wanted, yet He wanted not, for He had them."—TRAHERNE.

OUR argument led us to a belief in God as Creative Will, originating and sustaining all that is. As such, He has His being apart from all else, and in no way depends on the created universe for His existence. He is not merely the spiritual aspect of the universe, nor the sum of its values, nor even its totality, except in the sense that He is the ground of its totality which therefore falls within the scope of His will. This is what is represented in classical theology by the doctrine that the universe is not of the divine substance but proceeds from the divine will. If God ceased to be, the universe would immediately cease also; but if the universe ceased to be, God would still be God. His existence is independent of all else; He *is* absolutely.

This does not mean that creation is capricious, as represented in the words attributed to the Almighty by the youthful Shelley.

> From an eternity of idleness
> I, God, awoke ; in seven days' toil made earth.[1]

On the contrary, the Love which prompts creation is the very nature of God. Because He is Love, He is

[1] Shelley, *Queen Mab*.

274

and must be self-communicating; in principle (ἐν ἀρχῇ) there is, and always was, the Word, eternally in close relation with God, eternally God.[1] In this sense the universe is necessary to God. Being God He must create. But there is no reciprocal interdependence. The way in which God is necessary to the universe is utterly different from the way in which the universe is necessary to God; for in each case the ground of the necessity is in God. God is necessary to the universe in the sense that apart from God the universe would not exist: the universe is not necessary to God in that sense at all; it is necessary to God only in the sense that, being what He is, His nature leads to its creation.

It is this essential self-utterance of God which St. John calls the Word, and the necessity of it, grounded in the moral character and being of God, is called the eternal generation of the Son. The reasons for attributing to the Word a distinctness sufficient to warrant such an expression will appear later. At present the point to notice is that what is rooted in the moral character of a spiritual being is that being's act; so that to say the generation of the Word is the act of the Father and to say that God is such that He must give Himself in love is to say one and the same thing. The love in which He gives Himself is known to Christians by the name of Holy Ghost. Father, Son, Holy Ghost—each name stands for the divine love in one of its necessary aspects.

But these are not only aspects. The Father is the ground or fountain of all being, and in Him all is implicit; to Him all is present. But " present " is here a misleading term, used only because the limitations of human experience and language prevent the discovery of a better. " Present " is distinguished from past and future; and when we say that to God the Father all is present, we inevitably suggest to our

[1] St. John i. I.

minds the thought of One who *now* comprehends the future. But that is precisely what is not intended. *Now* means *not then*; *then* means *not now*; but it is neither then nor now that God comprehends all time; it is eternally.[1] This is something altogether beyond our apprehension, but our experience is not so utterly lacking in analogues that we can attach no meaning to the words. When we watch a play of which we know the plot already, we have an artificial imitation of an eternal comprehension; we see each episode and action in the light not only of its occasion, but of its consequences. Now imagine that the play is being acted by the children of the dramatist, and even composed by them as they act it, according to gifts of which he as their father is the source, and that he knows them well enough to be sure of the general course they will take —then his experience, as he watches, is something still nearer to the eternal comprehension. Christ taught us to think of God as Father, and we can conceive an ideal father who is a perfect artist in the living material of his children, so that, never infringing their freedom, he yet can guide them to a harmonious exercise of it. So we come still closer. It is true that all analogies fail; they ought to fail. If we had a conception of God which made His mode of being perfectly comprehensible to the finite mind, we should know for that reason alone that it was false. But we have in our experience indications of a superiority to Time which show us the intelligible possibility of an eternal comprehension, though such comprehension is itself for ever beyond our reach.[2]

The difficulty of apprehending the divine comprehension of the world would be greater if it were an act

---

[1] Cf.   Oh, if indeed that eye foresee
            Or see (in Him is no before).
                    TENNYSON, *In Memoriam.*

[2] Coleridge says that the only safe form of the doctrine of Omnipresence is, not that God is present to all things, but that all things are present to God.

This, perhaps, helps us further to see what is meant by an eternal comprehension.

of contemplation only. But it is not this. God, we have found, is Himself active in the process which He comprehends. That process is His own self-manifestation, wherein He Himself is active. Israel·had learnt to trace His activity in the events of the nation's history; Christians have learnt supremely to find His positive act in the Birth, Life, Death, Resurrection, and Ascension of Jesus Christ, and the subsequent gift of spiritual power to His disciples. But in that supreme act of self-revelation we do not find One remote from all forms of trouble or exempt from disappointment. We see Him pleading, sometimes in vain; loaded with the weight of disappointment; amazed at the path marked out for Him; overwhelmed with despair. God, who eternally grasps the whole universe that He has created in all its extent of space and time, also acts at a particular part of space under the conditions of time, and so acting His struggle and effort are profoundly real—so real that in time and for a time they are sometimes genuinely frustrated; if any soul is ultimately lost, then God's purpose for that soul is finally frustrated.

Now we must use human language and human thoughts, because we have no other; and it is clear at once that while God, as we have been led to conceive Him, is certainly personal, He is as certainly not *a* Person. To attribute to *a* Person at once the eternal comprehension of the universe and the disappointment of Jesus Christ over Jerusalem or His cry of desolation on the Cross is to talk nonsense. It is one God; but it is two Persons—so far as human terms have any applicability at all. Here we find the ground for that degree of distinctness in the divine Word or self-manifestation of God in time, which makes it appropriate to speak of Him as begotten of the Father rather than as merely emanating from the Father.

Before all worlds, or eternally, He is begotten of the Father. Into this world He was born. It was no act of man that led to His birth. It was that active energy of Divine Love which is called the Holy Ghost. God's love, not man's will, caused His birth.[1]   Here already we find a divine activity within the process of time, which yet is other than the only-begotten Son. Disciples of the Incarnate Son, moreover, found within themselves a power which was so plainly that of the Incarnate Son that they called it the Spirit of Jesus; yet it is not personally identical with Jesus, for it points to Him and bears witness of Him.   Moreover, it is a personal influence, more fitly called " He " than " It."   Here is a third activity of God; so we reach the Christian faith in three Persons who are one God.

In the period of preparation the distinction could not be drawn. It is a common but intellectually disastrous error to identify the Yahweh of the Old Testament with the First Person of the Christian Trinity. But, apart from all other modifications in men's thought of God to which the Incarnation led, the Yahweh of the Old Testament is the undifferentiated unity of the Godhead, and in as much as He is God self-revealed, He comes far nearer to corresponding with the Second Person in the Christian Trinity than with the First.[2] But such discussions are very futile. It is only the full Christian revelation which brings the complete knowledge of God, so far as men can receive it. What is so revealed has, of course, always been true; it did not begin to be true at the beginning of our era. We can read back our fuller knowledge into the earlier religious history, but we must not identify the terms of our fuller (though still utterly inadequate) terminology with any particular terms of the less full and distinct apprehension possible to the ancients.

The Holy Spirit, as made known to us in our experience, is the power whereby the created universe—

[1] Cf. St. John i. 13.
[2] So Coleridge (*Formula Fidei de Sanctissima Trinitate*) speaks of the Second Person as " the supreme reason; the Jehovah; the Son; the Word. . . ."

which the Father creates by the agency of the Son, His self-revealing Word — is brought into harmonious response to the love which originated it. The divine self-utterance is creative; within the thing so created the divine self-utterance speaks in Jesus Christ; the divine impetus which is in the created thing by virtue of its origin is thus released in full power to make the created thing correspond to the Creator's purpose. Love creates; Love by self-sacrifice reveals itself to the created thing; Love thereby calls out from the created thing the Love which belongs to it as Love's creature, so making it what Love created it to be.

This already lets us form some faint conception of the Divine Love itself. But there is first another question the answer to which will help us further. We said that what the Incarnation revealed had always been true. But this requires modification. The whole gist of our argument is that we must be thorough-going in our insistence that God grasps the whole universe in an eternal comprehension, and equally thorough-going in our insistence that He is at work in the process of time really doing particular things, really suffering particular things.[1] It is sometimes said that the Incarnation and the experiences of Jesus Christ on earth cannot have made any difference to God. But this is only a half-truth. Eternally God is what He revealed Himself in Jesus Christ to be; therefore to say that He then became this would be false. But temporally God passed from creation to creation—from the creation of Light to the creation of worlds, of animals, of man; He passed from training Moses to training Isaiah; and continually He passes from experience to experience. This does not make Him different, but it does not leave Him unaffected. He is indignant at cruelty; He yearns over His way-ward children; He rejoices in their love. If this is not

[1] The former conviction historically comes from Greece, the latter from Israel. Cf. Bishop Strong's *Religion, Philosophy, and History*, specially pp. 42-48.

so, the Bible is merely false and the Gospel story no picture of God. If He is thus affected by temporal occurrences, this must be true especially of the Incarnation.

God eternally is what we see in Christ; but temporally the Incarnation, the taking of Manhood into God, was a real enrichment of the Divine Life. God loved before; but love (at least as we know it) becomes fully real only in its activity, which is sacrifice. Temporally considered, we must say that the Love, which eternally God is in full perfection, attained its temporal climax when Christ died on the Cross; so that the Cross is, as Traherne called it, the " Centre of Eternity." [1] The act of sacrifice enters into the very fibre of love and makes the love deeper and stronger; for love at its fullness is not a disposition, it is rather " the consciousness of survival in the act of self-surrender." [2] At that time God put forth His power; but also God therein fulfilled Himself. The Father is eternally perfect; the Son, sharing eternally the Father's perfection, temporally fulfils Himself in the historic process, which is the temporal expression of God's eternal being. Thus God is both absolute and relative, both transcendent and immanent: as transcendent He is the eternal *One*, unchangeable because all change falls within His perfect Being; as immanent, He passes from glory to glory, from love to greater love—not changing in nature but more perfectly actualising His nature, adapting His activity to changing conditions so as at all times to act in love and, so acting, to add to the love.

At an earlier point [3] the doubt was raised whether the grounds for recognising a personal distinction in the Godhead between the Father and the Son did not apply also to the Incarnate Son, so that we must accept

---

[1] *Meditations.* First Century, § 55.
[2] Nettleship, *Fragment on the Atonement.* For this point cf. St. John xiii. 1 (R.V. margin).
[3] Cf. p. 143.

a Nestorian theory of a human Person subject to many limitations side by side with a divine Person, who takes the human Person somehow to Himself.   If God the Son, the Word of God, is at once the sustainer of the universe and the Babe in the manger, does not this involve duality of Person in Him, on precisely the same grounds on which it was said that there must be more than One Person in the One God? [1]   No, not necessarily.   The distinction within the Godhead we take to be fundamentally that between the eternal perfection and the progressive realisation which is its temporal aspect.   But the Divine Word and Spirit we take to be essentially temporal and progressive energies, which are everlasting and are also eternal because, but only because, they are the (temporal) energies which both express and constitute the eternal perfection.[2] Between the experience of the Son subject to human limitations in Jesus of Nazareth and the Son as progressively ordering the world according to the Eternal Purpose of the Father there is not the same distinction as between the eternal and temporal modes of the divine.   It is true, as has been said already, that we cannot expect to understand the Person of God Incarnate.   We only plead that our theory places the difficulty where we ought to expect to find it.

Thus temporally regarded God is known as Son and Spirit; as Son He achieves the perfect sacrifice; as Spirit He prompts and enables us to enter into it. God is thus our Leader in the way of life, and also our companion as we follow where He leads.   Father, Son,

[1] Cf. p. 116.

[2] What such philosophers as Bradley and Bosanquet call " the God of religion " does not closely correspond with anything in which I was taught to believe, nor with anything in my own thought or experience; but it comes nearest to what the Second Person of the Trinity would be if the First did not exist.   It has long seemed to me that the doctrine of the Trinity solves the problem which these writers propound to the religious consciousness as insoluble.   I ought to add that I am not aware of any former attempt to relate the doctrine of the Trinity to the problem of Time and Eternity as I have done.   I therefore submit this suggestion with some diffidence, and with perfect readiness to withdraw it if it be found incompatible with the intellectual and spiritual positions which it seeks to harmonise and safeguard.

and Holy Spirit are Three Persons, for what we know
of each is incompatible in one personal life with what
we know of Others. Yet these incompatibles are
personal activities of an identity, which is perfect Love.

There is, no doubt, a danger lest such a conception
may lead men to fix all attention on the Son while
they fail to lift up their minds to the Eternal Father.
There is an easy attractiveness and a fatal delusion in
a religion which worships an Invisible King who is
at work in History, while giving a perfunctory ac-
knowledgement to a Veiled Being who abides in a
remote Eternity. But to adopt any such attitude
would be false to all man's deepest religious experience, which is always that of communion with the
Eternal; it would also be contrary to the whole course
of the argument by which we have come to this
conclusion, for that argument consists in the double
contention that Eternity must be conceived as requiring the actual historic process as part of its own
content, and that History can only be understood in
the light of Eternity. The Son is Lord of History
only because He is the self-manifestation of the
Eternal. Only through Him have we access to the
Father; to Him, therefore, our immediate loyalty is
given; but He claims that loyalty precisely in order
that He may present us with Himself to the Father,
so that, just because of our loyalty to the Son, the
Father is Himself the supreme object of our adoration
and service.

We have often used the word Love, but have
attempted no definition. Nettleship's phrase lately
quoted is not a definition but rather a statement of one
element in Love. But Love cannot be defined; it
can only be named; and its Name is threefold—Father,
Son, and Holy Spirit. It abides constant in itself, and
all its activities, while they are utterly essential to it,
yet only express its constant nature; by its activities it
calls itself forth even from where its presence is un-

suspected. We know this quite well in our dealings with one another. What we have now found is that if we would understand God in whose Being all the universe is grounded, we must conceive that Value, which is real whenever two finite spirits find themselves in each other, raised to Infinity.

God is Love; therefore He seeks Himself in an Other; this seeking is the eternal generation of the Son, who is Himself the Other that is sought; the Son as the Divine Self-utterance is the agent of creation so that in Him all the universe is implicit;[1] within the universe the Creator-Son lives a human Life and dies and rises again, so declaring to the universe the nature of its Creator; thus He calls forth from finite spirits the love which is theirs because He made them, though by self-will they had obscured it; so the creature becomes worthy of the Creator; and the same love which the Son reveals to men and elicits from them everlastingly unites the Son to the Father; this is the Holy Spirit. And this whole complex of related spirits is the Supreme Value or Reality—the Love Divine.[2] In God it begins, in Him it ends, and in Him moves whatever moves. His perfection is not coldly static; it is wrought out in struggle and agony and uttermost self-sacrifice. But neither is it precarious, for the historic process is the temporal form of an eternal perfection to which that process is essential.

To say that we can understand this Supreme Reality would be false; and if our view seemed utterly complete that would condemn it. But we find what we have a right to hope for; we find that, though the Supreme Reality transcends our grasp, we are not

---

[1] " The world is a hymn sung by the creative Logos to the glory of God the Father " (Inge, *Outspoken Essays*, second series, p. 20).

[2] Perhaps it is worth while to point out that for the full realisation of all the Values comprised in Love, triplicity is indispensable; there must be the Lover, the Beloved, and the Friend who rejoices in their mutual love. In the full reality of perfect Love, the three parts are interchangeable. Each is Lover; each is Beloved; each rejoices (as the friend of the bridegroom rejoices) in the others' mutual love. It is not true, therefore, as is sometimes supposed, that in principle only two centres are needed for the perfection of Love. Perfect Love is in principle Tri-une.

ever merely baffled. As we move in thought from point to point, the mind is never checked by a sheer obstacle. In thinking of God as Christians have learnt to believe in Him, the mind is always free; it is the finite before the Infinite, but its freedom proves its kinship. We are His children, and cannot fully understand Him; but He is our Father, and we know Him enough to love Him. As we love Him, we learn, for His sake and in His power, to love men. So loving, we become partakers of the Divine Nature, sharers in that divine activity whereby God is God.

Thus nothing falls outside the circle of the Divine Love. The structure of Reality when regarded analytically is a stratification wherein the lower strata facilitate the existence of the higher, but only find their fulfilment as those higher grades inform them. The structure of Reality when viewed synthetically is the articulate expression of Divine Love. God loves; God answers with love; and the love wherewith God loves and answers is God: Three Persons, One God.

God is Love. But we miss the full wonder and glory of that supreme revelation if we let the term Love, as we naturally understand it, supply the whole meaning of the term God. There is a great danger lest we forget the Majesty of God, and so think of His Love as a mere amiability. We must first realise Him as exalted in unapproachable Holiness, so that our only fitting attitude before Him is one of abject self-abasement, if we are to feel the stupendous marvel of the Love which led Him, so high and lifted up, to take His place beside us in our insignificance and squalor that He might unite us with Himself. " When I consider Thy heavens, even the works of Thy fingers, the moon and the stars that Thou hast ordained— what is man, that Thou art mindful of him? " It is a defective Christianity which has no use for the *Dies Irae*:

Rex tremendae majestatis,
Qui salvandos salvas gratis,
Salva me, Fons pietatis.

To omit the thought of God's Majesty, and to rebel at language of self-abasement in His presence, is not only to cut at the historic and psychological root of all man's religion, but it defeats its own object, for it belittles the Love which it seeks to enhance. If our first thought of God is that He always has a welcome for us, there is less thrill of wonder in that welcome than if we first remember His Eternity and Holiness, and then pass to the confident conviction, which remains a mystery commanding silent awe—" Our fellowship is with the Father."

But no; it does not merely remain such a mystery; this is itself the climax of mystery, which we apprehend (if at all) in an agony of joy and a rapture of fear. For the joy is shot through with the sense of our unworthiness, the rapture intensifies the fear that is our response to overwhelming greatness. So it is only half the truth to say that we must worship the Transcendent that we may appreciate the Immanent. God is never so transcendent as when He is most immanent. It was in the consciousness that He came from God and went to God that our Lord performed the act of menial service. It was when He acknowledged His earthly Name that the very soldiers went backward and fell to the ground. Nor is there any more august and awe-inspiring symbol of the supremacy of the Most High than the sublime and dreadful solitude of the Figure on the Cross—a spiritual loneliness made more intense by the physical proximity of dying malefactors and mocking crowds, for whom in His agony He prayed.

Christus Veritas: " This is the true God and eternal life."

Printed by LOWE & BRYDONE (PRINTERS) LTD., London, N.W. 1.